Social History and Issues
in Human Consciousness

SOCIAL HISTORY
AND ISSUES
IN HUMAN CONSCIOUSNESS

Some Interdisciplinary Connections

EDITED BY

Andrew E. Barnes and Peter N. Stearns

Under the auspices of the History Department,
Carnegie Mellon University
and the Pittsburgh Center for Social History

NEW YORK UNIVERSITY PRESS
New York and London

Library of Congress Cataloging-in-Publication Data

Social history and issues in human consciousness : some
    interdisciplinary connections / edited by Andrew E. Barnes and Peter
    N. Stearns.
        p.   cm.
    Includes bibliographies and index.
    ISBN 0-8147-1130-8 (alk. paper)
    ISBN 0-8147-1144-8 (pbk)
    1. Social history.   2. Social history—Psychological aspects.
    I. Barnes, Andrew E., 1953–   . II. Stearns, Peter N.
    HN8.S58   1989
306'.09—dc20   89-12277
                         CIP

New York University Press books are printed on acid-free paper,
and their binding materials are chosen for strength and durability.

Contents

Preface

This book is an attempt to build a bridge between research in history and psychology, the latter seen both as a discipline and as a collection of issues. Three major topical categories are used: first, treatments of religious trances and related religious rituals; second, analyses of the cognitive dimensions of literacy; and third, approaches to emotion. Varied geographical areas and time periods are covered, to encourage a focus on topical themes rather than on the unities that historians more frequently favor.

The emphasis is on problems in interpreting human consciousness. The enterprise is primarily designed to stimulate theoretical and methodological concerns, with a historial component arising from the growing interest on the part of some historians in adding a serious "mental" dimension to the study of social history, on the grounds that deeply held attitudes in the past can be assessed and that these attitudes reflect a wider social experience and are causes of social and individual behavior.

The effort to relate history and psychology is not new. Two decades ago, the genre of psychohistory commanded considerable attention from historians and psychologists, and while its full promise by general admission has not been fulfilled some reverberations linger. Psychohistory focused primarily on the study of past individuals, most of them "great men." This reduced its salience for a number of historians because of the growing interest in group behavior and in lower classes as well as in elites. It relied heavily too on Freudian theory, or on some close derivative, and this reduced its salience for many psychologists because of a growing movement away from detailed Freudianism as the basis for personality interpretation.

The present attempt to rekindle romance between history and psychology (and other disciplines concerned with problems of consciousness) rests on different bases. Social historians, by definition, focus on groups, and so spontaneously incline toward more general statements about cognition and social dynamics. Although certainly interested in fundamental Freudian concepts, social historians today generally take a more flexible approach to psychological theory. Often, indeed, their interchange with psychology focuses more on specific problems, such as religious ecstasy or emotion definition, than it does on sweeping personality statements. The new historical courtship of psychology, in sum, derives from the transformation of historical research over the past two decades, plus more recent movement of social history itself toward problems of beliefs and values.

The relationship between research on popular mentalities and psychology builds, of course, on other linkages that have been constructed, however imperfectly, between social history and other social sciences. The essays in this book confirm the importance, for example, of anthropological concepts and findings to the practice of the social history of culture; some, indeed, considerably prefer anthropological formulations to psychological approaches that veer too close to biological determinism. The historical study of emotion interacts extensively with the growing field of emotions research in sociology, sharing findings and common problems of method—including how usefully to define (or whether to define) basic emotions and how to relate emotional standards to actual experience. The attraction for social historians of dealing directly in psychological concepts within the newer, social dimensions, is strong. If, as the bolder social historians of mentalities are now asserting, we can use history to get some sense of past mental states—cognitive and emotional, diseased and normal—then they would argue that we should be able to interact with the discipline that studies these states most centrally. Certainly, from the historians' side, borrowings of findings and definitions are increasing, as these essays surely suggest, and a sense of shared problems is beginning to emerge.

The interest of historians, of course, does not assure the response of the psychologists. Unlike the disciplines of sociology and anthropology, in which there is some experience with the problem of change, psychologists in their work tend to look for constants. The old psychohistory, whatever its limitations, did tend to offer a respectful willingness to take psychology as a given and simply apply its relevant findings to the past. There was no clear appeal to an idea that psychological dynamics themselves might change in more than surface ways. The newer historians of mentalities, including some modified Freudians interested in shifting patterns of childhood and childrearing, keep change as a central concern, and so implicitly challenge psychologists to join in its assessment. Compounding the problem is the structural inability of historians to reproduce laboratory settings or neatly replicable experiments.

The essays in this book, while sketching important new work in several areas, make no pretense at final statements about a history-psychology relationship. Psychology emerges in different ways and degrees in the several essays, and the historian-authors display varying degrees of commitment to a real integration of theory into their work. Interesting distinctions emerge among the three topical sections, quite apart from their contact with different branches of psychological inquiry. Historians and anthropologists working with religious experience thus confront a possibly standard psychological experience with strong biological determinants; their task is to explain changing cultural configurations that allow this experience to come to the fore, as well as the consequences of the experience in the dominant religious system. This framework itself allows important distinctions among formulations. The three main essays in the religious experience section differ notably in the extent to which, in an attempt to explain phenomena, they place emphasis on psychological constants as opposed to shifting social and intellectual climates. All three, however, at least touch base with an experience that, although highly variable in incidence over time and in impact on larger groups, does have some common components.

In contrast, historians working with literacy or emotion use historical categories as their starting point. They emphasize pronounced changes over time, often assessed through the standard historian's conceptual tool of periodization, as their means of grasping the experience in question, or at least (in the case of emotions) the standards by which experience is evaluated. Psychological theory based on contemporary experience is utilized more selectively, since defining and explaining inconstancy is the focus of the exercise. This in turn establishes a different, perhaps more dynamic, relationship between historical and psychological research. Finally, of course, lest this seem a dialogue shaped by historians alone, the statements by psychologists and kindred social scientists expand the sense of gaps and dilemmas in the interdisciplinary endeavor, as well as encouraging more vigorous interchange. In improving historians' use of relevant theory across disciplines, quite apart from the possibility of developing more active interdisciplinary agendas in research and conceptualization, it is vital to bring attention to bear on historical work from outside history. A process of this sort, which the current collection hopes to encourage, deters anachronisms of the sort that developed in the earlier, Freudian version of psychohistory, and it compels historians to pay more attention to their own methodology and assumptions than is often the case. At the same time it is heartening to note a willingness on the part of some cognitive and social psychologists to incorporate problems of change and to propose more structural collaboration around newly shared research themes.

Interdisciplinary interaction is always difficult, and exchange between history and behavioral science perhaps particularly so. The initial essays in this book set a deliberately skeptical tone. John Modell raises new problems for historians, in documenting unusual vagueness in disciplinary definition, including the use of concepts borrowed from other social sciences, although he also sketches a remedy. Robert Levy points to the distinctions between the research styles of psychology as opposed to more cultural research, which distinctions he correctly sees as enhanced when historical uncertainties are added to the cultural mix.

This collection, in sum, is meant to stimulate and provoke, not to celebrate a task achieved. The intent is to take risks in debating new connections and their limitations, with the hope of attracting historians, psychologists, other social scientists and scholars of religion, into further discussion and collaboration. The tensions between a discipline devoted not only to understanding the past but focused on change, and a discipline typically interested in presumably unvarying human experiences, laboratory-testable where possible and sometimes (relatedly) rather narrowly defined, cannot easily be wiped away even when common topics suggest the need for new bridges.

Despite the difficulties and untested prospects, the potential intellectual rewards seem considerable. Historians of mentalities think they know a fair amount about certain kinds of changes in deeply-held mental structures, and know something about what causes these changes, as the essays in this collection on various aspects of religious, literate, and emotional experience, where new research is now accumulating rapidly, suggest. Much of the mentalities work helps relate present phenomena to dynamics from the past. The need, in this context, to come more seriously to grips with psychological findings is considerable, lest the mental dimensions open to change be exaggerated. The essays in this volume argue, though, that the results of mutual engagement can be considerable. In knowing which historical strands form a context for religious ecstasy; in applying a historical problematic for the assessment of the cognitive impact of literacy (more properly, the varied cognitive impacts); or in showing how definitions of emotional normalcy shift dramatically over time, historians and psychologists can join in furthering the understanding of how the mind works in social contexts. This book hopes to advance the dialogue.

Earlier versions of papers in this volume were presented at the first biennial Pittsburgh Symposium on Social History, 10–11 May 1988, sponsored by Carnegie Mellon University and the Pittsburgh Center for Social History. We are grateful to the many participants in the conference, whose contributions materially improved this selected collection. Special thanks to Dr. Susan Lewis, who coordinated the enterprise.

ANDREW E. BARNES

PETER N. STEARNS

Contributors

ANDREW E. BARNES is Associate Professor of History, Carnegie Mellon University and is completing a book on French religious confraternities.

MARGARET S. CLARK has carried through various research projects on the social expression of emotion; she is a social psychologist at Carnegie Mellon University.

EUGENE G. D'AQUILI is on the faculty of the Medical School of the University of Pennsylvania.

JOHN R. HAYES is a cognitive psychologist interested in learning processes associated with reading and writing.

RICHARD LANDES is a medieval historian at the University of Pittsburgh.

ROBERT I. LEVY, a psychiatrist and anthropologist, is widely known for his study of the Tahitians. He is in the Department of Anthropology, University of California San Diego.

JAN LEWIS teaches at the Department of History, Rutgers University, Newark, and is working on the history of motherhood in the United States.

JOHN MODELL has just published a book on life-course patterns in the United States from the 1920s.

CAROLE A. MYSCOFSKI is a historian of religions in the Department of Religious Studies, University of Missouri, Columbia. Her current research deals with women and religions in colonial Brazil.

DANIEL P. RESNICK has written on issues in the history of literacy and the history of educational testing.

LAUREN B. RESNICK, a cognitive psychologist, is head of the Learning Research and Development Center at the University of Pittsburgh. She is founder and editor of the journal *Cognition and Instruction*.

PETER N. STEARNS, Heinz Professor and Head, Department of History, Carnegie Mellon University, is editor of the *Journal of Social History* and author of *Jealousy: The Evolution of an Emotion in American History* (New York University Press.)

DONALD S. SUTTON, a Chinese historian at Carnegie Mellon University, has conducted extensive field work on religious practices in Taiwan.

PART I

HISTORY AND INTERDISCIPLINARITY

— 1 —

The Quest for Mind in Different Times and Different Places

Robert I. Levy

Introduction

How is *mind* affected by *history?* How does *mind* affect *history?*
These pleasingly cosmic questions are beset from the start by all kinds of
difficulties, beginning with the definitions of the key terms. Members of
that subspecies of anthropologist who are concerned with how different
kinds of community life affect and are affected by the individuals who
live in them are, or should be, the natural allies of historians concerned
with histories of private lives and of mentalities—using that latter term,
as we will throughout this chapter, in a broad and vague way.[1] This
essay is thus concerned with one anthropologist's thoughts about mind
in other places and times.[2] The first part of the chapter is a prejudiced
essay sketching positions on some problems and some possible solutions
in approaching comparative mentalities. It is a sampler of diverse problems chosen because of the particular concerns of the conference for
which this chapter was originally prepared and the stimulus of some
recent controversies in anthropology. The second part of the chapter is a
presentation of some ideas stimulated by my work in Polynesia and
Nepal on some aspects of the interrelation of "kinds of communities and
kinds of minds," in the hopes of illustrating the sort of explanatory and
theoretical enterprise which I propose would strengthen a comparative
psychological history and anthropology.

On Distortion and Ideology

We are periodically reminded, rather clamorously in recent years, that the *sciences humaines,* an indispensable term for the collection of enterprises I wish to refer to, are in the ideology business. Certainly, questions about the minds of the "other," and the relation of those minds to their environing communities and times are prime grist for ideological mills, as the recent Freeman-Mead controversy (more of which later) has recently reminded us.

In a less self-conscious age, in 1796, the British Admiralty confidently sent Captain Cook off "to observe the Genius and Temper" as well as the physical "Disposition and Number" of the natives.[3] The Admiralty seemed to have assumed that Genius and Temper would be as unproblematic to observe and record as Disposition and Number. But once observed and recorded what to make of such idiosyncratic local Geniuses and Tempers? The peculiar and problematic behavior of the Indians of Virginia, for example, had long before, in 1609, been glossed in programmatic anticipation as "It is not the nature of men, but the education of men, which makes them barbarous and uncivil."[4] "Change the education of men," the tract went on, "and you will see that their nature will be greatly rectified and corrected." Conception, explanation and program were hand-in-glove. The abysmal failure of educational programs for the soon-to-be colonized other, based (in many ways fortunately for their objects) on a profound and enduring lack of understanding of how and what people really learn from their "cultures," discouraged such liberal (and imperial) hopes, and stimulated other ideologues and other attempted solutions to the problem of the other and us. Among such solutions were the Romantic anti-Enlightenment valorization of the incommensurable spirits of different and places (a precursor of one popular contemporary trend in American Cultural Anthropology) and, turning back to "man's natures" for explanation, evolutionary or polygenetic racism.[5]

It is useful for illuminating the prejudices and the areas of clear and dim vision in contemporary anthropological theory of mind and culture to remark that "culture theory"—given its seminal historical articulation by Franz Boas[6]—was, *inter alia,* an attempt to replace racist explanations of presumably biologically based differences in the mental *processes* of the others, processes that seemed to imply inbred and immutable (or, in some evolutionary theory, glacially evolving) biology, with another sort of explanatory claim about behavior, and thus of the interrelations of individuals and their societies. Boas tried to split the peculiar local *behaviors* of the other from the psychological *essence* of the other. "We recognize that there are two possible explanations of the different manifestations of the mind of man. It may be that the minds of different races show differences of organization; that is to say, the laws of mental activity may not be the same for all minds. But it may also be that the organization of mind is practically identical among all races of man; that mental activity follows the same laws everywhere, but that its manifestations depend upon the character of individual experience that is subjected to the action of these laws."[7] For Boas the locus of the differences ascribed to the other was in "the variety of *contents* of the mind as found in the various social and geographical environments," not in the *organization* of that mind.[8] The now critical variable, the informational *content* of minds, was more or less isomorphic with what was taken to be people's "cultures," conceived of as local systems of definition and information.

A further (and congruent) move splitting being from behaving was made in the social and cultural anthropology of Boas's time. It came to be assumed by many anthropologists that one was not watching people being themselves but rather playing "roles," the universally similar actors were simply following the differentiated scripts of their culture—as if the life of a tribe were somehow a play by Shakespeare, a play whose script did not express the nature of its performers, as though the inhabitants of some strange corner of the world were not, say, Hamlets but players of Hamlet.

With the exception of an often embattled group of "culture and personality" theorists (later to evolve into "psychological anthropologists"), mainstream ethnographers lost professional interest in such aspects of exotic actors as genius and temper and an associated host of questions about loves, hates, terrors, and bodily experience. Insofar as the private life of individuals was still of concern, the investigator was concerned with such matters, to quote a popular field handbook for anthropologists which flourished for several decades beginning in the 1870s, as "daily routine, training and education, life cycle from conception to marriage, sexual development, marriage, and [finally] old age, death and the disposal of the dead." This represented a shift from interest in personal "mental" organization to the "Social Life of the Individual" as the particular chapter in the handbook whose section categories we have just listed was called.[9] Histories of "private lives," which have proliferated recently also seem largely concerned with accounts of social lives in small arenas—sequestered spaces, privacy, the life of the household, leisure—set off in various ways from a larger, "public" world.

If we try to move further beyond such private social spheres toward the small inner voices at the center of history's whirlwind and of the scripted life of communities, to ask how the larger community *and* its private social spheres are experienced, thought about, known, connected to people's feelings, motives, and personal moralities, then when we try to think about the human subject, when we try to imagine a *history of mentalities* and not a history of acting and of drama and of conditions of life, we abruptly reopen a can of most lively worms, which culture theory had, it was supposed, sealed. We are back on the frontiers of ideology.

On Limits to Distortion

Among passionately contested contemporary positions about the individual, biology, culture, and society, positions whose passion suggests to some of us old programs and ideologies in modern masks,[10] can we find any solid high or firm middle ground in a search for understanding?[11] Are there better and worse ways of navigating the tight-rope we must walk as we try to understand, defend, and construct ourselves at the same time?

Derek Freeman's recent attack on Margaret Mead's earliest work in Samoa forced many of us to try to think more or less deeply yet again about the implications of conflicting ethnographic claims and the ways that Freeman proposed for their resolution.[12] Richard Feynman has an essay on bad, or as he calls it "Cargo Cult," science.[13] The examples of the doing of bad or false science he presents are not the work of flat earthers but of scientists centrally placed within the academy and research institutes. But these Cargo Cult scientists are people who fail to have something essential—to wit, "a kind of scientific integrity, a principle of scientific thought that corresponds to a kind of utter honesty—a kind of leaning over backwards." Failing this, one will produce famous findings but, Feynman says confidently, "We've learned from experience that the truth will come out. Other experimenters will repeat your experiment and find out whether you are wrong or right. Nature's phenomena will agree or they'll disagree with your theory." There's the rub for us.

Freeman argues that in ethnography the facts speak for themselves and that a battle of conflicting truth claims can be joined. To most commentators on the argument, the establishment of and nature of ethnographic facts (and the conclusions drawn from them) seems much more complicated.[14] In the *sciences humaines* we may, once we get beyond elemental statements, have to settle for something different from truth, at least of the kind which can be disconfirmed by a Popperian disproof. A good piece of work is probably to be characterized as something like *authentic*. That is, it draws not only on the "scientific integrity" of the worker, but on his or her widest range of cognitive and emotional responses to the subject, to the situation, to honest knowledge of himself or herself as an experiencer and an advocate. Out of authentic ethnographies come contributions to that ongoing discussion which continues to build human knowledge out of an encounter of *subjectivities* in some sort of a relation to a *nature* rather larger than that of the writer's inner world. From the inauthentic ones come muddles, confusion, and the wasting of time and resources in attempts to get things straight again. The trouble with judgments about inauthenticity is that they must be ultimately ad hominem, directed towards the scholar. This is, rightly, troubling (some inauthentic types happily exploit our discomfort in doing this, particularly when they are using, as they often do, the impersonal rhetoric of science and scientific method), but we are without the experimenter's convenient and seemingly impersonal guillotine, and must ultimately judge the scholar along with his work. We simply learn not to trust him.

But granting the possibility of an authenticity of encounter and report, granting even a relatively enlightened awareness by everyone concerned of the possible distortions produced by their conscious or unconscious fears, desires and defense mechanisms, we come smack up against another major challenge to seekers for the middle ground. Even if we enter authentically into another world through a kind of progressively corrected intuition can we then *translate* from our sense of some systematic way of life, world view, or whatever to another? Can we use our cognitive and discursive categories to think discursively about, talk about and write about theirs? Furthermore, when we look at their ideologies, and their dazzling constructions of reality out of gossamer, wish, fear, and anxious hopes of just keeping everything going, we are increasingly aware that we are doing the same sort of shadow crafting among ourselves and in our uses of them. We learn to distrust our own language and thought. What then?

The attack here comes not from the science mongers but from the nihilistic wing of postmodernism. One escape route is suggested in a hint of Gregory Bateson's. Like his contemporaries Bateson worked with certain *kinds* of communities, possessing what the prescient anthropologist Edward Sapir once called "genuine" as opposed to "spurious" cultures, genuine being characterized by relatively coherent and extensive traditional structures of meaning.[15] Bateson studied the nature, acquisition and maintenance of local systems of cultural and mental convictions which were true, as he put it, because everyone believed them. He called such convictions "deutero-truths," the results of a "second-level" or "deutero" learning, a learning depending on the way primary learning tasks (how to walk, how to dance, how to speak correctly, and so forth) were locally structured and contextualized. Second-level learning and the local truths built of it have many distinctive characteristics which contrast markedly with primary learning and knowledge. Once formed it is very difficult, for example, to disprove secondary convictions by ordinary experience. People simply select out of the miscellaneous flow of events those which confirm their understanding, and they ignore or devalue others. Much of culture, of folk categories, and the like is so built and maintained. In a few passages of an essay on "levels of learning"[16] Bateson asks what happens to individuals when two such systems of culturally constructed local certainty are brought into contact in such a way that an individual comes to the understanding that not only the other's exotic system, but his or her own is built out of congealed dream. Now a "third level" learning begins to take place, entailing alterations of consciousness, of self-consciousness, of personal epistemology—the individual's sense of the relation of his or her experience and perception to what he or she takes to be reliable knowledge. There is an interesting variety of possible responses to the crisis produced by a challenge to one's system of deutero-truths—self-doubting nihilism is one—but another is a kind of triangulated third-level knowledge which has some interesting characteristics. In a quotation from Tolstoy's *Anna Karenina* (which I find myself putting to repeated use) the Princess Myagky says to a group of women trying to evaluate Anna's husband in the face of their husbands' establishment-bolstering opinions, "And my husband says the same, only I don't believe it. . . . If our husbands were not so fond of talking, we should see things as they are." The husbands are *doing* ideology and folk culture, creating order through the manipulation of symbols. The wives, out of the main game, off to the side, triangulating all sorts of information and contexts, subversively (for here is some of the cultural significance and threat of women, along with adolescents and lower classes and other tribal enemies) know, or struggle to know or to intuit something which in some sense transcends local culture—and which is akin to the anthropologist's or the historian's critical understanding. The husbands are our exotic object of study and analysis, the wives are our collaborators. Out of an encounter of positions (including our own) we and the wives are achieving a third-level knowledge which is more analytic, more free of local culture[17] and ideology, a basis for a less parochial metatranslation, and a place to stand for some selected human purposes.

We can put Princess Myagky to further uses. When certain kinds of historical and spatial situations encourage encounters which threaten the provincial certainties of "genuine culture" what happens then? Will Princess Myagky become an intellectual (Tolstoy, in fact, treated her as a muddled scatterbrain) or will she try to overcome her confusion by a leap into a religious commitment, to the derision of the husbands? Can we make her paradigmatic of certain populations, in certain positions, at certain times, in certain places? That would bring us to positive proposals about space, time, and mentalities, to questions of typology and explanation. We will return to her choices below in our discussion of the contrast between some people in Nepal and in Tahiti. But first there is something to be said about the encounter of the deutero-truths— the truths that are true because members of a group believe them—not of cultures but of *disciplines*.

On the Encounter of Disciplines in the Study of Mind

In our approaches to mind illuminated or obscured by being else-where in space or time we bring together various disciplines—history, anthropology, psychology, psychoanalysis, and anything else of possible relevance, The use of such a chaotic toolbox has its own problems, and I wish to comment here and in subsequent sections on some which have particularly concerned me.

Breaching the walls of disciplines even ever so slightly by trying to bring two such disciplines, paradigms, or just plain approaches together, disturbs the peace of shared, often covert, assumptions within the walls. Thus, in an illuminating example, the attempt to bring psychoanalysis (about which more below) and cultural anthropology together in the "Culture and Personality" studies of a few decades ago turns out to have been an attempt to bring an essentially conservative or tragic view of human nature into partnership with a very different, a passionate opti-mistic, world view.

Lionel Trilling, in the Freud Anniversary Lecture of the New York Psychoanalytic Institute in 1955, phrased exactly the kind of tragic hope, if that is the proper phrase, implied by the theory:

We must, I think, recognize how open and available to the general culture the individual has become, how little protected he is by coun-tervailing cultural forces, how unified and demanding our free culture has become. And if we do recognize this, we can begin to see why we mainly think of Freud's emphasis on biology as being a liberating idea. It is a resistance to and a modification of the cultural omnipotence.

We reflect that somewhere in the child, somewhere in the adult, there is a hard, irreducible, stubborn core of biological urgency, and biological necessity, and biological reason, which culture cannot reach and which reserves the right, which sooner or later it will exercise, to judge the culture and resist and revise it.[18]

One can imagine what the culture theorists of the day made of this. That theory was the very mother of soft liberal utopias, as Freeman's conservative rage against Franz Boas, Margaret Mead, Alfred Kroeber and all recently reminded us. The responses of American cultural anthropology and of psychoanalysis to early twentieth-century crises in the relations of individuals, society, power, restraint, freedom, and rationality and its limits were in many ways antagonistic.[19] One may imagine some of the problems to bring the two together.

Ideological problems aside there are also logical problems in attempts to hold conversations through cracks in the disciplinary walls, let alone to build some inclusive metatheory. Terms are taken out of context; one may not know if one is talking about the same phenomenon in different languages or different phenomena using some common term, as *self* is differently used, for example, by the anthropologist and the psychiatrist. When one tries to connect two ways of explaining a phenomena, are we trying to connect two different descriptions of the "same event" occurring at the same time, say the neurophysiology and psychology of a "mental" event, or the chemistry and the perception of a flame, or are we dealing with two different phenomena which are connected by some causal network operating in time—the interrelations between, say, community disorder and the symptomatic psychophysiological stress of the community's members? The encounter of anthropology and psychology, of "cultural processes" and "mental processes" is full of these kinds of potential muddles.

Encounters: History and Anthropology

The interdisciplinary encounter of history and anthropology has its specific seductions, stimulations and irritants. Some anthropologists think to themselves that historians seem to have simpler kinds of data to deal with and less with which to work. Historians seem to them to have the working strategy of waiting till something is beatified by being long dead, and then sifting the ashes. Time transforms and simplifies much more deeply than distance. We can, for one thing, travel in space. The cultural anthropologist (for the most part) thinks he or she is somewhat closer to reality, closer to flesh and blood, to feeling and thought than the historian.

The satisfied conviction of superiority (inverted into respectful awe during times of failure of nerve) is mutual. Consider Indologists and anthropologists who work in South Asia. To the Indologists the anthropologists are amateurs who do not control, to put it mildly, the historical depth, classical languages, sources and special techniques necessary for understanding Hinduism, Buddhism, the nature and uses of deities, customary law, and so on. The Indologists believe, furthermore, that these amateurs are working with deteriorated cultures, whose Hinduism, Buddhism, or whatever, is the result of the contamination and degeneration of what the Indologists take to be (and more or less secretly venerate) as the true, the classic, the real and great contributions of South Asia to universal culture. They find the anthropologists' work both irrelevant and irreverent. The anthropologist on the other hand suspects that the Indologists are dealing with a purified fantasy world, with texts and artifacts which were even as they were written and created idealizations and distortions of local realities. Thus they think of Indology as a meditation of alien intellectuals on native intellectuals; a meditation on a world which never existed, and believe that their own dirty, imperfect, confused, field community is an infinitely better clue to what really once was—more, in fact than a clue, a coelacanthic survival. The anthropologist wonders why historians do not rush to experience his community. He sees that if one happens to do so he only uses it to look backwards through it, to filter its reality to reconstruct a cleaner, transcendent past.

The anthropologist working in South Asia sometimes gets the impression that the local species of historian, the Indologist, is impatiently, passionately, waiting for the surviving communities to die (as literary critics seem to wait for the death of their poets) and to pass into the strangely elevated and methodologically accessible purity of history. Of course this is what new-wave historians try to overcome. But even Montaillou, even the private lives of classic Greeks, keep their purified historical aura, the aura of those now exempt from death and corruption. The anthropologist, of course, begins this escape from contingency in his analytic stance, his distancing of himself from the "native," and above all in the writing of his ethnographies, ethnographies which become potential materials for historians. But a historical work is further, much further removed.

What is left behind in the filtering of social life into history? That, of course, is an elementary methodological concern for historians. What, I ask myself, would I know about the mentalities of people in the two communities in which I worked—"Piri," a Tahitian village, and Bhaktapur, a traditional Nepalese city—if I had only historical precipitates? For historically nonliterate rural Tahiti we have the "base line" accounts of

Westerners, a few fragile ruins, and the artifacts that survive for the most part in distant European and American museums. For literate Bhaktapur we have two millennia of local texts, setting out chronicles, myths and legends, theology and philosophy. Strangely, perhaps, out of such residues I would know more about Tahiti. By reading the accounts of such figures as Bougainville, Cook, Banks, and Captain Bligh and doing some triangulation I get closer to the intimate experience of the "natives" than I do in the Newars' (the cultural group which Bhaktapur represents) elaborate texts, texts which had no place for Princess My-agky's sort of knowledge, and were in fact the sort of gab that helped drive it out of the realm of knowledge into merely womanish hunch. I get no help either from Europeans' first bedazzled encounters with the three-ring cultural circus of the Kathmandu Valley. It is, at least in this case, *harder* to understand a literate high culture and its people, to penetrate its enchantments. That tells us something about such cultures. I trust the base line Tahitian accounts because I can interpret them, not only by relating them to each other and their own contexts (the contrast between, say, the reports of Bougainville and Bligh, for example, being prime material for a study of eighteenth-century French and British national characters) but in relation to the presumed historical continuities and discontinuities in the Tahitian villages of my day. Without my experience of those villages, I should have been on shakier ground.

Native literacy in itself transforms everything. There is a new opportunity for the razzle-dazzle of self and other in the writing of texts, even in private diaries where there is a dialogue between a more inchoate, preliterate self, and a more public, culturally standardized, literate one, in an activity where an apology of some kind is being crafted.

Mentality lies at various levels, none of them should be privileged. There is a complex inchoate infrastructure (variously sliced and bounded by different psychological theories), there is a private internal discourse (sometimes honored as mind itself), there is the transformation produced by discussion and interaction with others, and the further literate transformation through the production and use of written texts. Psychologically minded anthropologists, at least of my sort, are able to watch some of the relations of these levels in action. They can watch behavior characteristically occurring in one or another context, and they can watch (and watch for) expressive, kinesic, paralinguistic and organizational indexes; for false starts breakings off, association of themes in verbal speech and slips of the tongue; for clues to fear, irony, doubt, lying, insincerity, and to the gamut of emotions—for all the things, in short, that *give clues about the relation of the speaker to his or her utterances and to his or her culturally prescribed behavior,* clues that are lost in most written records, and that severely limit the psychological information of such records.

This is only to say that the study of mentalities by historians seems particularly difficult, and that the usual tasks of interpretation of historical documents are even more subtle here than it may be for other kinds of historical problems as the losses of critical information are more serious. It is not to argue that the difficulties are fatal, and not at all to argue that the attempt is not of great importance.

On Encounters of History and Anthropology with Psychology and Psychoanalysis: The Problem of Borrowed Theory

The quest for a comparative history of mind must work with faint clues under the distorting pressures of ideology and with an often uncertain methodology. This difficult enterprise would be strengthened if the study of individual cases became steps toward a comparative theoretical inquiry, if local phenomena were brought into an encounter with some empirically grounded theory. There would then be some working basis for an interpretation and evaluation of faint clues, an enterprise to be ideally restrained by the sorts of necessary self-consciousness we have urged. One needs a theory, no matter how modest, of mentalities in regard to something, no matter what, encompassing both the historians' processes of change and the anthropologists' "synchronic" dynamic order.

Theories seem to be close at hand in the neighboring "sciences of mind," but the borrowing of models and problems from those fields lead to the familiar interdisciplinary problems—the encounter of different languages, different ideologies, and different imperialisms. There is also the temptation to overestimate the accomplishments, the confidence, the superior sophistication of the other field. There is the further danger when one makes use of a neighbor's theoretical and methodological tools and their substantive propositions that one is giving up what the scientist or scholar (as opposed, say, to the physician, engineer or other technician) does (or should do), that is, the correction and modification of received theory in the face of data as well as the passive use of theory in ordering data. In the use of borrowed theory there is a danger that the productive readjustment of *both* data and theory is thrown off. It is difficult to challenge and change borrowed theory, one simply applies it. If one does stumble across a challenge to *their* theory, or even if one comes to understand something they do not and are puzzled about—the chances of being heard, let alone having any effect across boundaries, is minute. One needs, in short, just the right amount of arrogance in the face of these neighbors. They provide tools of be used, not shrines for worship.

The investigation of the relations among history, community, and mental matters depends radically on whose purposes are to be served. There are two very different modes of relation of history and anthropology to the theories and data of the mental disciplines. First, the other times and spaces which the historian or anthropologist knows about may be used to test or validate neighbors' hypotheses, in an attempt to show the parameters within which their data and conceptions hold. This produces, say, "comparative psychology," "comparative psychiatry," "comparative cognitive theory," or (try this on your local Psychoanalytic Institute) "comparative psychoanalysis." This mode is the loan of the space or time one "controls" (and often some of one's own time) to these disciplines. The second mode is, ideally at least, quite different. This is the use of selected tools, ideas, and data from these neighboring fields for one's *own* purposes towards the construction of a psychiatric *anthropology* or psychiatric *history,* a psychological *anthropology* or psychological *history,* and so on. Here we bring aspects of mind, or thought, or psychodynamic organization, or psychopathology into intimate relation with some theory of aspects of place and time. It is essential to note that for these special purposes the categories and kinds of relevant mental phenomena (what concerns us about thinking, feeling, moral controls, mental breakdown, psychodynamic structure, or whatever) *may* (to take a particularly vulnerable example) be different from those dear to, say, the latest edition of the *Diagnostic and Statistical Manual* of the American Psychiatric Association.

Academic psychology, for example, has its own more or less covert assumptions about what mind is, how it is bounded and separated from nonmind, how it must be measured, its own ideas about valid and reliable statements. All this has lead to its successes and limitations. Whatever their strictures about our data's replicability and our claims for its validity, our (for the crypto-Compteans still in their midst) metaphysics versus their positive knowledge, we must at the very least remember that we glimpse clues to aspects of mind which their discipline prevents them from seeing or remembering. Most historians and anthropologists, of course, study the structure and dynamics of a limited number of cases, not very large abstracted statistically treatable universes of "comparable data." The psychologists, insofar as they are experimentalists, can only deal with certain sorts of problems, those which may be illuminated by comparatively large numbers of what they take to be equivalent or replicable examples, made equivalent, often, by means of a considerable and often rather violent simplification. The mind we are concerned with is not the same mind, necessarily, as theirs, our methods are necessarily different, we play a different game. We can, at best, interchange suggestions and hunches.

Another even more troubling neighbor is psychoanalysis, converging as it does in some of its concerns on many of the issues concerning historians and anthropologists interested in the historical and contextual aspects of mind. Its insistence on self-knowledge, on the investigation of detail, on the treatment of surfaces as clues to structure and process; its sensitivity to the dynamics of conflict, defense, and unstable compromise; its emphasis on passion and on the economics of "energy"; its attention to the personal uses of symbol and of culture and of social structure; its sense of breakdown as an important clue to structure; its sense of the case; its sense of residues of the past in the present; its sense of the complex relations between what can be directly known and said and what acts in mute shadow and can only be deduced—all this is the summation and elaboration of some of the peripheralized concerns of the proceeding two or three centuries and an enrichment of them in a major offering to Western culture. It is full of useful methodologies, techniques, and ideas for the consideration of minds in different times and spaces, which we make use of both consciously—giving credit—and as part of our naturalized commonsense assumptions.

But something went complicatedly wrong within the psychoanalytic profession itself and in the dialogue between psychoanalysis and the social, historical, and literary disciplines. The official psychoanalytic enterprise has to a considerable degree—with due respect to the periodic reinvention of ego and self theories and therapies—fossilized. This has much to do with the peculiar institutionalization of the "psychoanalytic movement," the kind of commodity and weapon that its theory and practice became. In the psychoanalytic institutes there was often a split between humble clinicians whose interests were primarily therapeutic and the defenders of the movement who often controlled the institutions, their training of candidates and their general educational functions. Psychoanalysis lost its early force as a relatively open investigatory strategy, a procedure which not only called attention to previously neglected phenomena but used such phenomena and the problems in investigating them for ongoing and repeated corrections of theory.[20] It became involved internally and in the hands of at least some of its Freudian followers in the social sciences and humanities in a battle for the defense of its in-group defining shibboleths. The defenders of psychoanalytic orthodoxy use a canon carefully selected among Freud's work, ignoring

the embarrassing and deviant texts as well as the open-ended investiga-
tive implications of some of Freud's early clinical papers—treating the
later as hallowed steps in the development of the final theory rather than
as a model for continuing theoretical change.

The problems such an unreconstructed psychoanalysis poses for comparative mental history and anthropology are diverse. Here are some
examples. The medical emphasis on the closed and bounded "personalities" of patients, equivalent to the concern of physicians dealing with
organic disease with similarly bounded "bodies," creates problems when
the model is exported into inquiries about community and mind. In the
various traditional personality theories the open, mobile, context-
embedded aspects of mind are played down, as are those aspects of mind
which only arise or exist in complex interactions, emerging among as
well as within interacting people.

The classical model forces the consideration of the ways history and
community and culture are held to affect individuals and individual
minds into some much too simple channels—superego, the local shaping
of drives, the cognitive content of the mind unproblematically representing an "external reality" which the "mature ego" somehow "under-
stands" perfectly in some species-wide way but distorts for its motivated
purposes.

The psychoanalytic model is, as has often been pointed out, biased by
its origin in the study of neurotics. For neurosis can almost be defined as
the inflexible determination of behavior by a rigid and "deeply internalized" psychodynamic structure of remote origin, rather than by the
mobile interplay of a situation and a more flexible and open kind of
mind. The generalization of this bias contributes an a priori sensitivity
towards privileging the influences of childhood experience and its resulting "internalized" psychic structure in the explanation of differences in
behavior. And (a related difficulty) with all its emphasis on early experience classical psychoanalysis did not have any developed theory of individual learning (let alone of cultural learning) although it has a very
important theory of development. (Recall that the embryo, an influential
model for Freud, develops but does not learn anything from the variable
aspects of its environment except that that environment is *adequate* for
ontogenesis.)

Finally, the psychoanalytic enterprise in its search for a solid ground
of human, species-wide universals tends to ascribe shallow import to the
differential effect of history and community on mind, although it has
had much to say about the universal mental forms which history has
had, presumptively, to take account of.

In short, the historian or anthropologist is left again with the difficult task of demystifying and making selective use of psychoanalysis as he would any other set of ideas and tools he wishes to use. Psychoanalysis, whatever its claims to universality, like all the mental sciences is limited not only by its historical and institutional context but by its purposes. We must be open to the possibility, as with all the mental sciences, that what we might see and have to attend to in our historical and spatial quests may be aspects of mind different from those psychoanalysis tried to deal with, aspects of mind calling for their own theoretical articulations.

And more than irrelevance is at issue, for insofar as the issues, variables, and universals of the other mental disciplines are selected so that they resist being sensitive to what they take to be the *accidental* contingencies of time and space, they are specifically shaped to be problematic for our enterprise.

On Where to Look for Mind

Let us turn from problems in the use of neighboring disciplines to some of the problems shared by historians and anthropologists in their particular ways of considering mind. *Where* should we look for clues to "the mental"? One area, of course, is in the realm of the *private*. We have recently been reminded that the nature and extent of this realm is an important historical as well as spatial variable.[21] Any direct and simple equation of "private" and "psychological" is, of course, problematic, but forms of privacy, the structure of relations between (relatively) public and (relatively) intimate worlds surely affect in some differential and fairly regular way such "psychological" phenomena as the internal structure of moral controls, aspects of emotionality, of self, of defensive and adaptational mechanisms, of motives and the like. A consideration of what is learned and taught at different levels of the local public-private hierarchy, the conjunctions and disjunctions of private and public modes of instruction and of educational tasks, would be equally revealing.

The question of the relation of psychological matters—mind, self, personality or whatever—to the patterns of relation of public and private spheres is another way of phrasing the question of the relation of *outer* and *inner* lives, something which was at the center of those early ideological positions on the relation of the other's—the native's, the savage's—curious *behavior* to his *being*. We do know from our own private experience that the relation of dancer to dance (in Yeats's exact formulation) varies for each of us from moment to moment, from situation to situation.

O chestnut-tree, great-rooted blossomer,
Are you the leaf, the blossom or the bole?
O body swayed to music, O brightening glance,
How can we know the dancer from the dance?[22]

A once seductive claim that act and actor, natural and supernatural, thought and object were condensed among the primitive in a mystical participation in the world and the allied conception of a primitive ego (shared by dreamers, psychotics, the brain-damaged, infants, and savages) in which there was no distance between inner and outer, is—for savages at the very least—our own dream.[23] But its opposite, the idea of the self-conscious dancer always doing (instead of being) the dance for his or her own utilitarian, calculating purposes is a counter-dream. An intriguing documentary film, *Holy Ghost People,* of a meeting in West Virginia in the 1940s of the poor-white members of a poisonous-snake handling, Pentacostal group shows people who are possessed by the Holy Spirit, speaking in tongues and undergoing classical "hysterical" epileptoid convulsions. Among them is one man, at least, who (at least to my certain conviction) unable to become possessed is dancing around *pretending* to be possessed. The others, in contrast, are—whatever this may mean—not pretending. We have the difficult but possible task of seeing how in different epochs, in different places, and in the microscopic shifts in the ongoing life of a community, various kinds of dancers and their various kinds of dances are joined. This is an important task, for the way dancer and dance are joined is significant for what happened, or is going to happen, next. The question of dancer and dance is very closely related to the sociocultural and historical conditions for different forms of consciousness and of self-consciousness. Hamlet, if we may give him life, and Lawrence Olivier as Hamlet have rather different kinds of awareness of their acts, although the differences are hardly simple.

Another of the ways that one is tempted to go from public forms to private mind is via the symbolic forms of community life.[24] Such forms, and not, say, economic and subsistence activities, were taken in conjunction with the idea of *projective culture,* as being—as dreams were for individuals—royal roads to ethnic unconsciousness. There was an ideological undercurrent here. For the very use of symbolic thought seemed to enlightenment types to imply an inferior mode of thought, a prejudice which has strong echoes in psychoanalytic theory. "If we follow the formation of symbols in the course of evolution," wrote Herbert Silberer in a psychoanalytic journal in 1911, "we find that they appear when

man's mind reaches out for something which he cannot as yet grasp."
The next sentence insures the evaluation. "Symbols come about also
when a once greater power to grasp is decreased in the dream or in
mental disorder."[25]

But what does any culturally organized symbolic activity tell us about
any particular actor's mentality. Not much in itself without considerable
further description. This seems to be a problem similar to the one behind
Stuart Clark's remark, that "in advance of findings about the . . . significance [of beliefs and practices] for agents it is not clear that labels such
as 'religious' or 'magical' refer to any actual historical entities" and his
caution about placing a retroactive interpretation on such behaviors.[26]
But how are we to know the significance of such behaviors for agents?
For one thing we need as much context as possible, descriptions of
associated and relevant behaviors of various different kinds. For another
we need some kind of theory to force our "facts"—more accurately our
clues—to speak to something beyond themselves, to give us some ground
for nurturing them or being suspicious of them, to tell us whether or not
they are relevant.

Theory requires some sort of classification of events, some kind of
typology. We will soon return to theory and typologies, but we may
introduce here—to be put to some further use below—a rudimentary
typology of symbols as *marked* and *embedded* ones. In recent extensions
of the idea a "symbol" may be anything, porridge and cathedrals, papa
and Jehovah, lumped into one category of signification with often obscure reference. I have found it useful to distinguish a sort of symbolism
which is *marked* and set off from ordinary banal common sense and
mundane experience as special, dramatic, and compelling forms, which,
so to speak, call attention to themselves, from another sort of symbolism
which is *embedded*, that is trivialized, naturalized, and blended into the
ordinary course of life.[27] The second is present as a general mode everywhere, the first effloresces and is put to certain specific kinds of personal
and communal use under certain historic and sociocultural conditions.

If the marked symbolic behavior characteristic of a time or a community
is taken as being more than and often different from the direct expression of individuals' inner needs, what are its social uses? Historians,
among others, seem to hesitate about this. Robin Lane Fox talking about
pagan "cult acts" writes, "the older, nineteenth century view that the
ceremonies themselves had created . . . [a specific urban social] order,
defining the members of a family, the citizens of a city, and the orders of
its 'guilds' and corporations, is no longer convincing: cults alone did not
define these groups, although they did sustain and give them a public

expression."[28] A few pages earlier in the same book Lane Fox also states that "processions and festivals did not 'legitimate' or 'justify' the pre-eminence of the leading notables. . . . Implicitly, however, they rein-forced it: *we should remember how even the bigger cities were remark-ably underpoliced*"[29] (emphasis added). If festivals are associated in some causal way with "remarkable underpolicing" they are doing some-thing important. In distancing himself from the nineteenth century, Lane Fox seems to want to limit an explanation of such powerful ordering to some "emotional" rather than "intellectual" function. He is probably wrong.

If symbolic forms have, say, for the last pagans a socially ordering force, once again we have the need for differentiating questions. Under what social, historical, and communal conditions do dramatic symbolic forms effloresce (for they are always around), what do they do, and how do they work on and for individuals in the community to produce, if they do, social order or orderly change? And, perhaps less obvious a question, do the conditions of a certain time and place produce individ-uals whose minds are so constituted that they *need* and attend particu-larly closely to such symbolic forms, so that their mental peculiarities must be allied to the socio-cultural and historical context as part of an explanation of the extent and nature of the symbolic order?

The Need for Theory: Typologies

The problematic, dimly glimpsed, and slippery realities out there, the possible clues to comparative mind in historical residues and in the more accessible vivid collective forms and individual behaviors of people in contemporary communities do not speak for themselves. They must be chosen, interpreted, and made to speak out in continuing interaction with some theoretical approach, one which is somehow proper to mind in interrelation with history, space, community.

When, for example, we look at the materials in some historical efflo-rescence of diaries or of letters for clues to their writers' minds we must remind ourselves that it is precisely the transformations of mentality which are connected with literacy and diaries, the reciprocal causal relations between aspects of mental being and the availability and use of these forms that may well be most centrally important. It is not only what is in diaries that is interesting, but *why* diaries, why now, who produces them, and to what effect? What kinds of social and mental events have occurred (and why) to make diaries now useful and, per-haps, commonplace? Such an approach to literary *forms* is useful for the decipherment of particular examples, and as such indispensable for what

I take to be a productive sort of mental history.[30] That is, we should be interested not only in the history of some favored aspect of mind, but in a larger slice in which the delineation of psychological phenomena is an important element in the understanding of historical processes—in part explained by them, in part explaining them. This is the implication of a psychological *history* or psychological *anthropology* rather than a historical *psychology*, and so on.

We need a working set of possibilities. What are the particular aspects of mind, kinds of actors, sorts of historical and communal situations which may prove to be interdependent? *Interdependent* implies some kinds of necessity and the possibility of some kind of explanation.

My own studies of Tahitians and Newars suggest discernable and interesting differences between aspects of such mental sorts of things as (of course) cognitive "contents" (what people know) and cognitive processes (the way they think); of personal as well as communal forms of moral ordering; of structures of, as well as the more obvious differences in doctrine about, selves; of favored defense mechanisms; of ways of putting or keeping things out of awareness, and thus differences in aspects of unconscious content and processes; of people's sense of the relation of what they think they perceive to what they believe they know—that is, their unreflective epistemology—and thus (in one sense of the word) consciousness. All this and more varies in different kinds of communities, and seems to vary not just as the infinite (albeit within firm limits) possibilities of cultural invention, but in some regular, understandable, and explicable way. Or to put it more modestly, one senses that this is the way a member of this particular community *has* to be (in such and such aspects) if he or she lives, learns, and interacts with others in a place like this—or in his or her particular differentiated position in a place like this. And, conversely, these particular aspects of this sort of place are the way they *must* be if such kinds of people live here.

"A place like this," "such kinds of people" require that we come to terms with "kinds of places" and "kinds of times" as well as "kinds of people." We need a working set of types and a working taxonomy suggesting the relations and implications of those types.[31] This, as the earlier comments on middle-grounds should have made clear, is not to urge the substitution of a search for abstract and pale laws for richness of description and for the "clinical analysis" of each particular case, but to add a shifting (and potentially unlimited) variety of guiding theoretical considerations to the uses and understanding of each case.

The making of typologies in the *sciences humaines* is vulnerable to all the sorts of ideological misuses and methodological tangles we have been discussing. But there do seem to be in the flow of time interesting sorts of momentary—sometimes very long moments indeed—resting places, pools in the river. And these resting places are not infinitely varied. In regard to certain characteristics, at least, they seem to represent a limited number of discrete types. There are, for example, stable sets of typical sizes, of kinds of relations with the environment, of kinship organization, of social ordering, and of other more elusive ways of being, which in some sense seem "comfortable" for the ordering of the lives of communities and their inhabitants. The transitions from membership in one such resting place to another seem to be—and to be felt by their inhabitants to be—disorderly, unstable, and accompanied by a consciousness of not knowing what the future will be like, or of having to get somewhere else in a hurry, or of making progress and having the excitement of becoming, or of a sense of falling back with involutional regrets.

I will presently make use of two communities in Tahiti and Nepal to illustrate what I take to be some of the theoretically interesting typological characteristics of the two communities and their people, to suggest how kinds of places and kinds of minds may be correlated. But first a final excursion, this time some remarks on comparative time and comparative breakdown.

Ways of Being in Time

One significant and indeed fateful comparative difference in mentalities on the frontier between the concerns of history and anthropology is in local orientations to time itself. Different stances towards change and stillness are not only those vaunted oppositions, of, say, historians and anthropologists, with their sense of progress or decay or at least adventure on the one hand, and of Edenic, cool societies free of time on the other. Different communities or cohorts among their members not only *think* differently about "history" but seem clearly to *be* in history, in time, in different ways. Not to take this into account is to risk positing a fiction of an "historical man" similar to the economists' reified universal "economic man" that so distorts the economic analysis of the Third World. South Asians traditionally (and still in Bhaktapur), constantly edit linear temporal processes into an annual cyclical *eternal return,* constantly struggle to change change into a preexisting *structure,* and in so doing are often successful in their attempts to make change illusory and to forestall it. Bhaktapur was able some centuries ago to construct elegant spatial, social, artistic, and ceremonial urban forms and to begin a long-lasting, stately, endlessly reprised dramatic performance in a struggle to convince itself that it was finally out of history and at rest.

This influenced, in fact, as similar stances did throughout all South Asia, its "real" history. History played itself out differentially over the various South Seas Islands, not only because of differences in what Europeans and Americans were trying to do to them, and because of their preexisting social forms, their preadaptations to contacts with *their* others (the subject of once-popular "acculturation" studies), but also because of their different kinds of mentalities, because of what they thought and felt was going on. I was always struck at how when Tahitian villagers did better than they had expected in, say, fishing or horticulture, they would take it as an accident, an unexpected windfall, not (like the kind of ambitious, change-creating people I had come from) as the urgent and exciting stimulus for an optimistic search for new techniques in the service of a newly augmented goal, the establishment of a new norm to be expected and consistently reproduced. How you think and feel about change and stasis (note the pejorative tone for us of the latter term) and how your "psychodynamic structure" of moral controls, defense mechanisms, unconscious content and so on induces you to respond to them,[32] derives from what has happened to you over a rather long past and in turn affects what is going to happen to you in the immediate and extended future. It determines what you take to be a problem, what a victory, what a call for action, whom one looks to for advice and leadership. There are clearly more ways of being in history, of having history, or actively sharing, resisting, modifying the effects of time, than are suggested by the dichotomous characterization of societies into static versus change, cold versus hot. Many anthropologists are becoming interested in both local concepts of history and their outcome. A history and anthropology of mentalities can take this further in a search for the various psychological phenomena, the aspects of mental and personality organization, which are significant for different ways of actually being in history and ask what causes them to arise and what are their exact consequences.

Pathologies of Different Times and Places

Another typological possibility for the study of mind and its context is "pathology," clues to structure from the way things fall apart, a familiar medical tactic borrowed by Freud as the justification for the investigation of psychopathology in a quest for "normal" structures. The humanistic wing of contemporary consciousness worries about the misuse of "pathology" as an excuse for mystified evaluations at the service of one or another motive of power. But one can discipline the idea by using the once-familiar tactic of agreeing to agree more or less rigorously on some idea of minimal functional requirements for various kinds of social units—things like producing and distributing food, educating children to carry on the life of the community, creating basic conditions for sanity—and agreeing that if they are not fulfilled the unit is somehow "pathological," that it does not work right. (The biologists' problem in defining pathology is much simpler. They have the advantage of being able to use death as a rhetorical figure.)

If we entertain the possibility of some sort of "transcultural" or "metacultural" judgment then we should distinguish the idea of a "pathological" society or culture or period from the related idea of a "pathogenic" one. The term *pathological culture* (society, period, and the like) emphasizes the disturbances in the system or level under consideration in itself. A *pathogenic* one is one which produces problems of some sort in some other system. If that other system is the bodies or minds of individuals then the bodies or minds affected may include most[33] or, in some cases, some special category of individuals, who are, as the Public Health people would put it, at risk. If those individuals are sufficiently isolated, the pathogenic process may keep the culture as a whole "healthy" in itself, in analogy to the way the walled off infection in a boil may allow the rest of the body to remain healthy. One can infer pathology in a community even without obvious disorder among individuals in the presence, of some marked rigidity and of costly social defenses erected, consciously or not, against the production of or the effects of individual disorders.

As we are interested in mentalities, it is specifically psychopathology and the effects of community life mediated to the body via mind which may be of interest for an elucidation of comparative mental phenomena. There is a sprawling field or fields of variously called comparative-, transcultural-, or social-psychiatry, whose activities have waned in recent decades after a large efflorescence in the 1950s and 1960s.[34]

There seem to be (to pursue the question of mind in its social context) some psychopathologies which may characterize *any* extensive social disorder, anywhere in space and time, and others which seem to be the characteristic implications of *particular types* of sociocultural order. Extensive disorder, anomie, seems to be very generally associated with unbound anxiety—raw fear—and its consequences. Unbound anxiety means not only that people are chronically afraid because the sociocultural order is not working properly, but also that the sociocultural devices for dealing with that fear, for "binding" it, are inadequate. The consequence is "psychophysiological stress," which includes not only the experience of fear, but its bodily consequences in sleep disturbances, gastrointestinal disturbances, dry mouths and various other vegetative nervous system discomforts and, probably, greater vulnerability to some kinds of diseases.[35] All this is so uncomfortably familiar and banal in our experience of the contemporary world that we hardly think of it as a correlation of mentality and history. This is the stress which "revitalization movements" and a wide range of dramatic political and social and religious movements arise to assuage, in competition with other competing forms of folk self-treatment—drugs, alcoholism,[36] and other cures which (like many of the social movements) generate their own pathologies, to the great anxiety of those on the borders of the waste land.

If considerable psychophysiological stress is an index of any kind of extensive historical and social disorder there are other kinds of psychopathology which may be characteristic of particular sorts of historical periods and social orders.[37] Depression and hysteria are of interest here, and so are aspects of the mysterious schizophrenias.[38]

Kinds of Places and Kinds of People: A Tahitian Village and a Nepalese City

The first non-Western community I studied, Piri, was small, insular, nonliterate for the most part (although the people could read and write for some limited purposes),[39] Polynesian, with a subsistence economy based on horticulture and fishing. I chose for a contrasting study Bhaktapur, a city in Nepal's Kathmandu Valley. Bhaktapur was a sort of sacred city,[40] literate for millennia, continental, a significant center of Newar culture (a little-known, South Asian high culture), rich by premodern standards, with wealth based on highly productive year-round agricultural production in irrigated and terraced fields. From the fourth century A.D. a high culture made possible by the Valley's wealth began to effloresce (See the Appendix for notes on the history of the Newars.)

In the autumn of 1962 Piri, the Tahitian village, had about 284 people living in fifty-four for the most part thatched-roof houses constructed of wooden planks and bamboo. Bhaktapur in 1973 had more than 40,000 people living for the most part in often elaborately embellished four-story, brick, tile-roofed houses in an area of about one-third of a square mile, with, thus, an astonishing density of more than 100,000 people per square mile within its built-up urban area. Astonishing to those who know the city not only because its density is enormously high on a world scale, but because the city does not seem crowded. The population, their settlement and their movements is distributed through the city's space and time so that—in contrast to say downtown New York or Calcutta (both cities with less overall population density)—there is no disorderly massing except on the occasion of certain city festivals, when such massing is one of the points of the festival. The distribution of people is one of many indications of Bhaktapur's extensive order.

Shortly after arriving in Bhaktapur I was standing in one of its extraordinarily ornate squares with an acquaintance. We saw a middle-aged man strike a boy near him, and yell something. "Who is that," I asked my friend, "and why did he do that?" My friend, a leading Brahman priest and civic leader in Bhaktapur, did not know the answer to either question. I suddenly realized that I was surrounded by a quite different sort of order from that of Piri.

The order of a tiny relatively isolated and largely self-sufficient place like Piri where everyone knows everyone else is largely built out of a shaping of common sense and common moral understandings, shapings which are continuously rehearsed, experienced and enforced in the face-to-face theatrics of the tiny community—where even things going on inside the huts can be publicly heard. I had tried to portray the structure of that locally constructed village reality, of those local truths which were true because everyone experienced them, as well as the psychological implications of living in such an order. To know who is doing what to whom is the very basis of the maintenance of order.

But this sort of community construction does not work for Bhaktapur. Bhaktapur is too big. Yet Bhaktapur *is* ordered.[41] But what kind of order does Bhaktapur have? How is it created, integrated, maintained? What are the relations of that order to the personal qualities of its people, to their mentalities?

It takes only a few minutes to sense the difference between Kathmandu the intermittently modern, chaotic capital city of Nepal, and Bhaktapur. Bhaktapur is, by most conventional criteria, a city, but it is a city of a certain type. In a valuable paper (and one most stimulating for a theory of communities and their inhabitants) Robert Redfield and Milton Singer attempted to classify types of cities in their relation to "the development, decline, or transformation of culture." Among those types, they delineated one group of cities in which cultural heterogeneity and secularity were of central importance. These are cities in their words, where

> one or both of the following things are true: (1) The prevailing relationships of people and the prevailing common understandings have to do with the technical not the moral order, with administrative regulation, business and technical convenience; (2) these cities are populated by people of diverse cultural origins removed from the

indigenous seats of their cultures. They are cities in which new states of mind, following from these characteristics, are developed and become prominent. The new states of mind are indifferent to or inconsistent with, or supercede or overcome, states of mind associated with local cultures and ancient civilization. The intellectuals of these . . . cities, if any, are intelligentsia rather than literati.[42]

In contrast there is, they argue, a kind of city which they term "administrative-cultural" cities, "which carry forward, develop, elaborate a long-established local culture or civilization. They are cities that convert the folk culture into its civilized dimension." Redfield and Singer claim that the first cities in early civilizations were such cities of "orthogenetic transformation" as they called them, where local culture is carried forward, rather than broken down in the transforming and transcending internal clashes of the secular, heterogeneous, cities familiar to us at least since classic Athens through most of the Western urban history of recent millennia. Bhaktapur is such a city of orthogenetic transformation, in my own terminology an *archaic* city.

Let us sketch Bhaktapur's typological characteristics in its contrasts with, say, village Tahiti on the one hand and modern cities on the other before turning to the implications of those characteristics for the mentality of its citizens. In Bhaktapur, in contrast to the low-key workaday life of Piri, a resource which is used in Piri only on special occasions is greatly elaborated. This is marked symbolism, the kind of symbolism that calls attention to itself as belonging to some special realm, which is isolated from ordinary life by arrangements of space, by special practitioners, special doctrine, and special forms. Extremely compelling and extraordinary symbolic resources of this kind are employed to organize and maintain a very large component of the urban life of Bhaktapur and to engage individuals with it.

Let us take a ballet as a metaphor for the life of Bhaktapur. The bounded city space, a magic circle or mandala in local conception, may be thought of as a minutely marked stage. Beyond the city, in the wings, offstage, is another bordering world, a noncivic world, a nonmoral world, represented by its own proper symbols, ideas, emotions, divinities, and rituals. The civic stage within the city's boundaries is marked out (points, axes, boundaries, nested areas) through imagined divisions imposed on the "real" physical space of the city—concentric circles ringing a royal center; city halves; nine "mandelic" sections bringing into the city and under the city's control the dangerous chaotic but generative powers lying just beyond its borders; bounded neighborhoods acting as villages in the city, arenas for personal communities and moral controls; various kinds of interstitial areas—crossroads and public spaces, with meanings derived from their transcendence of ordinary spatial orderings. Each space is invested with meaning in part through the particular deities who inhabit it and the symbolic enactments grounded in it, and takes further meaning from its relations with other areas and from the semantic possibilities of the kind of space it is. Each space is marked by appropriate gods, shrines, and compulsory ritual activities. The large number of city gods (about forty deities of various kinds) are grouped and differentiated into interrelated sets of profoundly meaningful "signs," such as can only be provided by a polytheistic pantheon and can only be put to use when concretely embodied in discrete "idols." Most roles in the civic ballet are assigned to the city's inhabitants through descent, not through personal achievement. There are more than three hundred clanlike units which in large part determine what ritual and occupational roles their members will play in the city. These are ranked in some twenty or so status levels, in a hierarchy of statuses from king and Brahman to untouchable.

The flow of time, the temporal aspect of the ballet's score, is marked off so as to bring each actor on stage to witness or to take part in various performances—performances which are traditionally located in specific significant spaces and centered on specific deities. The annual calendar marks time in more than eighty festivals, many of great complexity. These constitute the annual round during which each division of space and of the social system is systematically enacted and interrelated and during which many intellectual and emotional responses useful to the order and well-being of the city are evoked in its citizens. Another sort of tempo is ordered by the rites of passage determined by the sequence of the life cycle—birth, maturation, menstruation, marriage, and so on, providing a dozen occasions during life, and a large number on dying and after death which insure the encounter of actor, space, time, and symbol in the city dance. Still another kind of time and another tempo, astrological time, is used to coordinate decision and chance into the system. Distributed by status, time, and space, minutely prescribed ritual enactments insure individuals' encounters with extremely powerful marked symbols, for example, blood sacrifice, demonic female figures, and a wide range of other such archetypical symbols which derive their canonic meaning from, for the most part, the South Asian Hindu tradition. The personal power of these forms for people in Bhaktapur is based in part on presumably pan-human "response tendencies," in part on specific features of Newar education and early experience, and in part on their location in a context of other symbolic forms.[43] All combine in a complex ongoing performance which is aesthetically compelling, continuously instructive, a dance of civic order. If one knows what a person's surname (the designator of his or her clan) is, his or her age and sex, what day of the lunar calendar (for some purposes, the solar calendar) it is, and where the person lives in Bhaktapur, one has a good chance of knowing where he or she is, what he or she is doing, what he or she is learning or reaffirming, and something of what he or she is experiencing in his or her private mind.

This should serve to suggest that the conditions of life in Bhaktapur are different both from Piri and from Brooklyn where I was born. And, if we are to follow the suggestions of Redfield and Singer, we may reiterate the proposal that Bhaktapur (like Piri and like Brooklyn) may be in these and other features a representative type of historical community and would contrast—in those particular features—with other types.

But what about mentalities? The argument is that not only are Piri and Bhaktapur different kinds of places but that their citizens tend to be different because they live where they do.

How does one know where one is and who one is in such a place as Bhaktapur? The coherent shaping of local reality which pervades the life of Piri provides one component of organizing importance in the life of households and to some degree of neighborhoods. But the understanding derived from the structured face-to-face interactions of small groups is complexly related in Bhaktapur to people's experience in the city's larger order, which sometimes supports it and sometimes opposes it. The intimately shaped small world generates one aspect of common sense—but experience in the larger world of the city will transform that common sense. That larger world is, we have asserted, controlled and made coherent not through laws and and the relatively unmediated effects of politics and economics (as is the larger world of Brooklyn), but through dramatic symbolic forms and enactments.

There are striking differences in discourse and behavior in Bhaktapur and Piri (including *discourse behavior*, the significant forms within discourse) bearing on "mind" and "personality." Let me give an example first of how one elicits such discourse, and in so doing introduce a matter of importance in the private responses of people in Bhaktapur. Everywhere in Bhaktapur there is blood sacrifice. One can witness it and ask informants to describe it. Certain aspects of its cultural form are striking. Blood sacrifice is mostly a matter of male animals being sacrificed to very frightening autonomous female goddesses. The sacrificial animal is consumed by an extended family group, along with alcoholic beverages. And everyone has a great time, one kind of great time, at least.

Once there were, in fact, also human sacrifices. The particular component of the pantheon which may and must be given blood sacrifices consists of anthropomorphic but inhuman deities which are placed and made use of in a special way. These particular deities represent the *outside* forces—outside of the ordinary life of the city and the ordinary self of its citizens—forces whose control is necessary for the maintenance and protection of the ongoing inner moral life of the bounded city, a moral life which has its own set of gods. These internal civic gods are, in contrast to the gods of the outside, idealized social actors. Among them the male deities are dominant, the goddesses among them being the properly subordinated consorts of those male deities. To offer these familiar neighbors blood sacrifice would be a sacrilege.

There are all kinds of echoes of dream, of the unconscious, of universal mythology and cult here and these echoes give clues to the personal meanings of these forms. But one can augment these useful echoes by shifting gears, by asking one's informant: "What do you *really* feel about sacrifice?" "What did you think and feel about it as a child?" "Did your feelings change as you grew up?" "How?" The *informant* about cultural forms now becomes a *respondent*, a subject for the study of the embodiment of community experience in himself or herself. "I loved the goats. We kept them in the house." "I could feel the knife against my own throat." "I thought if the adults did that to them, and they ever got mad at me, what might they do to me." And:

> I used to think the adults were hypocrites and liars. They pretended
> the gods wanted the sacrifice and that the animals would go to heaven
> ... but they just used the ritual as an excuse for a feast. They were
> just murderers. . . . But as I grew up [and went through certain rites of
> passage at the entrance to adulthood] I came to understand.

Such respondents came, in short, to make a commitment of faith to the city system of meanings which they had previously felt to be hypocritical, counter to common sense. They assented to the sacred mysteries, that is to the community of faith which defined them as citizens of such an archaic city—under the pressure, in part, of sacrifice itself. They had to choose, of course, to be a sacrificer in solidarity with other citizens or risk becoming a sacrificial animal.

The city needs this adherence to its system of marked symbols, for that is how it builds its community. But so do its citizens. In a mutual interaction the city's mode of integration produces problems, personal psychological problems, which that mode of integration then seems to solve. Such tautologies are the stuff of stability.

· · ·

Tahitian response to the question "Who are you?" is puzzlement at the question, although the nature of the Tahitian self can be deduced from other kinds of discourse and action.[44] The same question asked of a Newar elicits self-conscious analysis.

Newar informants were liable to say that the question of self was an interesting problem for them, that they had discussed it with their friends. They then went on to define themselves self-consciously in terms of relationships, of occupation, of descent, in terms of conflicting definitions that various segments of society hold about them, all in motion, dependent on context. As one respondent answered,

> There is a saying in the Gita, I do not know it by heart, the verse where Krishna talked to Arjuna, but I understand the meaning of what he said. He said that he [Krishna] was everything *other*. And so, to a great extent, it seems that I am everything other also, because whenever I cook, I am a cook; whenever I love some girl, I am a lover; whenever I have a son or a daughter, I am a parent, I am a father; whenever I am with my father, I am a son; whenever I am alone with a friend, I am a friend; whenever I am with foes, I am an enemy.

Note here that self is a problem; it is a problem which has been consciously and discursively realized; the problem has something to do with a multitude of roles; the "solution" to the problem is phrased in part by reference to literature, religious literature in fact.

I then say something like, "but then who are you," and he says, "I am someone who does all these things well."

Concern with self, self-consciousness, is one kind of heightened awareness. Another is something perhaps more subtle, an awareness of what "culture" does, a personal distance from and a standing against its propositions (or if you prefer a special awareness about "ideology") in contrast to our ideal typical Tahitian who is built of it.

Thus a Newar farmer, pushed on contradictions in his ideological justification for the repression of untouchables (a repression which serves to assure that they will continue to serve their traditional social roles) finally says in exasperation, "If we eat with them, we will lose our whole caste system. We will lose the whole system of hierarchy in our society. And people will be able to do whatever they want, there will be chaos."

There are many examples of this kind of analytic awareness.

A farmer: "Shame and embarrassment must exist everywhere in the world, but, of course, exactly what you feel ashamed and embarrassed about varies."

A member of a moderately high caste: "People accept their caste position not because other people make them but because of their [internal] images of themselves."

A high caste man: "Gods are representative of human feelings and activities."

A potter woman: "Girls cry during their wedding ceremonies because custom requires that they do it."

There is something strange about this high frequency analytic discourse to anthropologists used to the discourse of simpler communities.

Living systematically in an integrated but enormously complex system of shifting and contrasting worlds, citizens of Bhaktapur are forced into an epistemological crisis—forced to the understanding that external reality, as well as self, is constructed, and in some sense illusory, or in the Hindu philosophical expression, *māyā*. They are now in position for a kind of critical analysis which transcends the ideology of their culture, and they become like the Princess Myagky the anthropologist's potential collaborators in analysis, rather than, as in the case of Tahitians, the naive subjects of analysis.[45]

In contrast to village Tahitians, Bhaktapur's Newars are "sophisticated," in its dictionary sense of "altered by education, worldly experience, etc. from natural character or simplicity." If sophistication, taken as the index and result of a profound shift from the conditions which nurtured Tahitian life and mind, characterizes the majority (as I have reason to believe) of the people of Bhaktapur, there is a next step, a *response* to that epistemological shift which has made knowledge problematical, which in turn distinguishes the citizens of Bhaktapur from representative (or ideal) moderns.

For Bhaktapur is precisely as Redfield and Singer characterized the genre, a city of literati and not of intelligentsia. The insights which the above quotations illustrate are generated by the mind working over the contradictions and contrasts in the culturally proffered certitudes of various sectors and phases of a complex culture. Those contradictions and the awareness they generate are potentially subversive to the society, and to the self. Something must be done. The West institutionalized, isolated, and harvested this subversion in certain privileged and eccentric segments of the population as philosophy and as science and its precursors. But Bhaktapur deals with the crisis of analytic awareness by a kind of enchantment, a movement through a leap of faith into a commitment to the extraordinary and fascinating forms of marked symbolism. One can trace in the reminiscences of some individuals about their intellectual development this movement from naiveté, to skeptical sophistication, to a leap into assent to communal religious symbols and postulates after an initial period of doubt, under great emotional pressure towards solidarity (much of it focused and phrased in relation to blood sacrifice). Thoughtful people in Bhaktapur become *addicts* of their culture, literati—in Redfield and Singer's example "clerics, astronomers, theologians, imans, and priests"—rather than critical intelligentsia (a move which would signal the transformation of the city's particular order as well as the minds of its inhabitants), and they are like all literati, precisely, the technicians and consumers of marked symbolism.

In Bhaktapur it has all rested there. An elaborate symbolic system works to make community possible and to bind doubting individuals to the community through compelling, fascinating and mysterious forms. The symbolic system provides an essential chaos-reducing order in the face of doubt, but it reflects a different kind of order, an extraordinary order, different from the ordinary and problematic one which individuals experience at other mental levels.

Afterword

This essay began with an inventory of problems associated with the investigation of—and claims about—the relations of history, community, and human nature (or human natures). It argues that a withdrawal in the face of these problems into atheoretical description, into contemplation and hermeneutic interpretation of the other, although an understandable reaction, is unwarranted. It argues that the enterprise of a theoretically based comparative history and anthropology of those aspects of mind which may turn out to be sensitive to time and community, and to different kinds of times and communities, although a difficult and easily corrupted enterprise is possible.

My remarks on Piri and Bhaktapur, thus, are meant to suggest that there is an interrelation, indeed a causal nexus, between the kinds of communities their inhabitants live in, the kinds of lives they lead and at least some aspects of their minds, and to imply that such interrelations can be generalized beyond these particular communities and used as theoretical probes in the investigation of other places and their inhabitants which, although variously located in time and space, resemble Piri and Bhaktapur and their inhabitants in certain features.

All this, finally, is simply to make the modest proposal that we regain the middle position, that we bring empirical materials, methodological restraint and the construction of theory into balance in the high-stake enterprise of understanding the human experience.

APPENDIX 1. THE KATHMANDU VALLEY AND THE NEWARS

Traditional Nepal was largely confined to the Kathmandu Valley. People of this valley came in time to call their territory Nepal, themselves Newars, and their language Newari. Archaeology has not yet fully clarified their prehistory, but it seems that at an early period (perhaps the eighth or seventh century B.C.) a predominantly Mongoloid, Tibeto-Burman speaking people settled in the valley where they may have encountered an aboriginal population speaking an Austro-Asiatic language. In perhaps the first or second century A.D. a political organization emerged which was to characterize the Kathmandu Valley until the late eighteenth century. A succession of ruling elites, kings and courts of North Indian origin, speaking and writing Sanskrit for sacramental and literary purposes and a Sanskritic North Indian language (a Prakrit) for everyday purposes, were repeatedly and progressively woven into an underlying society and culture with Himalayan and central Asian features. Gradually a new language (Newari) and culture (Newar) synthesizing these elements arose. Although the Sanskrit culture of the priests and court persisted, it became more narrowly concerned with traditional and ceremonial segments of life. Through the centuries more and more of religious, political, literary, social, and daily life was expressed in the Newari language and in Newar forms.

There were dynastic disputes and confusion but the Newars flourished. The valley soil is exceedingly rich, the bed of an ancient lake. A complex system of irrigation—the collection of rainwater through a system of canals on the slopes of the surrounding hills—was inaugurated some time prior to the establishment of the first North Indian dynasty. Rich soil and irrigation permitted highly productive farming. In time the valley found itself on some of the major trade routes between India and Lhasa in Tibet, and trade and services established a series of important cultural and economic interactions among India and the two young and flourishing Himalayan civilizations, and became the basis, along with tolls on the trade routes and rich agriculture, for considerable surplus wealth. This made possible, and was developed through, a sociocultural efflorescence.

Stimulated by Indian ideals, ideas and images throughout a very long period, the Newars began, perhaps from the fourth century A.D., to elaborate their society and culture in urban centers. Three of these, Bhaktapur (founded in the twelfth century), Patan, and Kathmandu, became variously principle or secondary royal centers. They became highly organized, concentrated, bounded (eventually walled) units, each surrounded by a hinterland of farmland and villages. In time the three cities became politically separate. The hinterlands became dependent territories, and three small states developed, each with its central royal city, its king, its particular customs, its dialect. In these Kathmandu Valley cities there was an elaboration of a particular kind of society, culture, and person. This had much to do with Hinduism (in its widest sense as a set of peculiarly South Asian understandings, images and methods), and much to do with the structural necessities and implications of a certain kind of organized urban life.

In the late eighteenth century the Newar kingdoms, divided and inward-looking, fell to the attacks of the armies of the small Indianized mountain state of Gorkha in the western Himalayas. The consolidation of the Gorkhali alliances and conquests defined the territory and state of modern Nepal. The Newars were no longer *the* people of Nepal. They were only one of some (in recent estimates) seventy linguistic and ethnic groups, and a conquered one at that. The Gorkha alliance put its capital at Kathmandu. But Bhaktapur, only eight often muddy miles away from Kathmandu (a long enough distance for those who walked or were carried in palanquins) was left more or less alone. Gorkhali policy, variously motivated, was to encourage Newar traditional life. Bhaktapur ran on in very much the old way, like a clockwork mechanism assembled long ago which no one had bothered to disassemble. The first serious shocks of modernity did not begin until the early 1950s when, following a political revolution, Nepal opened itself to the West. Bhaktapur still ran on for many years in xenophobic, self-protective inertia. But its fragile archaic forms are now more and more rapidly fading into the history the city once tried to hold at bay.

NOTES

1. This essay began as a response to a set of issues proposed by Peter Stearns. It derives from two papers presented separately to the Pittsburgh Symposium on "Social History and Issues in Consciousness and Cognition." I am grateful to Peter and Carol Stearns and several of the conference participants for suggestions and to Helena Lepovitz, Roy Rappaport, and Ann Rappaport for critical readings of a draft of this chapter.

2. It may illuminate the positions and prejudices in this chapter to note that prior to working in anthropology, I was trained in and practiced psychiatry and psychoanalysis.

3. J. C. Beaglehole, *The Journals of Captain James Cook on His Voyages of Discovery*, vol. 1 (Cambridge, 1955), cclxxxiii.

4. A British tract quoted in Roy Harvey Pearce, *Savagism and Civilization* (Baltimore, 1965), 10.

5. Isaiah Berlin's *Vico and Herder* (New York, 1976) and *Against the Current* (Oxford, 1981), are useful for the "counter-enlightenment" roots of social and historical sciences. The best recent treatment of precontemporary anthropology is George Stocking's *Victorian Anthropology* (New York, 1987).

6. On Boas and culture theory in American anthropology see George Stocking, *Race, Culture and Evolution* (New York, 1968).

7. Franz Boas, *Mind of Primitive Man* (New York, 1911), 102–3.

8. It is important to emphasize for the later development of this splitting that Boas in 1911 accepted the assumption of the racial theorists that such "mental characteristics" as "inhibition of impulses," "power of attention," and "power of original thought," would be "hereditary" if they were taken to be qualities of the psychological organization of individual thinkers. Thus he alternatively explained such behaviors as responses of people whose minds—aside from their content—were equivalent, to different sociocultural *situations:* "The proper way to compare the fickleness of the savage and that of the white is to compare their behavior in undertakings which are equally important to each" (Boas, *Mind of Primitive Man,* 107). Adapted from Robert Levy, *Tahitians* (Chicago, 1973), 245.

9. *Notes and Queries on Anthropology,* periodically "revised and rewritten by a committee of the Royal Anthropological Institution of Great Britain and Ireland," six editions (London, 1874–1951).

10. Most of the *extreme* (and thus famous) dichotomized positions in the *sciences humaines* with regard to questions about mind in or versus culture and society seem to me to be evidently ideological. To make matters worse, we have recently been assaulted by American nihilistic naturalizations of French postmodernism which assert in their more intransigent moods that there is nothing else but ideology in the human sciences, that all social analysis, all discourse is in fact the active, ongoing construction of reality out of soft signs at the service of power, not of knowledge. See James Clifford and George Marcus, *Writing Culture: The Poetics and Politics of Ethnography* (Berkeley, 1986).

11. "The middle ground," Isaiah Berlin tells us in an essay on Turgenev (and presumably on himself) "is a notoriously exposed, dangerous, and ungrateful position. The complex position of those who, in the thick of the fight, wish to continue to speak to both sides is often interpreted as softness, trimming, opportunism, cowardice" (The Romanes Lecture 1970, included as an introduction to Turgenev, *Fathers and Sons* [New York, 1975]). The person in the middle of the battles in the *sciences humaines* tends to believe that one can spot ideology from the middle ground when the level of passion is too high, the fit between selected fact and theory is too tight, the countervailing phenomena and ideas too easily dismissed, and when the citation rates and book sales go beyond a certain decent level. He tends to find the partisan positions and *aperçus* useful in stimulating questions about the particular arenas and conditions in which their claims may actually apply (for they are not generally hallucinated out of unsupported fantasy) and in stimulating higher level questions about the sociocultural, historical, and psychological conditions in which such certainties are temporarily held by scholarly proponents, or some other class of people, or by everyone.

12. Derek Freeman, *Margaret Mead and Samoa: The Making and Unmaking of an Anthropological Myth* (Cambridge, Mass., 1983). My contribution to the debate was "The Attack on Mead," *Science* (April 1983), and "Mead, Freeman and Samoa: The Problem of Seeing Things As They Are," *Ethos* 11, no. 1 (1984).

13. *Surely You're Joking, Mr. Feynman* (New York, 1985).

14. Roy Rappaport ("Desecrating the Holy Woman," *The American Scholar* [Summer 1986]) wrote in the course of a long analysis of the moral climate of Mead's work and of Freeman's response that both positions on Samoa were to a considerable degree "myths," and that one should choose among such myths not by their truth, but by their human consequences, and thus he opted for Mead.

15. Edward Sapir, "Culture, Genuine and Spurious," in his *Culture, Language and Personality* (Berkeley, 1957).

16. Gregory Bateson, *Steps to an Ecology of Mind* (New York, 1972), 301–7.

17. *Culture* here is given a boundary, and is used for a subset of traditionally passed-on understandings, those which act specifically as a system of control for producing integrated, adaptive, sane behavior. I have expanded on this in "Emotion, Knowing, and Culture," in *Culture Theory*, eds. Richard Shweder and Robert LeVine (Cambridge, 1984).

18. Lionel Trilling, *Freud and the Crisis of Our Culture* (Boston, 1955), 53–54.

19. Accommodations were eventually attempted by the Freudian left—by such figures as Wilhelm Reich and Herbert Marcuse, by Erich Fromm and other neo-Freudians, and later within mainstream psychoanalysis by Erik Erikson and the ego theorists. But this always seemed—and still seems—to many influential psychoanalysts to be a watering down of the psychoanalytic truth of a costly "biological" resistance to culture and society, a resistance whose implications are not always as bracing as those expressed in Trilling's lecture. A useful essay on the "Freudian Left" is the book of that title by Paul Robinson (New York, 1969). Robinson also treats the once-influential anthropologist Geza Roheim as a member of this group.

20. This shift is in part a reflection of the medical-engineering stance of the medical psychoanalysts themselves, who are characteristically, as they say, "trained" not "educated" and who use the theory and protect it as a warrant for the practitioner's social and professional position. Serious criticism of the theory would threaten to undermine their status, would risk turning them not into innovative and thus respected scientists, but into apostates. And into apostates without any further audience, for an important implication of the institutionalization of psychoanalysis is that radical criticisms have had no effective internal disciplinary audience and are, thus, cranky and unproductive undertakings.

21. As represented for the nonspecialist in, for example, the volumes appearing in the series edited by Philippe Ariès and Georges Duby, *A History of Private Life* (Cambridge, Mass., 1987, 1988).

22. From his poem "Among School Children."

23. One of the most influential statements of this thesis with regard to

primitives (which ultimately contributed to the disrepute of the term itself), was the early work of Lucien Lévy-Bruhl. See, for example, Jean Cazeneuve, *Lucien Lévy-Bruhl* (Oxford, 1972).

24. In an influential formulation attempting to bypass the problem of judgment inherent in treating the relation of dancer and dance, a judgment based in part on something like *empathy,* Clifford Geertz argued that the approach to an "anthropological knowledge of the way natives think, feel, and perceive" should be based not on such empathy but "by searching out and analyzing the symbolic forms—words, images, institutions, behaviors—in terms of which, in each place, people actually represented themselves to themselves and to one another" (" 'From the Native's Point of View,' On the Nature of Anthropological Understanding," *Bulletin of the American Academy of Arts and Sciences* 28, no. 1 [1974]). This is a necessary and powerful aspect of description and analysis and a corrective to an earlier neglect of the constructive power of local systems of representation, but stopping at this point leads to an overestimation of the direct correspondence of the symbolic and intellectual forms of a community to local forms of mind. It follows Boas in emphasizing cultural content and its internal representations as being sufficient to reveal the differential implications of the life of various communities for mind.

25. David Rapaport, ed., *Organization and Pathology of Thought* (New York, 1951), 217. The essay, "On Symbol-Formation," from which the quotation is taken, is translated by Rapaport from Silberer's article "Ueber die Symbolbildung" in *Jahrbuch fuer psychoanalytische Forschungen* 3 (1911): 661–723.

26. Stuart Clark, "French Historians and Early Modern Popular Culture," *Past and Present,* no. 100 (1983).

27. The fundamental orienting Hindu concern with purity and impurity is an example of such naturalized and embedded symbolism.

28. Robin Lane Fox, *Pagans and Christians* (New York, 1986), 89.

29. Ibid., 81.

30. I have approached the problem of the sociocultural placement of horror stories and classical tragedies in "Horror and Tragedy: The Wings and Center of the Moral Stage," *Ethos* 13, no. 2 (Summer 1985).

31. A proposal about a type or a structure is not invalidated directly by particulate counter-examples. We know that gentle friends may get angry. If they do not they are more than gentle—but, rather, compulsive, neurotic or rigid. Their gentleness is not just an ideal type, it describes some quality of their general organization. A criticism of a typological claim has to be at its own level, in terms of what it tries to do.

32. It must be emphasized repeatedly that mind must include more than cognition for our present purposes.

33. This was the case, for example, in some of the worst encounters of Third World communities with imperious outside groups. There is a noteworthy and dramatic study by Ernest Beaglehole of the devastating "pathogenic"—social, mental and physical—effects of missionary rule on most members of a Polyne-

sian community in the Cook Islands, *Social Change in the South Pacific* (New York, 1957).

34. A convenient and important review of studies in comparative psychiatry, with a strong anthropological emphasis, is the quarterly *Transcultural Psychiatric Research Review,* now in its twenty-fifth year, published by McGill University.

35. E.g., E. Beaglehole, *Social Change,* and a large literature in the 1950s and 1960s on the association of community disorders and personal stress. Examples, among many others, are the work of Alexander Leighton and his associates in Nigeria and Nova Scotia (e.g., Dorothea Leighton et al., *The Character of Danger: Psychiatric Symptoms in Selected Communities* [New York, 1963]) and the work of Holmes and Rahe and others on the close association of life crises and consequent disease.

36. Sociocultural and psychological aspects of a wide use of alcohol associated with a dramatic *lack* of alcoholism in Tahiti (compared, say, to Native Americans) is discussed in Levy, *Tahitians.*

37. George Devereux suggested that the prevalent psychopathologies of a group are "model pathologies" which on the one hand reflect the particular psychological organization of normal people in the group, and on the other tend to mold a variety of other problematic behaviors into forms made culturally familiar by the model pathologies (*Basic Problems of Ethnopsychiatry* [Chicago, 1980]). Devereux's large and often idiosyncratic corpus of work is full of interesting proposals about the relations between psychopathology and different kinds of community culture.

38. Robert Levy, "Anthropology as Whose Handmaiden, Comparative Psychiatry or Psychiatric Anthropology?" in *Psychological Anthropology: Appraisal and Prospectus,* eds. Theodore Schwartz and Catherine Lutz (in preparation).

39. Not only is being able to sign one's name not a sufficient index of literacy, but, it can be argued paradoxically, neither is being able to read. That is, the Tahitian villagers had had their oral language transcribed by missionaries. The new written language, which almost all villagers were able to read, was used for many generations only for reading the Bible and other religious texts. This literacy was disconnected from the vast majority of their social concerns and its personal implications for literate individuals seem to have been very limited. On the contrary it is possible to be an illiterate individual in Bhaktapur and to be deeply affected by immersion in a profoundly literate culture. Compare the chapter by Daniel Resnick and Lauren Resnick in this volume.

40. "Sort of sacred city" because the term *sacred city* usually means something else, a religious center for a larger area, and Bhaktapur was a sacred space for, and only for, its own people.

41. I have described Bhaktapur's urban order in *Mesocosm: The Organization of a Hindu City in Nepal* (in preparation). Piri is described and discussed in Levy, *Tahitians* and in various articles.

42. Robert Redfield and Milton Singer, "The Cultural Role of Cities," *Eco-*

nomic Development and Cultural Change 3, no. 1 (October, 1954): 57. Emphasis added.

43. For a detailed analysis of the meanings of a complex ritual form in Bhaktapur see my "How the Navadurgā Protect Bhaktapur. The Effective Meanings of a Symbolic Engagement," in *Heritage of the Kathmandu Valley*, eds. Niels Gutschow and Axel Michaels (Sankt Augustin, Germany, 1987).

44. Levy, *Tahitians*, chapter 7.

45. See Robert Levy, "Mead, Freeman and Samoa: The Problem of Seeing Things as They Are," *Ethos* 11, no. 1 (1984).

— 2 —

A Note on Scholarly Caution in a Period of Revisionism and Interdisciplinarity

John Modell

Consider the arrogance of historians pretending that they can discover the characteristic mental structures of ordinary people in past times and convey these to contemporary readers. The very notion of *mentalities* is filled with definitional problems; evidence reflecting in an unmediated way what other than elites in the past even said, much less thought, is hard to find and harder to interpret; and in order to convey such things a primitivism of the left or of the right is a dangerous rhetorical temptation. And yet the arrogance in trying to do all this—and in claiming that we are doing it, even as we only think that we succeed partially—is the best characteristic of our discipline. We tell the stories that we think others should hear. We own a responsibility for the telling of the story, and at the same time we acknowledge a responsibility to the evidence. Our responsibility to the story allows us, perhaps commands us, to be eclectically responsive to the evolving world of social theory, as theory teaches us all to feel comfortable with, and uncomfortable without, asking new kinds of questions. We proceed iteratively, fitting story to theory to story. This is not displeasing, but it should be scary.

Our rules for responsibility to the evidence are a little fuzzy. Perhaps this is all to the best: perhaps it allows us more readily to fulfill our responsibility to tell the story. But I am not sure. What I am rather sure of, and a concern that *mentalities* raises acutely, is that the kinds of stories that historians believe that people should be told change according to what can accurately be called fashion, the fashions deriving in part from intellectual hungers developed outside history as discipline, and outside history as story. In the case of *mentalities,* these sources include European philosophical (and Marxian) anthropology and literary theory; in the case of the somewhat earlier historiographical fashion which formed my own sensibility (and the crotchets expressed in this essay), demography was the source. But it is not the alienness of such extradisciplinary sources upon which I am commenting here, but rather the urgency with which their categories have proposed new questions for our discipline, and the weakness of the methodological armorium with which our discipline meets this urgency. We have very little codified native wisdom that will indicate whether a given borrowing might be wise or not. We know very well what makes a historical account exciting, but we know far less well what makes it sound. In every discipline there must be a trade-off between reach and grasp, to be sure. But as we make an eager grab for *mentalities,* do we really capture what we describe? Do we do so as well as, say, I think we did when we discussed historical demographies? That personalizes it. To put it more grandiosely: just how does our discipline cumulate?

Historians in the United States have long been receptive to new ways of seeing things, *including those coming from (or centered in) the social sciences.*

> Few observers will deny that generation after generation history is becoming more of a science in the broad sense of the word. The steady accumulation of data, together with our increasing ability to classify and analyze facts bearing upon individual psychology, communal psychology, economic changes, and the growth of institutions and mores, enables us to lay down more "laws" and to do so less tentatively.[1]

But in the last several decades the social sciences themselves have formalized the way they carry on their investigations—first economics, political science, sociology, and the fringe of anthropology, by mathematicizing their methodologies, then anthropology and fringes of political science and sociology, by emphasizing hermeneutic methods. History, however, has on the whole rejected proposals of formalization, being, according to Barzun and Graff, "a piece of work which uses the terms of common discourse and which puts before [the lover of history], at no remove from his everyday mind, a spectacle to be attended simply by reading."[2] But yet, history seems to be as ready as ever to accept our neighbors' good ideas. Do we have a clearcut way by which we judge whether these good ideas blend well with our own? Do those of our disciplinary values and institutional structures that encourage revisionism perhaps also discourage methodological caution?

In the mathematicized social sciences, theoretically central concepts have been dimensionalized—seen to be more or less present in any given circumstances, rather than absolutely present or absent. In the hermeneutic, interpretive social sciences, the relationship between inner thought process and outer symbolic activity, including speech, has been seen as problematic. Historians attracted by the conceptual frameworks of social scientists have been confronted with highly formalized methodologies, said by their practitioners to be integrally related to the theoretical frameworks of those disciplines. What one can know, according to practitioners of these social science disciplines, is inseparable from figuring out how one can know.

Part of the methodological problematics with which social scientists are concerned have to do *with recognizing the presence or absence of the referent of a given concept* in a particular piece of evidence. And part of it has to do with *the combining of single instances of these referents* into appropriate characterizations of the conceptualized phenomenon's significance in a given society at a given time. These are admittedly hard questions for historians to deal with, precisely because of historians' necessarily distinctive relationship to their evidence: we do not make our own evidence, but rather find it, constructed according to the concerns of those we seek to analyze rather than according to our own conceptual frameworks; and we ordinarily cannot choose the distribution of our evidence, having to take it from where, and when, it happens to come. These two characteristics of historical research, it will be recognized, engage the central concerns of social science methodology, and obviously force historians to work with levels of certainty and reliability that are considerably lower than in the social sciences, but indeterminately so. There is simply no way that we can directly apply social science method to the evidence we choose to deal with. But if we did not deal with what evidence we happen to be able to find, we would not be historians. Perhaps these problems are so intractable that historians' methodological optimism is nothing but a sensible adaptation to conditions of great uncertainty. But we care too badly to know, and worry so little about what we actually do know.

The historical profession identifies relatively few discrete skills as requisite, and employs very little disciplinary jargon, apart from what it imports from other disciplines. Historians are good at reading handwriting and at bibliographical recall. We are good at figuring out the structures of loosely organized collections of data, from archives to newspapers, so that the apparently relevant elements can be efficiently extracted from the far higher proportion of dross, and we are good at anticipating what may be worthy of note, before having settled upon either story or conceptualization. We are good at discerning the historiographical thrust and the informational contribution of the secondary literature that we read. Historians are skeptics about any claims to discrete pieces of knowledge, and at the same time treasure even imperfect clues to historical knowledge, as if these were scarce. Our footnotes are the record of these skills in action, reflecting triumphs of organized scanning, collating, evaluating. These diffuse skills are mainly taught through the cultivation of attitudes rather than through explicit training.

When a historian collaborates with a social scientist, the historian asks the social scientist to theorize the historian's accounts, and seeks to discover whether the social scientist's techniques (as distinct from methodologies) include elements that might allow the historian to get something from a set of evidence that he or she knows to exist or already have gathered. The social scientist typically will ask the historian to listen to his or her account of the present, accept its conceptual framework, and tell him or her how the present got to be that way. And he or she sometimes will ask the historian whether there might exist past data sets from which, in the same way that the social scientist already infers things from current materials, the social scientist might learn about the same things in some past—any past—in order to compare it to the present. Historians are not well able, in interdisciplinary settings, to assert their own way of reflecting upon the world, but find it easy to temporarily inhabit those of their interdisciplinary collaborators of the moment. This asymmetry perhaps ought to give us some pause. A more symmetrical relationship might promote greater clarity on our part about what we really need from our partners.

Historians ordinarily understand their disciplinary distinctiveness in terms of a pair of related *perspectives:* an insistence on examining phenomena *in context,* and a strong preference for examining phenomena as they "unfold," not in a "natural history" sense of typical sequences but in particular instances of unfolding. The two in common represent a strong prejudice toward explanations that propose "meaning," seen in terms of synchronically environing phenomena, and of previous "origins" and subsequent "consequences." This is by no means the same thing as seeking to discern determinate sequences, and so it is shallow to say that historians "ought to" have a great deal to contribute to sociology's renewed focus on social change. Rather, it seems to me that (apart from data and archival skills) the historical discipline has to offer to the social sciences:

> a drive toward seeking previously undesignated common causes that might explain part or all of an apparently causal relationship between two phenomena—to search for larger patterns, that is, than social

science theory ordinarily does, using an alternate sense of causality that, if only for heuristic purposes, is looser than the social sciences ordinarily prefer;

and a suspicion that current states are not just entirely comprehensible through a current measurement, but rather must be understood in their *emergent* or *developmental* quality, in comparison with appropriate like measures at prior and subsequent moments.

Historians understand as their charge the imaginative reconstruction of swaths of the past, and their interpretation in categories meaningful to the general education of students and citizens in our own society. We are in effect enjoined to use whatever tools will clarify the past to actors in the present. As John Passmore says of historical explanation, it is nothing more than an exceptionally careful variant of ordinary explanation. And explanations are offered to people who are puzzled.

Being puzzled is a special sort of not knowing, not knowing "what to make of" a situation. The puzzling situation presents characteristics which are, from our point of view, unexpected; it interrupts the smoothness of our dealings with the world. The explanation, if we accept it, gets us moving again. . . . No situation is intrinsically puzzling. It is puzzling only to somebody who has not yet developed particular habits, particular forms of explanation.[3]

And, of course, people will still be puzzled if the explanation offered is too obscure, if it fails to add the right bit *to what they already knew*— and had to know in order to be puzzled by a situation. We are limited in how remarkable are the explanatory mechanisms we use, for they have to be rather comfortable for our audience. They cannot seem to get in the way. The ordinary methodological injunctions in our discipline do not argue against bringing in the interpretive framework of other disciplines, or their techniques, or their questions: we should be eclectic, "just so long as we really understand." And, of course, just so long as our readers will be comfortable with the explanations offered. They should not be too unfamiliar or technical. Thus, Barzun and Graff, surely no friends to the social sciences, make every effort to leave open the barn door to all callers deemed acceptable at the moment, and do so.

The historical method ascertains the truth by means of common sense. When that sense is systematically applied, it becomes a stronger and sharper instrument than is usually found at work in daily life. It shows a closer attention to detail and a stouter hold on consecutiveness and order. The exercise of these capacities turns into a new power by which new intellectual possessions may be acquired. For the historian's common sense must be understood to mean more than common knowledge and the cliches of ordinary thought. Methodical common sense takes in both what is usually known by the well educated and any special information relevant to the historical question being studied.[4]

The catch is, of course, that what is common sense of this sort is dependent upon the way individuals understand how individuals with motives are moved and constrained. Since, however, we also recognize that both the individual and society are imaginative constructs, and that their ongoing redefinition is much of what the social sciences are all about, an unfettered eclecticism constrained only by idiosyncratic, political, or aesthetic criteria seems to trade intellectual control of subject matter not so much for depth of interpretation—as the historical community ordinarily contends—as for a species of evocativeness. As a historian, I like evocativeness. But I wonder whether it is in any way a safe criterion. I wonder if, for instance, mentalities work will not stand or fall precisely to the degree that their exposition can be evocative. And I wonder whether that will not in the end depend more on the methods already used in intellectual history—the apt quotation, for instance— than on the technical hermeneutics appropriate to the explication of the obscure categories of remote cultures. (Closer to home, I confess to regularly favoring cross-tabulation over regression-based techniques of quantitative analysis when I wish to write history, because the former is descriptive, not inferential, in the way it "works.") Will we even employ the methods that best fit the theories we import?

To gain some perspective on how the American historical profession has dealt with innovation in a concrete instance, I examined those reviews that came to hand of a series of books in a "hot" historical field, American Negro slavery. The current generation of historians has successfully and cumulatively incorporated new perspectives on the peculiar institution that depend on different models of man in society, that pose and re-pose the institutional paradox of slavery within democracy the better to deal with contemporary biracialism. And they have done so with no formal—disciplinary—mechanisms for reconciling or even clearly recognizing the radically different notions underlying the successive cumulations of scholarship. The successive contributions have been superb, startling, brilliant scholarship. But their cumulation is left to mechanisms that are either idiosyncratic, political or aesthetic: I do not know which to call them.[5]

I chose from this substantial literature four books that, in the years between the late 1950s and the mid-1970s, were widely seen as having turned a field that was something of a sleepy byway of a somewhat quaint subfield—southern history—into a central question that all historians of the United States must treat. These books that not only challenged the substance of the way American slavery was understood, but did so by bringing new methodological perspectives to bear, perspectives developed by conscious attention to work being done (not on the question of slavery in particular) outside the historical discipline. I looked to historians' *initial* responses in print (whether in professional journals or in publications directed to a larger public) because these rather than ones given several years later would reflect the "standard operating procedure" by which historians confronted the question of how to incorporate the new. I make no effort here to distinguish between those reviews written in historians' professional publications and those written for broader audiences: for historians address broader audiences as an essential part of their work as historians, and there just as when they are addressing one another, the assumptions that bound their sense of "history" appear.

I am not concerned with assessing either American Negro slavery or the historiography that has come to surround it. My approach has been simply to use the reviews as data that presumably reflect historians' professional assumptions. My account is not intended to chart interpretive trends, but as an exposition of analytic tendencies. All I mean to do is to get a sense of what the discipline does when challenged, on a subject matter that it cannot ignore. A case could be made for including reviews of other books than those I examine,[6] and one could certainly make a point of examining the reviews with an eye to chronology, but I am not concerned with either here. My account is only suggestive. Even if professional reviews actually represent the discipline talking seriously to itself (and we may have doubts, for both history books and their reviews speak to several audiences at once), I have not looked systematically enough here. For coherence of research field, I have sacrificed representativeness; for suggestiveness of quotation, I have sacrificed explication of reviews' own inner logics. I have sought to describe overall range and tendency, however, and for this purpose my approach has perhaps been sufficient. And the exploration I carried out has persuaded me that a systematic monitoring of this channel of communication might well produce an excellent outcome.

The historiography can be summarized briefly. The great southern historian, Ulrich B. Phillips, in a series of monographs culminating in *American Negro Slavery* of 1918 put to rest for more than one generation the question of how respectable academic history would treat slavery. Phillips maintained that accounts of brutality toward and brutalization of the slaves were the gloss that biased northern historians had put on a view of slavery propagated by nineteenth-century abolitionists. Such a position could only fail to see the nobility inherent in the task of raising a vastly inferior race to a somewhat less inferior position. So strong was Phillips' mastery that it was only four decades later that a northern historian, Kenneth Stampp, gained sufficient familiarity with southern sources—especially plantation records—that he could credibly counter Phillips' interpretations, although Richard Hofstadter had earlier mounted a suggestive methodological challenge to Phillips. As was characteristic of the mid-1950s, Stampp attacked Phillips with the explicit assumption, one that would have been abhorrent to Phillips, that Negroes were and are "after all, only white men with black skins, nothing more, nothing less." Where Phillips found benevolent dominance, Stampp found cruel exploitation.

Stanley Elkins' *Slavery* (1959) is the first of the four books whose reviews I will discuss. Elkins identified a Phillips-Stampp standoff, arguing explicitly that new perspectives were necessary, and maintaining that most of what the historical discipline had so far offered was essentially source-mongering, and this would be insufficient to persuade either side, for the disagreement rested in the end rested on perspectives on race. The evidence was *in toto* ambiguous. Elkins' new perspectives were drawn from sociology, whereby he sought to characterize the relatively loose institutional structure of the United States, and the relatively modest restraints upon individual self-interest, on the one hand, and moral outrage, on the other; and from social psychology, from which he took a view of adult socialization that he argued might explain in terms of the peculiar institution of slavery the infantilized qualities that Phillips believed were products of the biological inferiority of the enslaved.

Elkins' work had only slight impact for a few years, but by the mid-1960s it had become central in a heated debate over the historical interpretation of slavery that helped push forward the work of four other historical scholars who wrote the books I treat here. These were Robert W. Fogel and Stanley Engerman, whose *Time on the Cross* appeared in 1974; Eugene Genovese, whose magnum opus, *Roll Jordan Roll* appeared in the same year; and Herbert G. Gutman, whose *Black Family in Slavery and Freedom* was published in 1976. Fogel and Engerman were neoclassically based econometric historians, who self-consciously and with great fanfare built their interpretation around a view of the slave plantation as a firm, and who took on a variety of topics having to do with the welfare of slaves that depended upon inferential quantitative techniques, most of which few historians understood, some of these methods depending upon chains of explicit assumptions. Genovese, by contrast, was a neo-Marxian, whose book both proclaimed and reflected techniques of textual interpretation drawn from Gramscian scholarship. Finally, Gutman was a labor historian of relatively conventional methodological persuasion, whose work had increasingly taken on a quasi-anthropological hue.

As most reviewers of *The Black Family in Slavery and Freedom* noted, the book is chaotic, reflecting among other things its author's obvious conviction that historical experience is somehow inherent and even palpable in historical evidence: his conviction along these lines is attested to by the unmediated apotheosis he provides for a photograph—his frontispiece—of a multigeneration slave family. But more relevant to the lively eclecticism of the historical discipline, Gutman imports some characteristic techniques of social anthropology, on which he bases the strongest part of his case.

By the time Gutman's volume appeared, the slavery field had been pretty thoroughly worked over, and this may lie somewhere near the heart of something that many of Gutman's reviewers felt to be a flaw in the book: its tendency to claim too much substantive novelty. Perhaps Gutman inclined to overlook relevant predecessors because he knew—as the reviews of his book reflect in their own organization even more than in their arguments—that a prime function of historiographical statement is to announce what interpretations in a given account add to the leading interpretation of a field. Thus a highly laudatory review of Gutman, Peter Wood's, notes that "the substance itself is straightforward" and is "In contrast to prior misconceptions," especially to prior generalizations, derived from Frazier and reflected in the Moynihan report. (Less laudatory reviews assert, however, that these generalizations were the same ones that most of the post-Elkins literature had already attacked.) Wood also remarks that the substance is in contrast to the tortuous organization of the book, which requires some explanation: "the book reveals something of the form, as well as the substance, of his arduous research."

Wood almost seems to feel obliged to create for his review—if it is to be laudatory—a framing argument to the effect that, so to speak, Gutman has told a new story, although less enthusiastic reviewers saw only new details, new methods, new evidence. Wood's paragraph most given over to flat-out praise of Gutman is telling in this regard. In it Wood's actual criteria emerge, from within the framing argument to which they are made highly relevant—though they really are not. "Few other historians of this generation have approached such a significant topic with so much discernment, imagination, and energy," Wood tells us, capturing very concisely Gutman's outstanding historianly virtues. "The new primary data, both written and statistical (not to mention the remarkable photograph that Gutman calls his single most telling piece of evidence) are the book's greatest strength." This is different, I think.

Wood accepts Gutman's claim that his book is addressed to Frazier-Moynihan; so does Nathan Huggins, in another highly favorable review. But August Meier, in a more mixed assessment, takes the Frazier reference more seriously than he believes that Gutman himself actually had, arguing that Frazier-Moynihan was just a "polemical" jumping-off point for Gutman, who "misses the point" of the key argument about matrifocality, because his real interests lie elsewhere, in realms like kinship in which Gutman "supplements and reinforces the recent work" of other historians. And yet Meier praises Gutman's book as "a brilliant achievement that charts new paths in the study of American social history." Meier has a hard time explicating the criteria by which he so values a book that polemically misstates its theoretical center, wanders, and repeats itself. He eventually explains that its contribution is a "methodological breakthrough, ... the pioneering reexamination of relevant plantation records, and the creative use of them to actually reconstruct the slave kinship system." But we learn from Meier's review nothing of the prior methodological limitations through which Gutman's work broke, nor even of the nature of the breakthrough beyond "extensive diagrams, analyzing in detail the exact kinship relationships over generations on the plantations he analyzes." This is better, far better, than prior "impressionistic use of traditional sources," and also than "dubious quantification," and this is the key to the book's genius, its value to the field. But why is it better? Meier (and I must emphasize that I agree with him) tells us that Gutman's story is a pretty good and valuable one, tells us what details he adds to what we previously knew, and celebrates a "characteristically creative" methodology without explicating it. So the failings in theory don't matter, and the triumphs in methodology don't need critique. How it modifies our story is what counts.

What imperatives led Gutman to cast his book as an argument against Frazier-Moynihan? Gutman's began his research when that perspective was quite timely. By the mid-1970s, however, it probably was not, and I would imagine, an obligatory revisionism directed the polemical structure of the book as much as any issue-oriented presentism. As historians, we should ask ourselves whether Gutman's book might have been better had he not been drawn into a struggle that by the mid-1970s was theoretically sterile.[7] This is surely the opinion of David Brion Davis, who, in a discerning short review, dismisses Gutman's counter–Frazier–Moynihan notion of "adaptive culture" for becoming "a meaningless cliché when deprived of social context—that is, the knowledge of who is adapting what to which, and why." Like other reviewers, most of them more favorable on the whole, Davis appreciates Gutman's "skill and imagination" in interpreting wide-ranging documentary sources. Would he really have been more pleased with a descriptive account that incorporated explicit methodological examination of what those sources could bear interpretively, how, and why? Perhaps such a book would have been disregarded, and Gutman was right?

The critical response to Genovese's *Roll, Jordan, Roll* was obviously (and justly) influenced favorably by his ability to embed his passionate engagement with his subject in a prose style and an organization of argument that properly suited them, in contrast with Gutman's book, which most charitably was read as a report on important research. Too, Genovese's thesis that the cultures of slaves and masters were interactive was able to synthesize much of what went before, whereas Gutman's book, appearing considerably later than early reports of his selected findings, appeared to many to be rather extreme in what it argued. But the reviews of Genovese didn't reflect much greater clarity about or concern with *how* he was able to work his wonders than they were with why Gutman ought not be trusted at the margins of his assertions. David B. Davis's review admits with equanimity that Genovese "covers so much ground and presents such rich mixtures of information and argument that its theme cannot be summarized without some distortion." Davis in some part sees the book as an ordered set of explications of diverse texts: "remarkably sensitive reading[s]" of slave narratives; "tak[ing] . . . seriously" slave weddings and funerals and Southern slave law; "discussing Afro-American language, clothing, and rhythms of time and labor." Yet embedded in Davis' list here are also explications of *social* relationships and *roles:* his paragraph on the slave narratives is followed by one on "Genovese's great gift. . . . his ability to penetrate the minds of both slaves and masters, revealing not only how they viewed themselves and each other, but also how their contradictory perceptions interacted"; his sentences on weddings, funerals, law, language, clothing, and rhythms of time and labor are followed in the same paragraph by a discussion of Genovese's "very best . . . tour de force," his analysis of the Mammy and the black slave driver. It is not that these are not shrewd judgments on Davis' part, but that even the way he categorizes Genovese's interpretational triumphs suggests that he feels no need to assess systematically how it is that these triumphs were achieved.

This is particularly striking, for Genovese takes some pains in an introductory section to discuss Gramsci's notions, and in early empirical chapters (as on the law) to explore a particularly clear example of the associated method at work. But Genovese also claims that in the end his purpose is to recreate and convey the *experience* of the slaves and the magnificent showing of the human spirit that represents, and apparently so excellent a go does he make of it that even the shrewd Davis doesn't feel impelled to ask how this can be done, only to show wherein it has been.

C. Vann Woodward's extensive review, similarly, is generous and perceptive, praising Genovese for having "done more than any other American historian to lift this tortured subject out of its culture-bound parochialism." How has he done so? By moving away from the narrower sense of Marxist history that he had previously practiced, by guarding against the current revisionist tendency to get so close to the nobility of the slaves that the peculiar institution is paradoxically romanticized, and by "patiently us[ing] the traditional canons of scholarship and rhetoric." What does this mean? "Not only does he marshal vast published sources, but extensively exploits manuscript sources as well. Of special importance is his use of slave and black testimony." Further, he makes comparison across place and time and category of working people. "To these endowments he adds a keen historian's sense of how things do not happen, of motives that do not motivate, a sense of the imponderable pace with which history moves, and an abiding skepticism of easy answers and quick solutions." As a historian, I certainly recognize what Woodward is talking about, and certainly concur that these are virtues in *Roll, Jordan, Roll*. But the unproblematic verbs in the first sentence quoted, and the unexplored nouns in the second, do suggest how easy it was for the historical discipline to accept what Genovese said that he did, as though he surely had accomplished it.

And what Genovese did was a thoroughgoing methodological innovation, no less so than the econometric approaches that Fogel and Engerman brought to the subject. His method claims of penetrating the social psychology derived from and maintaining a distinctive historical social structure by *finding like ambiguities of a particular kind* in multiple categories of texts: extensive verbalizations, speech acts, symbolic behavior, and, finally and crucially, purposive social action. The separate sides of these ambiguities—master and slave—he then must show to have been central to the continued reproduction of the peculiar institution, and to be analogous to those others have noted in other instances of extreme superordination/subordination, and to be at play in *subse-*

quent social actions of those—ex-slaves and their descendants—whose culture was formed under this domination, with this ambiguity.

Having done all this, Genovese may be perhaps forgiven for a method that obviously encourages the ransacking of evidence for exemplary rather than representative texts. But only one review that I read, that of George Frederickson, so much as makes a serious exposition of Genovese's method, although perhaps even more allusively than I just have. Frederickson's assessment, however, reveals his judgment that the discipline will not have to come to terms with the methodological question:

> This conception of the master-slave relationship is plausible and can explain a great deal. But some of the evidence that seems to support it can be interpreted in different ways. Moreover, slaves and masters often behaved or expressed themselves in a manner that is hard to reconcile with the paternalistic model. The term "model" is used advisedly, for Genovese's "paternalism" is as much an "ideal type" as Stanley Elkins' extensively criticized concentration camp analogy. . . . Like all models, Genovese's obscures the uniqueness of the phenomenon under study in order to subsume it under a more general category. . . . Existentialist philosophy with its concept of "the absurd" may be a surer guide to understanding it than Hegel or even Marx. But many historians of the South will not be satisfied with a fragmented reality. Efforts will continue to be made to impose a higher synthesis that will necessarily stress some aspects of the southern experience while neglecting others.

Read carefully, Frederickson's statement is that the chore of history is at once so massive and so undefined that even as we admit Genovese to the canon—perhaps dragging Elkins after him—we need not expect the next effort to understand slavery to employ or even come to terms with *the way* Genovese did his work.

Was Elkins' concentration camp analogy in fact extensively criticized in the review literature? I read six historians' reviews that came out shortly after the book's appearance. David Donald informed readers of his review that when Elkins had presented his thesis "before a seminar at the Newberry Library, . . . a group of experts were devastatingly critical of his" analogy, a response to which Elkins responded stubbornly and "clung firmly to his analogy, despite its poor taste and worse logic." Harvey Wish spent the largest of his five paragraphs on an exposition of the analogy, records that Elkins "is fully aware of the criticisms that can be leveled against his use of analogy as evidence," but found it "very plausible," except that slaves were more often rebellious than Elkins indicates. Frank Tannenbaum remarked only that "the issue of the impact of slavery upon the Negro's personality could have been made with a good deal less effort." H. L. Swint mentioned but did not evaluate the analogy, and Henry H. Simms ignored it altogether. The only review that wrestled with the analogy seriously is that of Earl H. Thorpe, an extensive but obscurely-published review-essay on the topic. Thorpe's substantive contribution, apart from rejecting the Sambo stereotype itself, was to evaluate specific ways in which the analogy fails, and the theoretical implications of these for slave personality. But he didn't question the use of analogy on methodological grounds at all. A decade after publication, Elkins noted that although certain objections remained, "it has been conceded that the use of analogy in itself, as an analytic device, is legitimate."[8] The overall impression I have is that despite the bluntness of Elkins' use of analogy as a rhetorical device for adding to the debate a new dimension, and a new theoretical perspective derived explicitly from social psychology, only splutter opposed it within the historical discipline, even at the start. Most wished that Elkins had been more polite, or had worked his analogy out more precisely.

As the second flight of books I have considered here were in gestation, Elkins presciently guessed that the coming wave of slavery scholarship dealing with slave personality-formation would emphasize "the ideological context" in which plantations operated, "their elaborateness, their complexity, the conviction and intensity with which they are held, their pervasiveness," which "should tell us a very great deal . . . about how coercive they might be upon all the individuals in any way concerned with such a system."[9] Elkins here foreshadowed Frederickson's identification of Genovese's with Elkins' "model," and we can hardly deny that through the easy incorporation of Elkins' questions into our analysis of slavery we have enormously enriched our understanding of the experience of slavery. But at the same time, such observations of potential methodological usefulness as Thorpe's comment that the concentration camp and the plantation had different mixes of adult and child socialization were never developed. In the late 1970s, therefore, Gutman was justly criticized for failing to develop such aspects of slave-family dynamics as child socialization patterns.

Donald ungenerously remarks that Elkins, in reasserting his analogy, "concluded that the experts [at the Newberry seminar] suffered from a lack of familiarity with the use of this 'kind of extended metaphor.' " I would guess that if Elkins so concluded, he was right, for in examining the reviews of all of these ambitious books on slavery, I have been repeatedly impressed by how often historian-reviewers are distressed not just by analogy but by indirect inferential approaches more generally,

and even by indirect indicators. without being able to oppose them with
very much more than their own prejudices. Their distress, perhaps, is the
other side of the already-mentioned tendency to assume that historians,
like Genovese, who handle personal documents are in some way in
essentially unmediated contact with historical experience.

The response to Fogel and Engerman, as might be anticipated, demonstrates this misapprehension the most clearly. Robert Engs, thus, in
an extensive and searching review, protested their use of data on misce-
genation to estimate the extent of sexual intercourse between master and
female slave, on the grounds that "it is . . . wrong to equate miscegena-
tion with sexual exploitation—the birth of a child is hardly an inevitable
outcome of intercourse." That the two may bear a ratio determined by
fecundability, efforts to control fertility, and fetal and infant mortality,
as the Fogel-Engerman method indicates, was not what Engs chooses to
debate, but their "equating" the two—perhaps because the two are,
somehow, morally on different planes. One can hardly claim that the
data presented constitute obviously excellent indirect indicators; but
they *are* indirect indicators, and their use is in the abstract only particularly "wrong" if historians ordinarily are somehow in unmediated contact with the past. It is hard to escape the thought that Engs's objection
was as much to *explicit* inference as to any special uncertainty it introduces: in his concluding paragraph he reminded the authors that the
computer is "only a tool," and that even though they have introduced
"a whole new set of techniques" of which subsequent historians will
have to "show awareness," their "final product" would only have been
"worthy of note" if they had displayed "the historian's skill, intelligence
and humanity." Of course, Engs's feelings were hurt by their arguments,
but *just what* are these qualities of some historians that Fogel and
Engerman did not show?

Other reviewers expressed analogous skepticism about Fogel and
Engerman's important indirect inference about family breakup in the
interregional slave trade depending on records on who was sold *with*
whom, because these records lack a direct indicator of marital status.
Few children were sold without older women with them, and few women
were sold with children with them *and without men of their own ages*.
John Blassingame made a check of these records, counting only about 4
percent that give data on families, and concludes that for the other 96
percent of the records "one would have to guess" about marital status,
just as "the authors guessed thousands of times and concluded always
that a slave over fourteen had not been separated from his or her mate."
It is obvious that they do not so *conclude,* but rather so *assume,* for
purposes of making indirect inferences. But Blassingame has liberty to

so misconstrue their analytic operation that he doesn't have to assess the plausibility *and impact* of the assumptions that they make. The inference that they make is surely not inescapable, but it is apparent that most historian-reviewers have trouble with the *fact* of the explicit inference. Only Allan Lichtman worked through the kind of hypothetical playing through of the multiplicative probabilities implied by these inferences. (Herberg Gutman did also in his scathing book-length review, not examined here.)

August Meier, in a balanced essay, remarked that "one may entertain a degree of skepticism about the degree of accuracy provided by the authors' data and methodology," especially noting that "I am struck by the fact that they so often must proceed on the basis of intelligent guesses rather than hard empirical data as their frequent use of the phrase 'on the assumption that . . .' suggests," and later cited but did not evaluate an inference to premarital sexual reserve from slave women's average age at first birth. That Fogel and Engerman argue counterfactually, on the same kind of "what if" basis that Lichtman employs in his "sensitivity analysis" of one of their indirect inferences, was particularly infuriating to several of the historians reviewing their work, although its heuristic purpose is much the same as that of Elkins' analogy, which, as suggested, had come to be easily accepted by this time. "The authors are practitioners of an anachronistic and thoroughly discredited form of historical inquiry known as the 'counterfactual' approach," Blassingame asserted, describing the approach "from the historian's perspective" as having "an Alice in Wonderland quality." No further reason for the purported discrediting of counterfactual method was offered. And, indeed, the whole set of reviews reveals considerable discomfort about the explicitness and reach of inferences, seen as a contrast to *what historians do*, when they distill a story from evidence from the past. Gerald W. Mullin's "own reaction to the great slouching beast of econometrics" reflects historians' sometimes unthinking fetishism of the document. Mullin will "adhere more resolutely to a narrative approach and . . . remain in the archives with magnifying glass in hand, as G. R. Elton once said, to become so familiar with the documents that I understand not only what the people in them are saying but what they are going to say next." *There are people in the documents,* so Mullin seems to believe, *historical* ones. Or maybe his method is to imagine people creating documents and then iteratively questioning the plausibility of each document's having been created by such people as he had to that point imagined.

In fact, historians' strongest commitments seem to be a particular scholarly task—that of recreating or uncovering experience—and to a particular resource, documentary evidence. We have already noted that Genovese proclaimed the recovery of experience to be the goal of his highly sophisticated interpretive methodology, and speculated that his enunciation of this conventional goal deterred critics from thinking very closely about how he got there. Charles B. Dew found documented experience in Genovese:

> Genovese has not looked at every surviving document dealing with slavery in the plantation South, but he has probably come as close to accomplishing this impossible task as anyone could reasonably be expected to do. He has also gone to the recently published slave narrative collection, . . . and his extensive use of this source enriches his presentation enormously. It sounds so deceptively simple—"to tell the story of slave life." To come as close as Genovese has to realizing that enormously difficult goal is a scholarly achievement of the first magnitude.

The earliest reviews of Fogel and Engerman, like Woodward's, which saw their book as "the start of a new period of slavery scholarship," were greatly impressed by the extensiveness of the evidence cited. Later reviews, less impressed with the extensiveness of the evidence, were also less impressed with what they understood to be the aptness of the evidence—as noted above—and less persuaded that the book was a pathbreaking contribution.

Commonly, evidence and historical experience are seen to be closely linked, without the nature of this relationship being explored. Eric Foner, like others, distrusted the "arithmetic averages" in Fogel and Engerman that obscure variation. Dew, correspondingly, expressed particular appreciation of Genovese's "amazingly sharp perception of the nuances that reveal so much," a product of his "remarkable understanding of the complexities, ironies, and paradoxes that characterize so much of human experience." I do not so much dispute either of these points, nor their application to the books at hand, as to wonder what principles underlie them? What are we to make of the implication that nuance reveals more of human experience than broad patterns reflected, or summarized, in averages?

We have already seen that numerous critics who sensed conceptual and organizational weaknesses in Gutman's book praised it nevertheless for the evidence that it presented. August Meier, quoted above for his skepticism about the "assumptions" that Fogel and Engerman proclaim on the way to making their inferences, announces that "the real methodological breakthrough" in Gutman "is the pioneering reexamination of relevant plantation records, and the creative use of them to actually reconstruct the slave kinship system." The "system" that Gutman produces is several large anthropological genealogies for historical slave families. Meier's "actually" is telling. It is obvious in reading these reviews that the method of cultural anthropology is more readily acceptable to many historians than is that of econometrics, with demography coming somewhere in between. Or, as Nathan Irvin Huggins puts it,

> Gutman's study frees us from Frazier's methodological straight jacket. Rather than begin with ideal types, he begins with experience and actual behavior. . . . He looked into the slave experience as none of the others have. He surveyed a vast number and variety of sources. . . . Focusing, thus, on the actual behavior and practices of slaves, Gutman . . . discovers in the slave experience an ingenious and courageous adaptation under conditions which might well have destroyed the family. Slaves attempted to find the locus of self within the family, to hold it together when possible.

Gutman, of course, actually looked at evidence, not experience, and, in fact, inferred the construct "culture" from evidence of behavioral patterns (like recorded assertions of specific kinship obligations), rather than any psychological quality like the locus of self. It hardly matters: Gutman has taken us through some very telling data, and this is doing what real historians do, and, evidently, should do.

Evidence may reveal experience in seemingly unmediated ways, then. The historian presumably "becomes the servant of his evidence of which he will, or should, ask no specific questions until he has absorbed what it says. . . . The mind will indeed soon react with questions, but these are the questions suggested by the evidence."[10] But, if some more powerful, even more unmediated experience should intervene, then perhaps inference, and maybe even evidence must be put aside. Thus, Blassingame states: "The so-called 'pecuniary income' of the slaves is such a theoretical construct that any one using it should probably spend some time chopping and picking cotton before applying it. Then, I predict that the 'return on labor' will not appear as high as Fogel and Engerman imply." Thus, Donald: "Genovese . . . does not know much about the South at first hand. . . . It is certain that southerners, both black and white, will find much missing in Genovese's work. . . . A little first-hand experience with fundamentalist Protestant sects in the South would have obliged Genovese seriously to modify his central claim for the distinctiveness of 'black religion.' " This is shallow, I think, if it expresses an actual methodological stance of a discipline contemplating which of a range of extradisciplinary alternatives to include within the corpus of new historical interpretation, rather than just a peevish moment. It may only be the latter.

Historians have rules governing the *employment of evidence* per se, as distinct from rules relating to *inferences from evidence*, which appear now and again in these reviews, although these rules are not quite used as matrix against which all works are compared. They strike the historian as close to common sense. One should read a great deal of the primary documentation on a phenomenon, in some kind of combination, not specified, with a respectful reading of the secondary literature in the same historical subfield. The latter seems especially important as an offset to the strong urge toward revisionism, as a way of posing alternative hypotheses and contrary evidence in analogous instances. Evidence used should be of many forms: this presumably serves in some measure to overcome some of the risks of the informal rules of inference with which historians seem in practice to work. Newly discovered evidence is likely to be particularly important evidence, although on historians' presumed assumption of a more-or-less coherent past, one would in fact anticipate declining returns to new evidence, as the proportion of confirmation increasingly outweighs that of disconfirmation, which should distress a discipline devoted to revisionism. In reality, of course, new evidence becomes admissable as new questions and new (usually implicit) ways of exploiting evidence appear: see the WPA ex-slave narratives so heavily relied upon by Genovese. And in fact, new evidence is not so much used to confirm or disconfirm what "we already know," or seem to, but as a still-inchoate but highly valorized mass to which new form can be put. "Sustained by an enviable command of the secondary studies, extensive research in manuscript collections, and new insights gained from a mastery of cultural anthropology and social psychology, Mr. Stampp marches to the fray with conviction and eloquence. The line of attack was foreshadowed by the studies of W. E. B. DuBois, but Stampp's conclusions rest on new evidence and are persuasive and original," as Frank W. Klingberg wrote.[11]

Critic-historians regularly display a concern for the *representativeness* of evidence, ordinarily meaning covering the *range* of likely variation relevant to the arguments the author makes, rather than some kind of quasi-statistical sense of a given confirming or disconfirming datum having an equal chance of appearing among the sources used by a historian. Historians seem by and large to recognize that the form, content, fact of production, and fact of preservation of documents all may represent statistically unrepresentative distortions that could be related to conclusions, and seem to carry out their informal "sampling" considerations according to how the documents might best allow inference to experience, in some contrast both to their inexplicitness in prescribing this (I can think of no instances of praise for careful sampling as distinct from having read nearly everything that exists) and to their reluctance to spell out rules of inference from evidence.

The most powerful methodological prescriptions present in these reviews—which I suspect are in fact close to the core meanings of the discipline to historians, and to which I personally respond strongly and favorably—are two: to examine phenomena over time, and to seek context. Foner, for instance, charges that what Fogel and Engerman have done is to construct "a system without any internal development." Just what is wrong with this approach is not articulated here by Foner, but Genovese's superb review of Gutman provides a related argument. Genovese argues that Gutman must go beyond describing the *structure* of the black family, or even explaining how it came into existence. "The family can encompass changing meanings over time." This relationship between the single institution and its context can be studied only by observing correlated changes in time, and *meaning* can be discerned only in the somewhat teleological sense of understanding *how* it actually proved adaptive to changing circumstances, not, as in Gutman, by asserting its generic adaptiveness.

Genovese's review of Gutman also provides a fine example of the second historianly posture, the quest for context.

> Since [Gutman] hardly mentions social relations of production and remains entirely silent about legal and political relations, . . . he abstracts family life from the day-to-day content of the lives of its members. Without attention to the economic, social, political, cultural and psychological content of family relations, the remarkable strength of the slave family and its attendant kinship networks [which is Gutman's empirical contribution] falls prey to contradictory interpretations.

Historical research, that is, is at core *configurational,* and where a single institution is extracted from the setting in which it operates, *meaning* cannot be discerned. "Although Mr. Gutman is probably correct in seeing the persistence of patterns as a testimony to the power of Afro-American culture, a less sympathetic student might argue that the persistence of the [family] institution rather demonstrates the crippling effect of all enslavement." In one sense, we are arguing here about which of two value statements, identical in their behavioral referent, we are to place on a given fact. Similarly, Foner criticizes Fogel and Engerman for constructing "a model of slavery totally abstracted from actual history," by which he means sectional conflict, world capitalism, poor whites.

. . .

And yet in looking through the review literature that surfaced promptly after the appearance of these four books, I found two startling reviews by historians, not discussed above, that asked quite explicitly what the historical discipline was all about, and answered quite boldly, offering formulations that searched beneath the ordinary day-to-day structures of professional beliefs of historians, and which have methodological implications. Seymour Mandelbaum's very brief review of Fogel and Engerman defended their book against attacks on its synchronicity, noting that the orienting question *ought to be* what the freedmen brought to Reconstruction. "What is neither trite nor obvious is the way in which the social system processed the 'output' of slavery in the 1860s and 1870s and was (or was not) transformed in the process." The question, Mandelbaum says, is not what slavery means to 1974 but what it meant to 1866: for this, the differences between, for instance Fogel-Engerman and Stampp matter. Daniel Calhoun's review-essay of Genovese faults his much-admired book for almost but not quite having escaped the trammels of the presentist question of what kind of Americans blacks are. "The model builders," like Fogel and Engerman, "seem compelled to accept the national or regional fences that define their units of measurement. The dialectician," Genovese, "seems to accept the national rubric because it offers to contain social process within safe channels. . . . The softening by Genovese carries a great reticence about the introspective side of theory, including the personal side of paternalistic theory." If we define the slave as a proto-black-nationalist and the black nationalist as a species of American, we cannot know the *other*, as Genovese almost let us.

Both of these lines of argument recall the dual concerns that underlie historians' examinations of slavery in the United States: the paradox of slavery within democracy, and the implications of this fact for a biracial society today. Both move for a reexamination of the former in the explicit perspective of the latter. But it is what they also do that may make them especially valuable as guides to an inchoate discipline: they seek to formulate the outlines of a methodology that could eventually include rules of evidence and inference, as well as the terms of theoretical argument—that would define the aspects of meaning of the historical paradox in terms of our current stance as actors—whether that stance be seen as political or technical. And for history's readers-as-actors, it would be precisely the elaborated contextual differences between *then* and *now* that would bind this meaning.

History as a distinctive discipline is ineluctably wedded to meaning and to context. To this extent, historians' treatment of mentalities will

differ from those of anthropologists, just as their treatment of population themes will differ from demographers'. Neither meaning nor context, however, is an imperative whose extent is defined by a priori theory
governing the treatment of a given sequence of past events; nor is it
defined by the historical record itself. Meaning and context are instead
imperatives derived from rhetorical or communicative concerns.[12] They
thus offer little "toehold" by which methodological concerns may assert
themselves as against concerns of story—as we have seen.

The suggestions derived from Mandelbaum and Calhoun, however,
are suggestive, for they posit a two-step process in critical historiography: an initial step forthrightly exploring the current cultural (or political) usefulness of the historical understanding being sought, and a subsequent step assessing the aptness and evidentiary and inferential reliability
of the meaningful, contextualized accounts historians compose to that
end. Reliability would be in this way provided a benchmark for measur-
ing adequacy: adequacy to the underlying use of the historical work
undergoing scrutiny, instead of implicitly having to be balanced directly
against the demands of story qua story.

NOTES

1. Allan Nevins, *The Gateway to History* (New York, 1938), 31.

2. Jacques Barzun and Henry F. Graff, *The Modern Researcher*, 4th ed.
(New York, 1985), 268.

3. John Passmore, "Explanation in Everyday Life, in Science, and in History," *History and Theory* 2 (1962): 107.

4. Barzun and Graff, *The Modern Researcher*, 168.

5. The fascinating and detailed account of the development of that debate by
August Meier and Elliott Rudwick has carried out that task more than satisfac-
torily. Their conclusion, that "the repeated crystallization of new perspectives
on slavery over the decades did not flow from intellectual interchange among
students of the subject," but rather from the way each historian, given his or her
own background, "responded to the social and intellectual climate of his generation," certainly leaves room for asking the question I ask here. *Black History
and the Historical Profession, 1915–1980* (Urbana, Ill., 1986), 276.

6. In fact, I did examine reviews of Kenneth Stampp's *The Peculiar Institution,* (New York, 1956) and John Blassingame's *The Slave Community* (New
York, 1972), but found that the *methodological* novelty of neither of these
books justified inclusion here. And the methodological implications of the oral-
history claims of Alex Haley's *Roots* (Garden City, N.Y., 1976), were not joined
by historians in the reviews I read, because they could and did treat it as a novel,
sidestepping questions of its value as historical evidence, or as history.

7. At this point, I should take the moral high ground of reminding the reader
that in two, critical contemporary published reviews of Gutman, one specialized

in its focus on demography, I left unchallenged his book's presumed organization around Frazier-Moynihan, and hardly could have done otherwise, having contributed just two years earlier to an essay organized around precisely this supposed theoretical framework. I must thus admit to have been the prisoner of the same disciplinary blinders that I presently criticize. See Judith Modell and John Modell, "Review of *The Black Family in Slavery and Freedom, 1750–1925* by Herbert G. Gutman," *Signs* 4 (1978): 380–81, and John Modell, "Herbert Gutman's *The Black Family in Slavery and Freedom, 1750–1925:* Demographic Perspectives," *Social Science History* 3 (1979): 45–55; also Frank F. Furstenberg, Jr., Theodore Hershberg, and John Modell "The Origins of the Female-Headed Black Family: The Impact of the Urban Experience," *Journal of Interdisciplinary History* 6 (1975): 211–33.

8. Stanley Elkins, "Slavery and Ideology," in *The Debate Over Slavery*, ed. Ann J. Lane, (Urbana, Ill., 1971), 349.

9. Ibid., 360.

10. G. R. Elton, *The Practice of History* (New York, 1967), 62.

11. Frank W. Klingberg, review of Kenneth M. Stampp, *The Peculiar Institution, American Historical Review* 63 (1957): 139–40.

12. J. H. Hexter, "The Rhetoric of History," in *International Encyclopedia of the Social Sciences* ed. David L. Sills, vol. 6 (New York, 1968): 368–94.

REFERENCES: HISTORIANS' REVIEWS EXAMINED

Of Stanley M. Elkins, *Slavery: A Problem in American Institutional and Intellectual Life* (Chicago 1959).

David Donald, *American Historical Review* 65 (1960).

Henry H. Simms, *Annals of the American Academy of Political and Social Science* 329 (1960).

H. L. Swint, *American Political Science Review* 54 (1960).

Frank Tannenbaum, *Journal of Southern History* 26 (1960).

Earl Thorpe, *Negro History Bulletin* (May 1962).

Harvey Wish, *Mississippi Valley Historical Review* 47 (1960).

Of Robert W. Fogel and Stanley L. Engerman, *Time on the Cross: Vol. 1. The Economics of American Slavery. Vol. 2, Evidence and Methods—A Supplement* (Boston, 1974).

Anonymous, *Times Literary Supplement,* no. 3769, 31 May, 1974.

John W. Blassingame, *Atlantic Monthly* 234 (August 1974).

Robert F. Engs, *Harvard Educational Review* 45 (1975).

Eric Foner, *Labor History* 16 (1975).

Allan J. Lichtman, *The New Republic* 171, 6 and 13, July 1974.
Seymour Mandelbaum, *American Political Science Review* 69 (1975).
August Meier, *Civil War History* 20 (1974).
Gerald W. Mullin, *William and Mary Quarterly* 32 (1975).
Peter H. Wood, *American Historical Review* 80 (1975).
C. Vann Woodward, *New York Review of Books* 21, 2 May, 1974.

Of Eugene D. Genovese, *Roll, Jordan, Roll: The World the Slaves Made* (New York, 1974).

Daniel Calhoun, *Agricultural History* 49 (1975).
David Brion Davis, *New York Times Book Review,* 29 September 1974.
Charles B. Dew, *Civil War History* 21 (1975).
David Herbert Donald, *Commentary* 59 (January 1975).
George M. Frederickson, *Journal of American History* 62 (1975).
Marion Kilson, *American Historical Review* 81 (1976).
Bertram Wyatt-Brown, *Journal of Southern History* 41 (1975).
C. Vann Woodward, *New York Review of Books* 21, 3 October 1974.

Of Herbert G. Gutman, *The Black Family in Slavery and Freedom, 1750–1925* (New York, 1976).

James D. Anderson, *Journal of Negro History* 62 (1977).
John W. Blassingame, *New Republic* 175, 4 December 1976.
David Brion Davis, *American Historical Review* 82 (1977).
George M. Frederickson, *New York Review of Books,* 30 September 1976.
Eugene Genovese, *Times Literary Supplement,* 25 February 1977.
Nathan Irvin Huggins, *Labor History* 19 (1978).
August Meier, *Civil War History* 24 (1978).
Allan Spear, *The Historian* 40 (1978).
Peter H. Wood, *William and Mary Quarterly* 34 (1977).
Bertram Wyatt-Brown, *Commentary* 63 (January, 1977).

PART II

MEANING IN RITUAL
AND TRANCE

— 3 —

Ces Sortes de Pénitence Imaginaires: The Counter-Reformation Assault on Communitas

Andrew E. Barnes

During the sixteenth and seventeenth centuries, prompted by the threat of Protestant competition and guided by the mandates of the Council of Trent, the clerical hierarchy of the Catholic Church sought to change and reform the nature of lay Catholic devotional life. The success the hierarchy experienced in this endeavor was tempered after 1750 by the Enlightenment which brought an attack on many tenets of Catholic faith from secular and secularized intellectuals, and—I would argue more important—a widespread decline in lay participation in Church-sponsored rites and rituals. These twin processes—intellectual alienation from Church teaching and lay alienation from Church ritual have been studied collectively by historians as *dechristianization*.[1] This chapter seeks not so much to offer yet another explanation of the process of dechristianization as to suggest that there existed another dimension of the process historians have ignored. Reflecting the materials available to them, historians have traditionally approached the devotional behavior of the Catholic laity from the institutional perspective, that is, from the perspective of lay participation in institutionally sponsored activities. Thus Lebras attempted to assess lay piety based on percentages of parishoners making annual confession and communion, while Vovelle attempted the same assessment based on the willingness of individuals to pay for post-mortem rites.[2] Implicit in this approach is the assumption that the rites offered by the church remained constant in nature, structure and in symbolic content. A growing body of research, influenced by recent strides forward in the application of anthropological theories to histori-

67

cal investigation, has indicated that the devotions sponsored and promoted by the Catholic clergy changed radically between the fifteenth and
eighteenth centuries in all three categories.[3] It is therefore valid to pose
the questions: "How and in what ways did the devotional experience
the clergy presented to the Catholic laity during the Counter-Reformation change? What influence did these changes have on the decline in lay
participation?"

The answer to the questions argued here is that the changes were all
in the direction of removing or limiting the type of psychic reward earlier
Catholic devotional experiences had offered. Anthropologist Victor Turner
coined the expression *communitas* to denote the psychic experience
collective participation in ritual engendered.[4] Psychiatrists Barbara Lex
and Eugene d'Aquili have sought to explain Turner's notion neurophy-
siologically as an altered state of consciousness induced by various sensory stimuli which can be and have been coded into the structure of
rituals.[5] Analysis of the types of ritual devotions permitted by the late
medieval Catholic Church reveals that most were structured in such a
way as to promote collective experiences of communitas. Analysis of the
types of ritual devotions permitted by the Counter-Reformation Catholic
Church reveals that most were structured in such a way as to deemphasize collective experiences of communitas. The discrepancy between the
psychic rewards for participation in the two types of devotional experiences is at the heart of the eighteenth-century decline in lay participation
in church sponsored devotions.

I

There seems to be consensus among researchers that all altered states
of consciousness involve some degree of alteration in normative patterns
of interaction between the left and right hemispheres of the brain, though
disagreement remains whether what is involved is right side dominance
or simultaneous activation of both hemispheres. Central to Lex's conception of altered states of consciousness, which she labels collectively
as *ritual trance,* is the notion that they involve more than alteration in
patterns of hemispheric interaction, that somatic and hormonal changes
are equally significant aspects of the trance state. She emphasizes that
ritual performance involves entrainment, i.e., the synchronization of
internal biological rhythms according to some external stimuli. Ritual
performance forces its participants to function in unison not only externally, but internally. Lex cites Chapple as to the effects the rhythmic,
patterned external stimuli utilized in the performance of ritual, which
she calls *driving mechanisms,* have on participants:

Voodoo drums, the regular and driving rhythms of revivalistic ceremonies, the incessant beat of jazz or its teenage variants in rock and
roll, must synchronize the rhythms of muscular activity centered in the
brain and nervous system.

Combined with the dance or with other rhythmic forms of synchro-
nized mass movement—stamping the feet or clapping the hands over
and over again—the sound and the action of responding as the tempo
speeds up clearly "possess" and control the participant. The external
rhythm becomes the synchronizer to set the internal clocks of those
fast rhythms.[6]

Driving mechanisms, which sometimes are combined with "adjunc-
tive aids—such as feasting, breathing vapors or hyperventilation," contribute, "to alterations in the biochemical environment of the body."
Further, "all of these physiological manipulations, complexly combined
in the context of a ritual, effectively generate stimulus bombardment of
the human nervous system."[7] In sum, Lex is making the case that even
without the attainment of ritual trance, ritual performance still induces
some form of psychic internal transformation.[8]

Continuous *stimulus bombardment* can induce various types of ritual
trance. To explain this process Lex makes use of Gelhorn and Keily's
construct of "central nervous system tuning." Briefly, this construct
involves recognizing a distinction within the central nervous system
between the *ergotropic,* or *energizing,* subsystem of nerves and the *trophotropic,* or *relaxing,* subsystem of nerves. Activation of each of these
subsystems entails secretion of assisting hormones and other internal
changes. These two subsystems normally function so as to counteract
each other, in this way keeping the individual on an even keel. In other
words, a sudden triggering of the ergotropic subsystem, such as in a *fight
or flight* situation will almost immediately trigger the trophotropic subsystem to return the individual to the status quo. During ritual performance driving mechanisms which entrain the central nervous system
"tune" the two subsystems into simultaneous discharge. Lex describes
the process:

In the first stage, response in one system increases while at the same
time reactivity in the other system decreases. Augmented reactivity of
the sensitized system continues; in the second stage of tuning, reached
after stimuli exceed a threshold, not only is inhibition of the nonsensitized system complete, but also stimuli that usually elicit a response in
the nonsensitized system instead evoke a response in the sensitized
system. Behaviors resulting from this second stage of tuning are termed
reversal phenomena. If stimulation continues, increased sensitization

in this second stage can lead to a third, wherein reciprocal relation-ships fail and simultaneous discharges result. The third stage of mixed discharges prevails as a product of chronic or intense excitation, as prolonged or excessive stress and as characteristic of normal physio-logical states such as orgasm and rapid eye movement (REM), or paradoxically sleep; learned behaviors, including Zen and Yogic med-itation and ecstacy states; and pathological states such as experimental and clinical neuroses, psychosomatic disorders, and psychoses.[9]

It is not clear in Lex's discussion how attainment of the third stage of central nervous system tuning fits in with right hemispheric activation. She takes the position that during ritual trance the right side of the brain is dominant. From her discussion it can be inferred that she accepts Ornstein's argument that right side dominance is triggered through the monopolization of the left side by some internally or externally gener-ated driving mechanism.[10] D'Aquili's position on this question is much clearer. He takes the position that during ritual trance both sides of the brain are active simultaneously. He argues further that Lex's distinction between the ergotropic and trophotropic subsystems can be extended to include the two sides of the brain, the left side of the brain being tied to the ergotropic subsystem, the right side being tied to the trophotropic subsystem. Thus the simultaneous discharge of both subsystems which occurs during the third stage of central nervous system tuning has as one of its aspects, the simultaneous activation of both sides of the brain.

Lex equates ritually induced trance states with Victor Turner's con-cept of communitas or the anti-structural movement at the heart of ritual performance. She focuses on what can be labeled the *experiential* nature of this moment:

Turner's concept of *communitas* hints at a perception of shared emo-tional states among persons having presently or historically, individ-ually or collectively, experienced equivalent conditions by common response mediated through human neurobiological structures. Ambiv-alence, created by oscillation between opposing emotional states, char-acterizes these "liminal" states wherein *communitas* prevails. More-over, whether in the transitional phase or in institutionalized deviant social roles, the liminal individual is simultaneously a part of and not a part of the ongoing social order: in like fashion alternation of categories of time, sacred and profane, constitutes the temporal pat-tern of a particular culture—neither category of time is less important or "real," for one cannot exist without contraposition of the other. Implicit in liminality is a recognition of contrast between part-whole (or figure-ground) perception of individual and collective experiences.

This schizoid state is the condition of man, for acknowledgement that both alternatives exist is necessary so that individuals or groups may deliberately shift from one mode to another; people return to the mundane world from the sacred and journey from their ordinary plane of existence to mystical realms.[11]

In stating this Lex is making two claims. First (in terms of its importance to us) is the idea that the journey from the mundane to the sacred world, from the "ordinary plane of existence to mystical realms" is psychically or emotionally therapeutic. Her argument on this point is an amplification of that of Chapple who states: "it seems quite evident, but little studied, that the rites have evolved, in part at least, as structured means through which equilibrium, in all its complex emotional-interactional patterns, is reestablished. In doing so they discharge the emotional tensions which the sympathetic nervous system has built up."[12] Lex goes on to conclude that "ritual trance is a form of catharsis."[13]

Her second claim, which is not so clearly articulated, is that this journey is culturally determined. That is the essence of her comment that, "*communitas* hints at a perception of shared emotional states among persons having presently or historically, individually or collectively, experienced equivalent conditions by common response mediated through human neurobiological structures." Implicit in her discussion is an argument for the existence of emotional or psychic grammars—particular to peoples and groups—which permit through the performance of rituals not only the articulation of emotional or psychic tensions, but relief from them.[14]

D'Aquili takes her argument and goes one step further. For him the performance of ritual has an explicitly biological motivation:

We are postulating that the various ecstacy states, which can be produced in humans after exposure to rhythmic auditory, visual or tactile stimuli, produce a feeling of union with other members participating in that ritual. This sense of union is diametrically opposed to intragroup aggression. In fact, the oneness of all participants is the theme running through the myth of most human rituals. . . . Although it is difficult to extrapolate from a human model to an animal model, it is probable that some sort of analogous affective state is produced by rhythmic, repeated behavior in other species. This state may vary in intensity, but it always has the effect at least of eliminating intragroup aggression and of unifying the social group.[15]

For Lex, ritual performance is "nature's way" to vent emotional and psychic tension. Trance states for her are a subset of the set of abnormal states of consciousness. These states are actively sought because they provide a means of both individual and group catharsis. Implicit in her argument is the belief that each group develops (presumably over a long period of time) a subset of rituals and trance experiences, a grammar of ritual trance as I have called it, to deal with their specific emotional and psychic needs. For d'Aquili the pursuit of communitas is more than just the culturally determined exploitation by humans of their neurophysiological makeup; it is a characteristic of what Turner, in his review of the writings of Lex and d'Aquili, labeled the *genotype*.[16] For d'Aquili ritual performance is a mode of communication employed by all animals including man. All animals which function in groups have rituals which lessen intragroup antagonism through the inducement of psychic states which positively reinforce both group identification and acquiescence to group expectations. Thus communitas is only a human variation on a biological theme.

A final topic worth consideration is the relationship between ritual trance and symbols. It should be obvious that the above explanation of the process through which ritual trance is induced, which focuses on central nervous system tuning, works without reference to symbols. For Lex this is a vexing problem, because she wants to affirm that symbols play an essential role in the inducement of ritual trance. Again she approaches an answer through the ideas of Chapple, who has described symbols as, "cultural shapings of neurological events."[17] In other words, symbols encapsulate past experiences. This approach makes symbols both historical and cultural phenomena. To give an example, the Christian cross as a symbol has no autonomous abstract meaning. Rather it is the specific set of past experiences, both positive and negative, undergone by an individual in contexts where the cross was used as a symbol, which gives the cross its value as a symbol during ritual performance. Such a definition of symbols fits neatly into Lex's conception of culturally determined grammars of trance states. Symbols, according to this line of reasoning, are encapsulated collective experiences. As such they serve, particularly in the context of learned patterns of ritual performance, as further stimuli for the inducement of trance experiences.

D'Aquili does not deal directly with this question. This makes sense because for him ritual performance is a mode of phylogenetic communication, ritual trance a phylogenetic phenomenon. For him, communitas is the end for which ritual is performed, and the reduction of intragroup aggression the end for which communitas is sought. Symbolic value ultimately is in the eye of the beholder:

often the very point of a human ceremonial ritual is precisely its anti-structural character and the generation of a sense of *communitas*. An example of a benign form of *communitas* is the Christian celebration of the Lord's Supper, a central aspect of which is the development of the sense of a people of God and followers of Christ among the participants, no matter what their social status might be. A malign example of the sense of *communitas* arising from ceremonial ritual is the sense of "one people" generated by Nazi rituals, particularly the famous torchlight ceremonies of the Third Reich. Whether for good or evil, the primary effect of human ceremonial ritual is very much in touch with the biological base of ritual, and it involves the elimination of intragroup aggression and the formation of a sense of group oneness and cohesion.[18]

II

Historians, following Turner, have operated for quite some time upon the assumption that ritual performance served as a vehicle for collective psychic and emotional release. In this sense all Lex and d'Aquili are providing is a neurophysiological explanation of a process long accepted as a given.

But their discussion of the process brings up a question historians have not considered, namely do all rituals have the same therapeutic value, i.e., are they equally efficacious in promoting experiences of psychic release? Implicit in Lex's discussion especially is a notion of a continuum stretching from a state of mild arousal, or ergotropic stimulation to use her terminology, induced by entrainment to states of ecstacy, equated with simultaneous discharge of both subsystems of the central nervous system and activation of the right hemisphere of the brain. Accepting this, are all rituals equally effective in inducing all states along this continuum? Or are certain rituals effective in inducing certain states? Arguably, affirmation of the latter conclusion is behind Lex's undeveloped conception of what I have called a grammar of rituals.

But which rites generate which states? Or to put this question in the context of our topic, which rites performed by late medieval lay Catholics generated the most psychic release for them? Neither Lex nor d'Aquili are forthcoming with answers to these questions. Thus it is necessary to push their arguments into new directions. For example, Lex observed:

> Alert attention to detail is required for perfect execution of rituals, and thus performance engenders a certain degree of ergotropic activation.

In addition, attention to detail in contexts requiring behavior explicitly contrary to routine patterns, whether in opposition to ordinary patterns or to behaviors essential in other types of ritual, further heightens awareness by interrupting the trophotropic responses that prevail in habitual acts. For the novice, such external and internal stimulations are necessary for experiencing requisite emotions and manifesting socially approved behavior; for experienced participants, who have internalized the essential configurations of behavior, evoked responses may appear less significant but are, nevertheless, indispensable for establishing the proper setting for the ritual.[19]

We can extract from this statement two things. First, unfamiliarity with ritual procedure and/or irregular or occasional participation in a rite generates higher degrees of anxiety about correct performance. This is important because, as the statement illustrates, Lex's model is actually one based on ergotropic stimulation and the inhibition of trophotropic rebound. In other words, ritual trance is attained through ongoing energizing of the central nervous system. Further, this energizing is more a factor in inexperienced or nonprofessional performance than in experienced or professional performance. If, as Lex seems to be suggesting a bit later, ergotropic stimulation is the factor governing psychic reward, the conclusion here must be that the therapeutic value of performance of a ritual is greatest for those who have performed it least or on the most irregular or occasional basis. Plugging this conclusion into our larger discussion it is possible to say that the rituals lay participants performed on an irregular or occasional basis, and thus with whose procedures they would have had least familiarity, would be those that provided the greatest psychic reward. In terms of lay devotions this would mean that rites performed on a cyclical basis, such as in patron saint celebrations, or rites performed during times of trouble, such as intercessory processions during famines or droughts, generate more psychic release than would weekly mass, monthly confession and communion, and so on.

Note that this argument implies that right hemispheric activation and simultaneous discharge of both nervous subsystems are distinct, even autonomous phenomena. Right hemispheric activation is a function of left hemispheric preoccupation. To the extent that the latter is the result of central nervous system tuning, then the two phenomena are related, but not in any automatic fashion. While Lex never says this, it is certainly consistent with her model. The argument also assumes, in line with Lex's reasoning, that tuning is the source of whatever psychic payload is delivered at the attainment of ritual trance. Lastly, it posits an inverse relationship (negative correlation) between ease of ritual performance, that is, familiarity with ritual procedure and a lack of anxiety over performance, and the psychic or emotional release gained from performance. Experienced performers of a rite may use it to attain right hemispheric activation with, in comparison to inexperienced performers, relative ease, but the therapeutic value of this attainment is also correspondingly lower.

Relating the amount of ergotropic activation involved in ritual performance to the amount of therapeutic psychic release to be gained from the performance raises the question of level of participation and its relationship to psychic release. In any ritual performance there is a distinction to be made between those performers whose participation is more central to the completion of the ritual and those performers whose participation is more peripheral, between those performers who are actively participating and those performers who are passively participating (observers). It makes sense to assume that those performers whose participation is most central to the completion of the ritual experience the highest levels of energizing over their performance and therefore experience the greatest degree of release through the performance. If this is the case, then it was those rites in which the laity themselves most directly participated, as opposed to those performed by the clergy with the laity as observers, which generated for the laity the greatest psychic reward.

In summary, to the question which rites performed by late medieval lay Catholics generated the most psychic release for them, the answer advanced here is those rites which were performed on an occasional or irregular basis and with whose procedures laypeople would be least familiar, and those rites within whose completion lay people played the most central roles would offer the greatest psychic rewards.

III

The attack of the clergy on ritual devotions during the Counter-Reformation had two aspects: an affirmation of literate piety as superior to ritual piety; a replacement of ritual performance by meditation among the devout laity. The Council of Trent, in response to Protestant attack, defined the rudiments of Catholic faith. Importantly, from Trent onward the expectation was that these rudiments could be and should be conveyed in written form. Thus the act of being a Christian became one of articulating or affirming ideas first communicated on a printed page. By the seventeenth century the catechism had become the chief vehicle of lay instruction, replacing the medieval reliance on preaching, theater, cathedral windows, and other didactic tools. Along with the catechism came a host of devotional books aimed at instructing the laity in the tenets of correct faith and the ethics of devout behavior. To exploit this literature a system of schools and colleges were created to bring literacy (if not writing) within the range of most lay Catholics. The results of the effort were mixed, but by the end of the seventeenth century, most lay people from the middle classes upward had some capacity to understand the printed word.[20]

The commitment to lay literacy necessitated a change in church policy toward lay piety. In the late Middle Ages churchmen had responded to, more than initiated, lay devotional acts. After Trent, however, church-men increasingly claimed the initiative in both articulating and develop-ing lay devotions, in this way introducing the laity to the new devotional program. It was in this area that the Jesuits excelled, developing net-works of interlocking lay devotional brotherhoods tied into the schools and colleges they maintained.[21] In Lille, for example, over the course of the seventeenth century, the Jesuits established a series of schools stretch-ing from boarding school for poor students, through a "collège" (sec-ondary school) for the sons of the local elite, to a seminary.[22] Next to these they created a host of brotherhoods, all under the patronage of the Virgin Mary, each aimed at a specific age or specific ethnic group. The goals of all these confraternities was the same, the pursuit *de la vertu et piété chrestienne,* which were attainable through a program of nightly examination of conscience, weekly attendance of religious discussion groups, monthly confession and communion and voluntary work at local hospitals and prisons.[23] Chatellier has argued that over the seven-teenth century, Jesuit confraternities experienced increasing success, not-ing that in Anvers, the number of men enrolled in the confraternity for married men increased from 320 in 1612 to almost 1,000 in 1664, that in the middle of the seventeenth century 4,000 of the inhabitants of that city were enrolled in one of the Jesuit brotherhoods, compared with 2,000 of the inhabitants of Lille, and 2,000 of the inhabitants of Co-logne.[24] He also explains how the members of these associations were trained in increasingly sophisticated meditative techniques leading up to instruction in the *Spiritual Exercises* of Loyola for the more devout among the laity.[25]

Secular clergy did not leave the initiative completely in the hands of the religious orders. Trent, after all, had put bishops in complete charge of the spiritual life in their dioceses, and bishops used this power to favor the spread of confraternities based in the parish and controlled by the parish priest. Parochial confraternities such as those in honor of the Holy (Blessed) Sacrament prospered and proliferated in the seventeenth and eighteenth centuries, often at the expense of older associations and associations established in monastery churches.[26] Parochial confraternities did not put as much emphasis on meditation as did Jesuit confraternities. On the other hand, they did stress proper devotional behavior and the dangers inherent in the "superstitious" (read ritualistic) practices of pre-Counter-Reformation associations.[27]

To Jesuit schools and parochial confraternities were added, beginning in the seventeenth century, missions, usually performed by religious orders such as the Capachins. The goal of these missions was not simply to fire the enthusiasm of the laity, but to introduce the less educated, especially peasants, to the cathechism and new spiritual values. To do this missionaries worked in teams of four or five and settled in a region for at least six to eight weeks, preaching, but also cathechising, establishing confraternities, and in France, teaching new religious lyrics to be sung to age-old popular tunes. Very often these missions were timed to coincide with the celebration of local festivals, as in Autun in 1647 and Anger in 1702, when missions were held during the period of Carnival, to which they were to be an antidote.[28]

The Counter-Reformation clergy did not expend all its energies in the implementation of the new program. A significant portion of its reforming zeal was directed toward regulating lay behavior not in line with the new values of literacy and self-discipline. This involved suppressing most of the festivals and ritual celebrations which had come to punctuate the rhythm of lay devotional life, and stripping the remaining celebrations of their superstitious elements.[29] There was no uniformity in this process, rites which were suppressed in one region being outfitted with new "Christian," (as opposed to pagan) garb in others. Thus the rites involved in the celebration of the feast of Saint John the Baptist, which included the ritual building and lighting of a fire to ward off evil spirits for the following year, were prohibited in Chalon-sur-Soâne, while those in Meaux were reformed—interesting enough by use of a cathechism which explained that the "fires of Saint John" were "ecclesiastical fires" useful in "banish[ing] the superstitions practiced at the Fires of Saint John."[30]

The fate of the fires of Saint John the Baptist is an appropriate place to begin an assessment of the Counter-Reformation from the point of view of the amount of psychic release the devotions it permitted afforded the laity. In general it can be said that the Counter-Reformation clergy feared any devotion which brought about high levels of ergotropic stimulation. Dancing, for example, was almost universally condemned. "Dancing around the fire" was first on the list of superstitions the ecclesiastical fires promoted in the *Cathéchisme de Meaux* aimed at banishing. The bishop of Autun, complaining about ritual dances, "from which are born many scandals," instructed his *curés* to neither display the host nor make processions to those villages where dancing was part of the ritual celebration.[31] Noel Chomel, *curé* of Saint Vincent's in Lyon, concerned about the "lewd gyrations" of participants in ritual dances, warned the parents among his parishoners to keep their daughters away from the potential "sexual sin" present at festival occasions.[32]

This point is important because it can be shown that the laity, when left to its own devices, took devotions exactly in the direction of further ergotropic stimulation. As William Christian demonstrates in his *Local Religion in Sixteenth Century Spain,* festive life in rural Europe grew out of *votive* devotions performed by villages in supplication of heavenly intervention against earthly disasters. Hailstorms on the feast of Saint Anne for five years running, a flood on the feast of Saints Cosmas and Damien, a fire in the church tower caused by lightning on the feast of Saint Barbara: the only way Spanish villagers knew to address these catastrophies was to show the saints on whose days these events took place that the whole village was listening and willing to do homage in return for protection. Homage meant celebration, the taking of time from mundane activities to show the saint they cared. Most of these votive celebrations usually involved rites of collective purification, such as fasting on the day before, rites of collective expiation, such as a procession to an image or shrine of the saint on the feast day, and a rite celebrating communal solidarity such as a distribution of food after the return to the village (a *caridad*).[33]

Since these rites were performed initially in a state of extreme anxiety, the psychic release they engendered was great. Over the years, however, the calamitous event which was the source of the celebration receded from memory, though it might still remain powerful as a symbol. Rather than leading to the decline of the celebration, this empowered the unconscious search for alternate sources of ergotropic stimulation. Over time the simple celebrations would become more complex: musicians would begin to accompany the processions and dancing would become part of the ritual performance; the free time after the end of the rites would fill with festive events such as bullfights or competitive games; the break in the daily grind would become an invitation to indulge in other forms of social interaction including mating, drinking, and fighting. The participants in the celebration would see no contradiction between the event and their activities because, after all, these things were done in honor of their heavenly advocates. For our purposes, however, these later developments are an illustration of how ritual celebrations, initially an ergotropic response to some collectively experienced trauma, under the control of laypeople moved further in the direction of ergotropic stimulation and greater psychic release.

In a world in which confrontation with forces outside human control was a daily occurrence, ritual performance provided the only available psychic comfort that these forces could have been appeased. The clerical suppression of rural festivals thus denied the one way peasants possessed for coping with the anxieties associated with premodern agriculture. And since these rituals were the source for whatever time from mundane concerns the peasants could snatch, their disappearance removed much of the excitement in the peasants' lives. Bercé summarizes the response to these developments:

> These modifications to the ritual practices of the countryside were resented by the majority as an assault against their innermost convictions, as an attack on their most time-honored and reassuring traditions. Changes in the liturgical calander never occurred without generating protests, provoking recriminations or petty acts of violence. Such spontaneous reactions usually disappeared without issue due to the lack of leaders to push and guide them. It is mainly through occasional mention in judicial sources that we know of them at all, and those reports were always thin. They were very important, however, and the study of the history of dechristianization and anticlericalism should start with them.[34]

The rural model does not work for the cities. There the clergy rarely exercised sufficient power to control lay behavior so totally. Urban social relations, however, were characterized by levels of competition and confrontation uncommon in the countryside. Thus urban religious life featured more rituals specifically concerned with reinforcing group solidarity. On an obvious level this can be seen in craft guild and *Corpus Christi* Day processions. But on a less formal, and arguably more effective level, it can be seen in the rites performed by confraternities. Ronald Weissman provides an example in his discussion of the rites performed by the flagellant confraternities of Renaissance Florence. As he explains, the rites were therapeutic in the way they permitted individuals to forego their differences and perceive themselves as brothers sharing the same goals and aspirations: "Through ritual self-abasement—the recitation of penitential psalms, the ritual reenactment of Christ's crucifixion, the adoption of garments symbolic of poverty and low status—and through psychic disorientation produced by mass flagellation, singing and wailing, the participants underwent a linimal experience that suspended the traditional social order and produced a spirit of concord and unity."[35]

As I have detailed elsewhere, the clergy's attack on the rituals per-

formed by flagellant confraternities was just as total as its attack on the
rituals performed by peasants. And the result was the same as in the
countryside—by the middle of the eighteenth century, members of flagellant confraternities, once the vanguard of the devout laity, were being
castigated by the clergy for their lack of participation in church sponsored activities. The experience of the flagellant confraternities can be
taken as representative of the experience of the urban laity in general.[36]

One last point emerges from the journal of René Lehoreau, priest and
chaplain of the cathedral church of Anger. Lehoreau relates the story of
an event which took place during a mission preached in Anger in honor
of the Grand Jubilee of 1702:

> A month after the opening of the mission, several laymen of differ-
> ent qualities sought to perform public penance at different hours of
> the evening, that is to say between eight o'clock and twelve midnight.
> In pursuit of this goal, for many nights, i.e., for six or seven in a row,
> the performed their stations, marching in procession, nude except for
> their chemises, to all four of the indicated churches, hoping in this way
> to make restitution (*amande honorable*) for their sins. They were
> followed by a large number of common people. They created quite a
> sensation in the city, which brought their actions to the attentions of
> Monseignor the bishop and the magistrates, who promptly ordered
> the cessation of these imaginary acts of penance.[37]

One hundred twenty years earlier, the *processions blanches* which
traversed the length and breath of northern France had been composed
of laymen performing the same imaginary penances. The difference then
was that they had been organized and directed by the clergy.[38] As for
the argument that Lohoreau's comments were motivated by an enlightened rejection of what may be seen as a superstitious practice, it is
worth pointing out that his journal records numerous occasions when
processions made their way around the city of Anger in supplication for
rain. Importantly, these processions were made up primarily of clerics.

The point here is not to condemn Counter-Reformation clergymen
for hypocrisy, but to suggest that in their eagerness to force laymen to
abide by the new spiritual values they overreacted to the threat posed by
lay devotional initiative and the directions in which this initiative went.
In an earlier age the acts of the public penitents—no doubt motivated by
the mission being preached in the city—would have been appreciated for
what they were, an effort by lay Catholics to relieve themselves of the
anxieties they felt concerning their salvations through the performance
of long-recognized rites of penance. The reaction on the part of the
bishop, simply to shut them out of the churches, is also indicative. The

Counter-Reformation church turned its back on what was for the laity an essential part of Catholic devotion. It is so surprising that the laity in turn turned it back upon the Church?

John Bossy has observed that:

> Cathechism was well designed to instill obedience and to mark out boundaries, between versions of the Reformation as much as between Protestants and Catholics, and it could be the foundation of a reflective Christian life. It was less well adapted to inspiring a sense of the Church as a *communitas,* a feeling for the sacraments as social institutions, or simply the love of one's neighbour.[39]

Bossy's comment reflects his argument that Protestantism chose as its battlefield the printed page and that the Counter-Reformation Church's implantation of a lay devotional experience based on literacy represents a successful response to the challenge. As his comment acknowledges, there were in this victory some tradeoffs, especially in the area of the psychic rewards to be gained from devotional participation. But as this paper has argued, the culprit for the decline of communitas in the Catholic church was not the cathechism, not the emphasis on literacy per se, but the clerical decision to deemphasize ritual. There is no natural antipathy between literate and ritual piety. In this sense perhaps the Catholic clergy conceded far too much to their Protestant competitors. Then again, literate clergymen have always been (and continue to be) both threatened by and alienated from the ritualistic devotions of the unlettered. So the Counter-Reformation may have been an opportunity for the Catholic clergy, as the Reformation was for the Protestant, to "purify" religion of its popular element, this element being, as argued here, a push toward some sort of psychic reward for devotional participation. Some support for this point comes from the fact that in the nineteenth century the Catholic clergy showed itself to be quite interested in a revival of religious ritual, though it is noteworthy that most of this ritual was created by them from history books.

NOTES

1. See John Bossy, "The Counter-Reformation and the Catholic People of Europe," *Past and Present,* no. 47 (1970): 51–70 and his *Christianity in the West 1400–1700* (Oxford, 1985); Jean Delumeau, *Le catholicisme entre Luther et Voltaire* (Paris, 1971) (Eng. trans. *Catholicism Between Luther and Voltaire* [London, 1977]); Jean Quéniert, *Les hommes, l'église et dieu dans la France du XVllle siècle* (Paris, 1978).

2. Gabriel Lebras, *Etudes de sociologie religieuse,* 2 vols. (Paris, 1956);

Michel Vovelle, *Piété baroque et déchristianisation en Provence au XVllle siècle* (Paris, 1978).

3. See M. H. Froeschlé-Chopard, *La religion populaire en provence orientale au XVllle siècle* (Paris, 1980); William Christian, *Local Religion in Sixteenth Century Spain* (Princeton, 1981); Phillip T. Hoffman, *Church and Community in the Diocese of Lyon 1500–1789* (New Haven, 1984); Louis Chatellier, *L'Europe des dévots* (Paris, 1987); Andrew E. Barnes, "From Ritual to Meditative Piety: Devotional Change in French Penitential Confraternities from the sixteenth to the eighteenth Century," *Journal of Ritual Studies* 1, no. 2 (1987): 1–26.

4. Victor Turner, *The Ritual Process: Structure and Anti-Structure* (Ithaca, 1966).

5. Eugene G. d'Aquili, "Human Ceremonial Ritual and the Modulation of Aggression," *Zygon* 20, no. 1 (1985): 21–30; Barbara Lex, "The Neurobiology of Ritual Trance," in *The Spectrum of Ritual*, eds. Eugene G. d'Aquili, Charles D. Laughlin, Jr., and John MacManus (New York, 1979), 117–51.

6. Elliot D. Chapple, *Culture and Biological Man: Explorations in Behavioral Anthropology* (New York, 1970), 38, as quoted by Lex, "Neurobiology," 122.

7. Lex, "Neurobiology," 124.

8. See discussion, ibid., 140.

9. Ibid., 137

10. Robert Ornstein, *The Psychology of Consciousness* (New York, 1972).

11. Lex, *"Neurobiology,"* 141.

12. Chapple, *Culture and Biological Man,* 317 as quoted by Lex, "Neurobiology," 141.

13. Lex, "Neurobiology," 141.

14. As Lex observes:

> Reports of fairly continuous alpha frequencies in the right hemisphere may reflect culturally determined inhibition; laboratory subjects in these experiments are almost invariably white, male, middle-class college students from a cultural background emphasizing sequential verbal-lobical reason rather than holistic synthetic perceptions. Although laboratory investigation has scarcely broached the subject, Ornstein analyzing ethnographic accounts of ritual trance, suggests that hemisphere alternation may be culturally influenced, and Bogen reporting preliminary findings from tests administered to Hopi Indians and blacks, considers that "hemisphericity," "a tendency to rely more on one hemisphere than the other," may be culturally determined. ("Neurobiology," 129)

15. D'Aquili, "Human Ceremonial Ritual," p. 23.

16. Victor Turner, "Body, Brain, and Culture," *Zygon* 18, no. 3 (1983): 221–45.

17. Chapple, *Culture and Biological Man,* 60, as quoted by Lex, "Neurobiology," 130.

18. d'Aquili, "Human Ceremonial Ritual," 27.

19. Lex, "Neurobiology," 140.

20. John Bossy, *Christianity*, 97–104, 117–21; Delumeau, *Catholicism*, 199–201; Quéniert, *Les hommes*, 94–102.

21. See Chatellier, *L'Europe des dévots*, 67–123.

22. Alain Lottin, *Lille: Citadelle de la Contre-Réforme? (1598–1668)* (Dunkerque, France 1980), 127–31.

23. Ibid., 265.

24. Chatellier,*L'Europe des dévots*, 68–69.

25. Ibid., 97–101, 163–167; Hoffman, *Church and Community*, 84. Also see Barnes, "From Ritual to Meditative Piety"; H. Outram Evennett, *The Spirit of the Counter-Reformation* (Notre Dame, Ind., 1975).

26. Ibid., 105–16, especially 110; Froeschlé-Chopard, *La religion populaire*, 143–71.

27. In addition to Hoffman and Froeschlé-Chopard, see Yves-Marie Bercé, *Fête et révolte: Des mentalités populaires du XVIe au XVIIIe siècle* (Paris, 1976).

28. On missions see Quéniart, *Les hommes*, 106–11; Delumeau, *Catholicism*, 189–94; Hoffman, *Church and Community*, 81–97. On the preaching of a mission during Carnival in Autun see Thérèse-Jean Schmitt, *L'organisation ecclésiastique et la pratique religieuse dans l'archidiaconé d'Autun de 1650 à 1750* (Dijon, 1957), 176; on Anger see René Lehoreau, *Cérémonial de l'eglise d'Angers 1692–1721* (abridged and annotated by François Lebrun) (Paris, 1967), 125–27.

29. See Bercé, *Fête et révolte*.

30. Delumeau, *Catholicism*, 177.

31. Schmitt, *L'Organisation ecclésiastique* 174.

32. Hoffman, *Church and Community*, 93.

33. See Christian, *Local Religion*, 23–66.

34. "Les modifications apportées au culte étaient ressenties par le plus grand nombre comme une aggression de leur for intérieur, comme une mise en cause des valeurs les plus assurées et les plus rassurantes. Les changements de calendrier liturgique n'allaient jamais sans susciter des désarrois, provoquer des récriminations, voire des sursauts de violence. Ces réactions spontanées restaient généralement sans echo et sans lendemain, faute de hérauts pour leur prêter un discours et faire retentir leur protestation. Au hasard des sources judiciaires, on est réduit à les deviner, et leur chronique pourrait alors paraître mince. Elle deviendrait immense, si toute l'histoire de la déchristianisation et de la naissance de l'antiicléricalisme devait luiêtre rattachée" (Bercé, *Fête et révolte*, 156).

35. Ronald Weissman, *Ritual Brotherhood in Renaissance Florence* (New York, 1982), 54, also see Bossy, *Christianity and the West*, 57–63.

36. Barnes, "From Ritual to Meditative Piety."

37. "Un mois après l'ouverture du Grand Jubilé, quelques personnes laïques de différentes qualités voulèrent faire à différentes heures du soir comme depuis huit heures jusqu'à minuit des pènitences publiques; et à cet effet firent plusieurs soirs, c'est·à-dire six ou sept jours de suite, leurs stations aux quatre églises marquées, tous nus en chemise, pour fair amende honorable. Ils furent suivis du commun peuple en grand nombre, ce qui fit bruit dans la ville, en sorte que Mgr.

l'evêque et les magistrats de la ville pleinement informés des dites choses y mirent promptement ordre et firent cesser ces sortes de pénitences imaginaires. (Lehoreau, 27).

38. See Denis Crouzet, "Recherches sur les processions blanches, 1583–1584," *Histoire, économie, et société*, no. 4 (1982): 511–63.

39. Bossy, *Christianity*, 120.

— 4 —

Ritual Trance in Brazilian *Umbanda*

Carole A. Myscofski

In the 1920s, a religious leader named Zélio de Moraes began a small religious center in São Gonçalo, across the bay from Rio de Janeiro. Under the guidance of his spirit, *Caboclo das Sete Encruzilhas,* or Indian-Spirit of the Seven Crossroads, Zélio drew on his Brazilian religious heritage through the Afro-Brazilian religion born of the Indian, African and Euro-Christian past and transformed it by means of French spiritist doctrines. There in São Gonçalo, *Umbanda* began and with it a new understanding of the relations between the human and spiritual worlds through trance.[1]

The subject of this chapter is the twentieth-century religious movement known as *Umbanda* and the new perspective it offers on religious trance experience. Although not well documented, *Umbanda* is a modern historical phenomenon; it has been minimally scrutinized by sociologists and anthropologists and offers to the scholar its own texts on history and doctrine. Since no field research undergirds the present study, these contemporary sources on *Umbanda* serve as the foundation for my analysis. This chapter will reconstruct the development, myth-history, and doctrine of *Umbanda* and investigate one of its central practices, trance or possession experience, as an individually complex phenomenon and in relation to the formation of this increasingly popular Brazilian movement.

The study will begin with the context, that is, with summaries of Brazilian history and Brazilian religious history, specifically including the noted antecedents to contemporary *Umbanda*; contextualization will be followed by the historical development of *Umbanda* itself, as suggested by recent non-Umbandist researchers, and by an account of the myth-history, doctrines, and rituals of *Umbanda*. After a brief description of trance in *Umbanda* ceremonies, the focus will shift to analysis of the trance state and comparisons of psychological and sociological theories with the Umbandist understanding of the religious meaning of trance. Throughout the preliminary discussion, the term "trance" will be used, in an operative definition based on Erika Bourguignon's studies of possession trance,[2] to designate an altered psychophysiological state expressed in a set of learned behaviors and religiously understood as an experience of contact with an independently existing spirit; the conclusion of this chapter will include consideration of the usefulness of this definition.

The intent of this study, through its emphases on historical traditions in religion and meaning in religious experience itself, is twofold. The first objective is to forestall the simplistic stigmatization of the Afro-Christian religions of Brazil as *syncretistic*. This adjective usually identifies religious movements perceived as different from large-scale religions —Christianity in particular—because of their apparent recombinations of religious forms discoverable in antecedent traditions. Designation of religious groups as syncretistic often also suggests that the participants lack a true understanding of the ancestral systems from which they have randomly borrowed a hopelessly jumbled combination of symbols, beliefs and rituals, and that they have entered a regressive state in religion and in cultural development generally. Underlying this unfortunate perception is an assumed separation of religions into "true" and "false," or "revealed" and "pagan"; the term at this time has limited usefulness. Noting that no historically known religion has begun in a vacuum but instead readily draws on valuable, available traditions, I hope to stress that the participants in Afro-Christian religions continue the aspects of existent religions in which they find meaning while recreating the religious cosmos in a radically new direction.

The second objective is to suggest reconsideration of the possession trance through religious interpretations, including those of the religious community under study. Trance has been investigated as abnormal physical or psychological behavior, as the remarkable result of whirling social forces in history and as the means for expression of the otherwise inexpressible frustrations of an oppressed underclass. The conclusions of such investigations inevitably reduce religious experience to something other than itself, and introduce no insights into religion, into the spiritual depth and meaning which sustain commitment. With the inclusion in this study of the voice of the religious community itself under the assumption that religion is a distinct phenomenon demanding separate and coherent study, this second objective expands the basis for understanding the persistence of trance in Brazil and other religious contexts.

Brazilian history opened with an ingenious but unsuccessful attempt on the part of King João II to export feudalism to the New World; between 1549 and 1821, the colony flourished under the dominion of a governor-general and, later, vice-regent appointed by the Portuguese crown and holding not only political but also religious leadership because of the papal grant of the royal right of patronage. Portuguese colonization was not the undertaking of families or communities seeking political, economic, or religious liberties inaccessible to them in Europe, but was the political and religious conquest of new resources for economic gain, primarily undertaken by individual men. The bloodless secession from Portugal was followed by the Brazilian Empire and Republic, the latter led until recently by military leaders or their collaborators.

Swept into an industrializing society in the 1950s, large and small communities in Brazil still preserve vestiges of feudal structures and relations engendered by slavery, maintained between the Euro-Brazilian owners and officials and the mixed-race working populace. Modern classes in Brazil now comprise the dominant Eurocentric urban upper class of industrialists and professionals, a new middle class, arisen from the urban labor force since World War II and a split lower class of farm wage-workers and urban industrial laborers.[3] This diversifying class structure is further complicated by the Brazilian perception of race, which is determined less by racial heritage than by the recognition and evaluation of distinctive physical characteristics, such as skin tone, hair texture and facial features, tempered by the individual's education, wealth, and social background. As the Brazilian populace is historically triracial, designation by race or color actually encodes a matrix of social designations.

Brazilian religious history, although not separable from economic, racial, and social history, also presents a complicated pattern. *Umbanda* itself preserves elements of four distinct religious strands, each tied to distinct social or racial communities; these four strands, considered consecutively below, are: (1) native Brazilian religions; (2) Portuguese Catholicism; (3) Afro-Brazilian religions *(Candomblé* and *Catimbó),* and (4) modern spiritism.

The first religious strand, from native Brazilian religions, is drawn from the dominant coastal tribes of northeastern Brazil and connects *Umbanda* with the Brazilindian past. When Portuguese explorers first encountered native Brazilian tribes in the sixteenth century, they variously reported that they found no religion, a religion distantly imitative of Christianity, and devil-worship. Gleanings from such colonial reports and mission letters and records, when combined with more recent anthropological investigations, reveal patterns of religious beliefs and behaviors common to the Tupí-Guaraní tribes which dominated north and central Brazil. Brazilian native religions focused on maintenance of proper ritual relationships between humans of a tribe and the spirit powers who controlled the physical and metaphysical environment. Communities relied on experienced visionaries and ritual healers to maintain communication with spiritual powers, guide human life and mend any breaks in the perceived relations. The tribal shamans were thus accepted and supported by the community as they were able to receive dreams and visions, or to experience spiritual journeys and thus receive guidance. Tupí-Guaraní and Gê mythologies are replete with images of encounters by shamans—and others wandering outside the limits of ordinary life— with supernatural beings of both benevolent and malevolent intent. Shamans were familiar with numerous intoxicants and hallucinogens and employed them to initiate contact with the spiritual world or to render themselves receptive of visions; tobacco, specifically, was used not only to encourage visions but also in healing rituals.

Community participation in religion among native Brazilians rarely consisted of adherence to doctrine, but rather enhanced daily life with many ritual observances, including group dances and celebrations of nature and the life cycle. Preparations for agricultural work or hunting, as well as for war, included invocations of imageless but named and well-known divine entities.

The religions of the Brazilindians cannot be said to have had a major impact on the remainder of Brazilian religions, primarily because the native population declined by an estimated 90 percent within one hundred years of the first encounter with the Portuguese. Native beliefs and practices have nonetheless continued in the mainstream culture in both original and remote stereotyped forms.

Indians converted to Christianity in the colonial era apparently preserved such belief in spirits and medicines as were compatible with Portuguese folk religious life, for the Inquisition records of the seventeenth century contain confessions of "magical" practices similar to traditional Indian healing. The Inquisition of 1591 uncovered an Indian-Christian religious movement known as *Santidade*,[4] whose participants worshipped an uncarved stone in which the holy power resided, anticipated the upheaval of the colony and reversal of power relations and "drank the smoke" of tobacco to catch a glimpse of the world to come.

More recently, anthropological reports detail modern belief in dangerous forest spirits and soul-snatchers, beliefs which are traced to indigenous religions, among villagers in the Amazonian region.[5] Further, one type of Afro-Brazilian religion, called *Pagelança* or *Catimbó*, has also transmitted indigenous ritual elements such as the invocation of spirits and intoxicant use of tobacco and the root *jurema;* this will be discussed further below.

While constituting one of the religious strands preceding the formation of *Umbanda,* Brazilian Indian religious traditions are not directly antecedent to it; no native community survived to offer such independent influence. Rather, elements of these traditions have been preserved, as noted above, in Brazilian folk beliefs—especially among the mixed Portuguese-Indian populace—and in Afro-Brazilian traditions.

Catholicism, although not the first Brazilian religion, is nonetheless the foundation for the religious history of Brazil and is the second religious strand woven into *Umbanda.* The Catholic church played an undeniable role in the conquest and colonization process over the centuries of Portuguese presence in the New World and facilitated the establishment of other European institutions in the colony. Its tolerance, indeed its incorporation, of elements of non-Christian religions has served as the mechanism for unifying Brazilians within a Catholic heritage and Catholic culture—even when those Brazilians are not practicing Catholics. The official religion of colony and empire, Catholicism in Brazil has produced a nominal and traditional religious adherence for as much as 90 percent of the multiracial Brazilian populace.

The Catholicism imported to Brazil, still practiced today, was formed under the peculiarities of medieval Portuguese culture and may be best construed as Portuguese—now Brazilian—folk Catholicism. In the absence of sufficient clergy to maintain ecclesiastical orthodoxy, this religion is one of domestic and village practices such as the cult of the saints, penitential processions, and lay religious brotherhoods.

The Catholic creed has survived historical permutations, so that belief in the Trinity, Mary, and the Resurrection of Jesus serve as the heart of Brazilian religion, but it has not prevented the accretion of both belief and practice from non-Catholic sources. The experiences of missionaries provide a clear illustration of the result of the interaction of faiths: the missionaries themselves borrowed native Brazilian examples of divinity and demon to instruct Indians on the concepts of God and Satan, only to discover later that the product of catechizing was a new religion, such as the *Santidade* movement. Similarly, evangelization of enslaved Africans in Brazil resulted not only in the incorporation of large numbers of new converts under the Christian banner, but also in new religions—the Afro-Brazilian religions called *Candomblé, Xangô, Batuque, Macumba,*

Pagelança, and so on. Three of these—*Candomblé, Macumba,* and *Pagelança*—seem to be historically precedent to *Umbanda.*

Although Portuguese-Brazilian colonial policy dictated that all subjects be Catholic and the influence of the Catholic culture on Africans was inevitable, the full conversion of slaves to Christianity was not an ecclesiastical priority. Social policy demanded the segregation of nonwhites even in religious observance, such that a black Catholicism emerged as a separate phenomenon in Brazil;[6] this branch grew from the Euro-Brazilian domestic model and supported, as did that model, at least the externals of Catholic cult. Characteristically, it also permitted the preservation of traditional African elements, as in the major procession dedicated to São Benedito, popularly proclaimed the patron saint of Africans. The procession followed the prescribed Catholic pattern of the exhibition of the saint's image through village streets followed by Mass for all participants; added to the event were dramas reminiscent of Bantu history and myth, including the crowning of the black community's king and queen. The *Congada* thus formed functioned not only as a religious confraternity in the eighteenth century, but also as the structural base for nineteenth- and twentieth-century Afro-Brazilian religions.[7]

The examples of *Santidade* and the range of Afro-Brazilian religions indicate the true meaning of Roman Catholicism in Brazil. It has been continued not as the strict orthodox doctrines and liturgical events preferred by elites of the ecclesiastical hierarchy of the colonial past, but as the foundation for religious understanding and experience in unparalleled forms. The wealth of the Catholic tradition, in its sacred stories, songs, symbolic and graphic images, and ceremonies, has served as a wellspring for Brazilian religious expressions; its resilience ensures that Roman Catholicism itself is still a living tradition.

The third religious strand woven into the fabric of *Umbanda,* Afro-Brazilian religion, is itself drawn from the two traditions discussed above, and enriched by its distinct though distant roots in the African tribal religions. Although Africans enslaved in Brazil came from disparate tribal clusters and tribal bonds were purposely destroyed, religions of the Sudanese (notably the Yoruba tribe) and the Bantu cultures (including Congo and Angola tribes) were preserved to a limited extent in the New World. As noted above, fragmented survivals existed under Catholic auspices, allowing the continuance of Yoruba tribal theology, ritual practice, and terminology along with Bantu concepts of priesthood and cosmology. Cloaked under or adapted to Roman Catholicism, these African traditions reemerged in the early 1800s in distinct religious communities. The Afro-Brazilian religions grew powerfully in the northeast coastal cities, where the concentration of descendants of Africans was greatest and where occasional links with Africa could yet be made. The distinctions between African tribal ancestries receded, to be replaced by regional differences between the Afro-Brazilian centers. Afro-Brazilian religion generally integrates Catholic doctrine with African—primarily Yoruba—structures. Its central ritual invokes gods and goddesses of the Yoruba religion, called also by Catholic names, to possess their dedicated followers in Brazil and dance, celebrate, or receive offerings or prayers. The mediums for divine possession, called *filhas de santo* (daughters of the god), enter religious service through complicated initiations and form the core of the religious community. From their ranks rise the leaders for the independent centers; until the last two decades the followers and leaders of Afro-Brazilian religions have been predominantly women. Of the numerous Afro-Brazilian religious groups, three regional types are relevant to this discussion: *Candomblé, Pagelança* and *Macumba*.

Candomblé emerged in Salvador, Bahia, and is traditionally heralded as the earliest recognized Afro-Brazilian sect because of the histories of the founded centers at Engenho Velho (ca. 1830), Gantois and Axé de Opô Afonjá. *Candomblé* centers have continued Yoruba priestly roles, language, and named gods (Obatalá, Oxalá, Shangô, Ogun, Oshossi, Exú) and goddesses (Yemanjá, Oxum, Yansan). Its skeletal theology parallels Christianity, as followers acknowledge a high creator deity, Olorun, but invoke patron deities for intercession in human affairs; any African mythology has been reduced to lists of divine attributes. *Candomblé* rituals are spectacular dramas of possession, as the mostly female mediums assume elaborate costumes after entering trance states and lead the participants in exciting dances and songs. *Candomblé* center leaders, the *mães de santo* (mothers of the god), perform animal sacrifices and divination rituals for individual consultants.[8]

Pagelança and *Catimbó* are the names of the Afro-Brazilian sects in the Brazilian states near the Amazon; these are heir not only to Christian and African traditions but also to the *caboclo* (backlander or Indian-European) traditions based in native religions. The *Catimbó* religious centers are simple buildings housing an altar, few statues, and seating; their rituals are performed by the *curandeiro* (healer) who leads the community in petitioning the spirits for health and a good life and drinking the intoxicant *jurema* to induce visions. Among most *Catimbó* groups, only the leader accepts possession by spirits; however, he or she may receive any spirit during a ritual. The invoked powers are Indian spirits whose names include the traditional Brazilindian Tupã and Ituapã, Christian Santo Antônio and Josaphat, African titles, and stereotypical Indian designations Iracema and Master Healer; these *encantos*[9] inhabit spiritual villages, states and kingdoms, aligned with similar powers. The native Brazilian influence on *Catimbó* has been muted by centuries of contact with Christianity, while the African influence derives primarily from the descendants of Bantu tribes and reflects the Bantu cosmology in geographic location of divinity and the centering of rituals on healing and possession trances.[10]

Macumba represents the more recent trend in Afro-Christian spirituality, blending Bantu (divine names, leadership roles, rituals), Christian (divine titles, theology), and Brazilindian (spirit names) traditions with spiritist metaphysics. *Macumba* centers are led by *embandas* or priests, employ spirit mediums for the vehicles of possession and invoke divinities and spirits known to *Candomblé* and *Pagelança* groups as well as souls of the enlightened dead. In Rio de Janeiro, *Macumba* rituals and teachings are quite similar to those of Bahian *Candomblé,* but are often reduced to simpler core elements by the fractioning of larger communities; there has also been division by intent: positive rituals remain under *Macumba* control while negative or evil-manipulating rituals are called *Quimbanda.*

This third religious strand represents the most diverse religious presence in Brazil, including many more regional patterns than may be described here, each of which consists of independent religious communities often separated by disputes over doctrine or leadership. The Afro-Brazilian religions were, before *Umbanda,* the first to interconnect the breadth of religious traditions in Brazil and give new vitality to the Brazilindian, Catholic, and African heritage.

The fourth and final strand woven into the Brazilian religious fabric is that of European spiritism, introduced by aristocrats of King João VI's court while resident in Brazil during the early 1800s. The most influential spiritist author has been Allan Kardec (pseudonym of Léon Hippolyte Rivail) who composed a doctrine of spiritual essences and manifestations in a cosmic hierarchy of powers. An eclectic scholar, Kardec was introduced to magnetism and positivism in European spiritualist circles in the mid-nineteenth century. From this background and the additional influences of Hindu philosophies and evolutionary theory, he developed a religious philosophy which became immensely popular in Brazil. In his 1858 volume, *The Book of Spirits,* Kardec explained that the human soul may achieve spiritual perfection through its successive incarnations in its admittedly degraded material form. His spiritual hierarchy included those striving human souls and—progressively higher—nonincarnate spirits, Jesus and, ultimately, God the Creator; these spiritual entities differ primarily in their proximity to and thus contamination by the material plane. Holding Christian charity to be the content of the highest act, Kardec also taught that superior disembodied spirits may be called upon for guidance through sensitives or mediums and that their generous actions entitle them, under the cosmic law of cause and effect, to higher levels of spiritual awareness.

The first Brazilian Kardecist group organized in 1873 to promote spiritual growth and social assistance for the poor. Since that beginning, spiritism in Brazil has been oriented toward receiving spirit messages and performing works of charity through ritually induced possession trances. Unlike most European spiritist groups, Kardecism not only proclaims the goal of salvation through participation, but also supports adherence to Catholic dogma; contemporary spiritists insist that Jesus was the incarnate form of the most highly evolved elemental spirit. Kardecism continues to grow in popularity and, by 1960, 3,614 Kardecist groups were recognized.[11]

The religious movement known as *Umbanda* grew from these four Brazilian roots of Amerindian, Roman Catholic, Afro-Brazilian, and spiritist traditions, and emerged in the 1920s in the industrializing urban centers of Rio de Janeiro and São Paulo. Although scholarly focus has not shifted to consider *Umbanda* until recently,[12] accounts of the new religion reached the Brazilian newspaper *O Globo* as early as 1937. Zélio de Moraes, named at the beginning of this chapter as an early leader in *Umbanda,* was contemporary to a small number of like-minded religious reformers who sought to relate the African core of *Candomblé* or *Macumba* to both Catholic and spiritist theology, while lessening the ethnocentrism of each of the traditions. José Amaro Feliciano, a religious leader in Pernambuco in the late 1930s, consciously removed African tribal elements from *Catimbó* and infused his teachings with both Kardecist spiritism and pantheism to meet the perceived needs of urban workers for a humanistic religion of greater spiritual content. Moraes himself offered new spiritual comfort and healing as part of his "more evolved" form of Afro-Christian spiritism.[13]

By 1941 sufficient numbers of *Umbanda* centers existed to inspire the first federating meeting of Umbandists, the *Primeiro Congresso Brasileiro do Espiritismo de Umbanda* (First Brazilian Congress of the Spiritism of *Umbanda*). Representatives to the Congress agreed to many statements of solidarity but none of unity. They finally published their agreements which, summarized, simply proclaim that *Umbanda* is a new and unique Brazilian religion with an ancient heritage, that Kardecism remains the guiding philosophy, and that the "primitive" rituals of many Afro-Brazilian centers—such as animal sacrifice—were unacceptable in

Umbanda. They acknowledged Jesus Christ as the Supreme Spiritual Master and affirmed the existence of disincarnate spirits bound to the material world through reincarnation and the laws of Karma.[14]

In 1961 a second Congress met and since that date *Umbanda* has spread widely, expanding from its primary base among people of color in the new middle and urban working classes to touch Brazilian life at all levels. Neither Congress succeeded in unifying the increasingly divergent *Umbanda* centers and doctrines: each leader and each center operates completely independently. As Pedro McGregor concluded, "*Umbanda* has no code, no ground rules, no homogeneity of rituals, and no defined aims other than to practice charity by doing spiritual and social works."[15] Nevertheless, it is possible to generate an overview of the *Umbanda* doctrine and ritual to which the many centers from Bahia to Rio Grande do Sul adhere, based on Umbandist treatises and anthropological reports.

According to Umbandist historians, *Umbanda* is both a recent Brazilian phenomenon and the most ancient of human religious impulses. As human beings themselves only achieved humanity by the descent of spirits into their material forms at the beginning of time, so spiritism is "as old as the world"[16] and has been the secret doctrine of all great religions. Spiritist teachings thus emerged with the human race on the primeval continent of Gondwana—a land formed by the conjunction of the later separated Americas, Africa, and the Indian subcontinent. As this parent continent broke apart, the spiritist teachings of *Umbanda* were maintained for millennia in the now-lost continent or kingdom of Lemuria. Spiritism was influenced by the ancient Hindu laws, by the erstwhile inhabitants of Atlantis, and by voyaging Mayans. Greek, Egyptian, and Jewish priests kept spiritist mysteries alive briefly, but the body of the tradition was carried into Africa and preserved there, albeit in rapidly degenerating form, while it died out or was suppressed elsewhere. Finally, Umbandists conclude, the importation of African slaves to Brazil in the sixteenth century marked the commencement of the revival of spiritism through the reuniting there of three branches of humanity: Indians, Europeans, and Africans.[17]

The doctrine of *Umbanda* and the cosmic history it relates rest on belief in hierarchic systems of divinities and spirits. The highest power is God the Creator, the transcendent divine and illimitable entity recognized by Christians and Africans (as Olorun); God the Creator is essentially unaffected by human behavior but is the source and destination of all spirits. His son Jesus Christ is the highest communicating power in the Umbandist system and is called the *Orixá Maior* (great deity, from the Yoruban title); subservient to him are other *orixá maiores* who have never been incarnate, *orixás menores* or spirits who had been incarnate but evolved to higher states of power, and the still-evolving spiritual entities undergoing incarnations now. Umbandist ritual doctrines present the same beings defined according to their roles in possession; they are the *orixás (maiores)* who never possess a medium in trance and the *orixás menores,* possessing spirits under their direction; these spirits include (1) *caboclos* or *caboclas,* spirits of dead Brazilindians; (2) *pretos velhos,* or *pretas velhas,* souls of dead African slaves; (3) *crianças,* the spirits of dead children; and (4) *pombagiras* and *exús,* spirits of malicious women and men, especially dead Europeans. These last four correspond with the category of once-incarnate spirits who, while now beyond human limitations, still choose to adopt the stylized personalities of their last incarnations during the rituals.[18]

As Umbandists further order the cosmic powers, each *orixá maior,* correspondent to a Christian figure, commands a *linha* (line) of spirits organized on a quasi-military schema with descending ranks of disincarnate and once-incarnate spirits. The most common pattern enumerates seven lines: (1) the *Linha do Oxalá* or Jesus Christ includes lesser male Oxalá-African spirits, popular Catholic saints and the *criança* spirits; (2) the *Linha de Yemanjá* or Virgin Mary includes female African and Brazilindian water spirits; (3) the *Linha do Oriente* or of John the Baptist incorporates Kardecist or universalist powers and is alternately called the *Linha de Oxum* or St. Catherine, or a vaguer *Line of Souls;* (4) the *Linha de Oxossí* or St. Sebastian ranks aggressive male and female Brazilindian spirits of the wilderness; (5) the *Linha de Xangô* or St. Jeronimo includes powerful or malicious entities and may be replaced by the *Linha de Omulu* or St. Lazarus with its *exús* and *pombagiras;* (6) the *Linha de Ogum* or St. George; and (7) the *Linha Africana,* with subordinate "old black" spirits, complete the list. Each major *orixá* represents a separate sector of activity and is ultimately subordinate to Jesus Christ, who in turn communicates with God the Creator; together they form the Celestial Court which rules the universe under Divine Law and guides human lives.[19]

The Umbandist doctrine of spiritual powers departs from Afro-Brazilian traditions under its Kardecist influence: the *orixás* are more remote deities, no longer clearly identified with African tribal beliefs, and there has been a new emphasis placed on communication with spirits of the dead and the enhanced antiquity of the religion itself. In analyzing the changes from *Candomblé,* Roger Bastide underscored the radical devaluation of genuine ethnic heritage from native Brazilindians or Africans, and Esther Pressel suggested that the new spiritual powers of *crianças* represent the multiracial Brazilian culture itself.[20]

While the hierarchy of powers seems far removed from human life, the spirits are in fact deeply concerned with the dangers and joys of the material world. Each human being is an embodied soul, protected by a lesser guardian spirit and overseen by a transcendent *orixá*. Humans stand in the lowest ranks spiritually, as incarnate spirits passing through many lives on a "journey toward perfection."[21] According to Kardecist philosophy, the incarnate soul is bound in each body by a sheath of spiritual fluids—the "peri-soul"—which both protects the evolving spirit and subjects it to disturbances. The soul or the peri-soul may be disturbed by one's own neglect of religious awareness, by the unresolved acts of past lives or by the undeveloped potential for mediumship. Spiritual sickness may also be caused by other humans through black magic or the evil eye, or by unhappy disincarnate souls.[22] These illnesses, the troubles of ordinary urban life, and the desire for greater spiritual knowledge bring participants to the *Umbanda* centers for nightly rituals. For the general followers, the mediums, and the ritual leaders, the purpose of *Umbanda* is to bring potent spiritual guidance and health to the needy and suffering. Brazilians, "lost in a life of agonies," turn to the *Umbanda* leaders to "supplicate God for a little light for them."[23]

The most important ritual activities in *Umbanda* are the *consultas* which take place in the centers, during which the spirits descend into the mediums and give advice on personal problems and illnesses. The spirits may specialize in the type of advice given—*cabocla* or *caboclo* spirits advise on work-related problems, *pretas velhas* and *pretos velhos* help with personal and family problems, and *exús* and *pombagiras* consult on misfortunes or love affairs—but all convey messages from the powers higher in the spiritual echelons.

Umbanda rituals are held at least twice weekly at the independent *centros*. The design of each *centro* is similar: near the entrance rests an altar to the *exús*, appropriately set as African traditions considered Exú a messenger to the deities and patron of entrances and access to the sacred. The ritual room is halved by a railing; one-half contains benches for the participants seeking spiritual guidance and one-half the sacred space for ritual dance. In the sacred space is a white-draped altar supporting statues of the *orixás maiores* in their familiar forms as Jesus, Mary, other Catholic saints, Brazilindian warriors, old blacks, and twin children; the altar is decorated with flowers and candles as well as with vases of water to draw out the evil fluids present.[24]

The *consultas* are part of the extended ritual called the *Gira* (dance; gyration), which begins with drumming in increasingly rapid rhythms as the ritual leader and as many as forty mediums emerge to meet the gathered followers. The mediums have prepared for their roles through extended fasts and herbal baths and dress in white with necklaces or ribbons in the representative colors of their own patron *orixás;* they begin the *Abertura do Xiré* by dancing in a counterclockwise circle and singing praises of the great powers. The ritual leader performs the *Defumação* with a censer of burning herbs, moving the smoke to the altar, the mediums and the audience. The mediums respond with the *Saravá,* a ritual greeting to the patron deity of the leader and to other spiritual powers, prostrating themselves first to the leader and subsequently to the sacred altar. The ritual continues with prayers *Para o Exú*—to honor and dismiss the potentially dangerous spirits—and with a collection, general lecture of advice, and short series of prayers in which all may participate.

The mediums then begin to enter a trance state, abruptly convulsing and calming as the spirits "descend into their horses" for the remaining two to three hours of the ritual. Each of the sessions is dedicated to a different category of spirit, such that at least once weekly in separate sessions, the *cabocla* and *caboclo* spirits descend and the old blacks' spirits descend; *criança* and *exú-pombagira* spirits descend less regularly but must be called at least once a month. As the spirits descend, they speak through the mediums, announcing their presence and greeting one another. They also transform the behavior and appearance of the possessed medium in conformance with a recognizable pattern: mediums possessed by Brazilindian spirits take on a brave, even haughty demeanor, smoke cigars and demand alcohol; mediums possessed by old black spirits become stooped as if bent by suffering, and their speech is slurred as if slowed by age; those accepting *criança* spirits behave childishly or playfully; and the mediums under *exú* or *pombagira* possession may speak with strange accents or give other hints of evil nature. Each medium is also transformed by the sex of the possessing spirit, assuming stereotypical masculine or feminine behavior during the trance.

After another series of songs and dances to confirm the possession state, the congregants approach the mediums, explain their problems and receive both general religious and moral admonitions and specific ritual advice from the descended spirits. The spirits give blessings, or cleanse the consultants with *passes,* sweeping hand gestures to drive out evil influences and resultant spiritual sicknesses. As the mediums tire or emerge from the trance state and the congregation thins out, the session is called to a close by the ritual leader. The mediums sing and dance as a group once more and undergo the violent convulsions signalling the departure of the spirits.[25]

The members of each *centro* may number in the hundreds, but the gathered audience for each night's *consulta* may only number between fifty and 100. The *centros* themselves are predominantly located in the working-class or new middle-class neighborhoods from which also come the majority of their usual participants. While *Umbanda* in the 1970s was enjoying enhanced prestige and nationwide popularity, it is still associated with the lower-class or Afro-Brazilian community and upper-class Euro-Brazilians may decline to admit participation. The participation by sex in *Umbanda* is increasingly balanced; women retain a slight majority in the medium's role, while the drummers and financial directors are nearly always male. Both men and women lead the centers, and the general membership seems so divided as well.[26]

For Umbandists, possession is consistent with three tenets central to the doctrine of the evolution of spirits. First, as detailed above, there exist separate levels of spirit entities ranked according to their proximity to the material condition, their understanding of the cosmic order, and their content of divine light. Accordingly, we humans as embodied souls are spiritually inferior, while spirits who no longer need material forms because of their advanced natures are quite superior to us. Second, all spirits are engaged on the journey toward perfection, toward God. We embodied souls must experience numerous reincarnations as part of the journey and seek help from the higher powers. Third, under Divine law, the higher spirits must help the less fortunate, and so may provide direct guidance through temporary repossession of a material form provided by *Umbanda* mediums. In the experience of possession, all entities benefit: the possessing spirits receive divine rewards for their charitable actions, mediums gain insight into advanced spiritual concepts because of their intimate contact with the more highly evolved spirits and their dedication to religious needs, and consultants receive transcendent advice for material problems.

The role of medium is undertaken by women and men who seek further spiritual commitment to their religion, who are advised that their illnesses or problems stem from the innate but undeveloped potential for mediumship or who spontaneously and repeatedly enter trance during the *Gira*. In any case, the mediums are taught their appropriate behavior by more experienced mediums, as their possessing spirit is also constrained by the ritual leader. Mediums learn the dances and songs, while undergoing training in trance induction; experienced mediums may teach them focusing techniques or simply spin them or rock them in order to precipitate an acceptable and accepting psychological state. As the novices are progressively instructed in the concepts of possession and the doctrine of *Umbanda,* they themselves initiate the concentration, spinning or rocking which for them allows the entry of a possessing spirit.

The spirit, too, must be instructed at length—in private or during rituals—in the expected stereotypical behavior. Esther Pressel has reported widespread presence of deep unconscious trance in the mediums, a state which lasts at least in the first moments of the possession, characterized by "glazed eyes . . . ; profuse perspiring . . . ; production of more saliva than usual . . . ; some difficulty with motor coordination; unconsciousness; and the need to be supported for approximately 30 seconds after trance."[27]

Most mediums continue possession in a light or "conscious" trance with fewer externally observable physiological changes; the mediums themselves report distortions in perception of themselves and their environment. The beginning and end of possession are characterized by shaking or convulsions, and following a trance the mediums experience a deep sense of relaxation and may not remember all events which occurred during trance.[28]

Before consideration of the analysis of the *Umbanda* possession trance, the ties of *Umbanda* with the four above-mentioned strands in Brazilian religious history and its unprecedented innovations require further clarification. First, the Umbandist myth-history has clear bonds with the Kardecist view of the universal and persistent presence of spiritualism in human civilization. Umbandists have, however, recentered the myth to include a unique role for African and Afro-Brazilian religions. Second, the form and content of the rituals of trance in *Umbanda* recall the Brazilindian and African tribal rituals; the function of the rituals, for mediums and consultants alike, is radically new and will be considered in greater depth below. Finally, the doctrine of the hierarchy of *orixás* most clearly demonstrates the emergence of Brazilian themes in the new theology. The structure of the hierarchy rests upon Bantu religious traditions which locate divinity in geographic space and spiritist and conservative Christian doctrines which rank entities according to their control of spiritual powers. The introduction of the spirits of Indians, blacks, capricious Europeans, and children reveals a creative religious process as the Brazilian Indian, African, and Christian pasts are, as personified powers, welcomed into a single doctrinal and ritual structure. The images of these spiritual entities represent not only the full complement of racial representatives, but also the Brazilian underclass attitudes toward them.

The historical and descriptive sections of the present study concluded, the focus now shifts to the *Umbanda* possession trance itself. My analysis begins with the general descriptions from physiological and psychological theorists and proceeds through sociological and combined theories concerning possession trance. Following a restatement of the Umbandist understanding of the phenomenon of trance will be my own conclusions on the meaning of possession trance in *Umbanda*.

Physiological and psychological analysis of the trance state provide enlightening descriptions of the event and confer a sort of scientific reality on the ephemeral experience but, in the study of religions, cannot advance our understanding beyond the merely descriptive level. Physiological descriptions of trance induction emphasize the need for radical changes in stimulation or alertness in connection with myriad other bodily alterations. Psychological descriptions furnish extensive details concerning the alteration in thinking, emotional control, perceptions, and suggestibility which qualify the possession trance state as an "altered state of consciousness." Psychology also illuminates the personality changes undergone, as "personality dissociation" through the loss of consciousness and control and the assumption of distinctly different patterns of behavior.[29] These descriptions lend precision to our analysis of possession trance and the vocabulary by which we may confirm that trance does indeed occur. We should not, however, mistake description for interpretation or analysis; physiological and psychological theories of the effect of trance on the individual human do not offer a meaningful basis from which to understand the place of trance in religious systems.

Analysis of the role of trance has been undertaken by sociologists and by recent theorists employing a combined theoretical base of psychological and sociological structures dependent on religious context. Sociologists accept the presence of the mechanism of personality dissociation as an adaptive function within a particular religion. The dissociation allows the assumption of a socially determined personality under which guise the possessed act as agents of social change in a smaller or greater field. I. M. Lewis, for example, suggests the connection between spirit possession cults and deprivation or social oppression, such that the deprived and oppressed—especially women—make use of possession trance to ameliorate both personal position and community circumstance.[30] Esther Pressel points out that *Umbanda* emerged during an early period of modernization in Brazil and is thus connected with widespread and significant social changes such as urbanization, the rise of the urban working class and new middle class, and the weakening of traditional familial and personal support. From this perspective she regards the possessing spirits as representations of the religious heritage of Brazil and the emergence of the central ritual *consultas* as the final result of the precedent in African religious traditions, the aloofness of the Roman Catholic church and the scarcity of health care in Brazil. The possession trance introduces the possibility for new interpersonal relations among participants and secures tremendous personal affirmation for the mediums. Above all, it serves as the mechanism for the reorganization of the personality of the medium by allowing expression of otherwise inexpressible desires and experimentation with other viewpoints.[31]

Roger Bastide categorizes *Umbanda* as social protest well within the tradition of the African cultures in Brazil. The destruction of the African kinship system and the continuity of religious observance had resulted in earlier Afro-Brazilian religions such as *Candomblé* and *Catimbó* and thus in their descendant, *Umbanda*. *Umbanda* presents both the valorization of African heritage and the rejection of African religion in genuine practice; these opposing moves were based in the need of Afro-Brazilians both to protest the dominant Euro-Brazilian standards and to merge with the general Brazilian society. Bastide asserts that "the creation of *Umbanda* is a purely sociological process dictated by social causes alone and to be explained only by the contact of civilizations"[32] and considers trance to be a device for the preservation of social cohesion, existing as a complex phenomenon only insofar as diversification of the Afro-Brazilian community is suppressed. Certain parallels are also to be drawn between the compartmentalized lives of the descendants of African slaves and the different categories of possessing spirits.[33]

Sociological perspectives of these sorts provide the irreducible social context without which religious activity is erroneously conceived to be only timeless or otherworldly. However, these perspectives avoid recognition of existential reality in personal religious experience. The theory proposed by Lewis is most flawed on this account. Participation in a spirit possession cult, rather than having inherent value for personal spiritual fulfillment, is reduced by his theories to its function as a (usually unsuccessful) means for social change. While social change and even social benefits may arise from participation, it is inconceivable that members utilize that function primarily. In the example of *Umbanda,* upper-class and Euro-Brazilian members may in fact deny their participation because of the social stigma still attached to the religion, especially in Rio de Janeiro. In addition, *Umbanda* resists categorization according to Lewis's labels of amoral/moral or central/peripheral. Amoral and peripheral from the viewpoint of the Catholic church, *Umbanda* nonetheless bears a clear moral message and—given the sheer numbers of participants—has become central to Brazilian religious life.

Pressel's contribution to the study of *Umbanda* is significant and only limited, I believe, by the consistent orientation to the themes of the collections in which her research has appeared. The theoretical stance there elaborated provides a solid foundation for the understanding of the psychological, social, and spiritual needs which *Umbanda* meets. But

Pressel's conclusions rely too heavily (as do Bastide's) on the mere existence of religious tradition as sufficient cause for commitment to a particular religious community. Umbandists are not drawn to *Umbanda* simply because it holds a collection of familiar religious motifs.

Finally, Bastide's perspective, exaggerated in the admittedly out-of-context quote above, focuses on the history of African-based religions in the Afro-Brazilian community as they confronted Indian and European beliefs and practices. Bastide is particularly concerned with emphasizing that the master-slave pattern of race relations has persisted in all social contexts and permeates the religious ideology as well. As an interpretation of culture conflict in Brazil, Bastide's work is without equal. However, from the perspective in the Afro-Brazilian community, he cannot account for the nearly fifty-percent Euro-Brazilian membership in *Umbanda* nor for specifically religious activity. Accordingly, his conclusions suggest that possession trance only exists in *Umbanda* because it has existed in African traditions before.

Erika Bourguignon and Robert Wilson have complicated the theoretical analysis of possession trance by adding the element of religious belief or commitment. These authors offer the richest analytic base for the study of *Umbanda*. Wilson emphasizes the positive valuation of possession trance, acknowledging its stereotypical behaviors as socially conditioned and nonetheless perceiving the core of genuine religious experience. As an element in religious belief, the phenomenon of possession trance allows the religious community to articulate its understanding of the result of contact between the human and superhuman worlds. The physiological and psychological changes which characterize the trance state as well as any socially acceptable variations represent the impact on a mere human when the door to otherworldly communication is opened. In Wilson's specific example of prophethood in ancient Israel, the trance state may only have been positively valued by a minority, yet it supplied the means for the improvement of a personal situation as well as for the enactment of validation of social change.[34] Bourguignon's theory of possession trance suggests a religious prerequisite for use of trance—the belief in active spirits. Her perspective posits not only a specific rigid social context of relatively fixed roles and a high degree of differentiation, but also a necessary religious context of rather flexible polytheistic beliefs. Possession trance cannot occur unless the religious community acknowledges both the independent existence of spirits and the reality of possession. Bourguignon draws from her Haitian case study the additional elements of resistance to possession trance and the undercurrent of sexual tension, elements recognizably present in *Umbanda* as well. Bourguignon posits the conjunction of the possession belief and acceptance of trance with social role conflict and theorizes that the learned behavior in possession trance functions as personality reorganization having an adaptive value where the individual must otherwise remain passive in a rigidly defined role.[35] These theories, from Wilson and Bourguignon, together establish a meaningful foundation for the understanding of *Umbanda* through their use of broader perspectives on the effect of religious commitment. However, neither takes the final step which my conclusions will encompass: the evaluation of the religious experience of the possession trance as meaningful in itself. In order to underscore the religious content of the phenomenon, I will now return to the Umbandist understanding of possession trance and the meaning therein before my own conclusions.

Umbandists recognize the nonspiritual benefits which arise from Umbandist membership and assumption of the role as medium. *Umbanda* exists as a source of personal and social assistance, to educate and regulate and to expand the limits of human awareness. Through *Umbanda,* changes in personal and social situation are made real and the means to them concrete, as Umbandist doctrine affirms that all goals are accessible through effort. Fontenele places the burden of social responsibility on the medium who, through great personal suffering, becomes a warrior for just causes and may initiate or support significant changes in Brazilian society.[36]

Yet the foundation of *Umbanda* is religious, offering spiritual assistance and development. The members or consultants receive the benefits of spiritual insight from spirits who seek to lift the veil of ignorance and promote the virtues of persistence, charity and justice. For most Umbandist theologians, the mediums themselves are superior humans, having the ability to contact disincarnate spirits and communicate with them because of their own advanced natures. Mediums benefit from the spiritual contact experienced in the possession trance, as they learn to further control their own spirits and coordinate with "irradiation" by a higher power. While Umbandists insist that the ritual trance brings suffering and personal confusion, mediums accept their duty to bring the possibility for spiritual growth to themselves and others through their greater understanding of cosmic reality and the nature of the nonmaterial world. Through the trance, through the medium, *Umbanda* renews its intimate contact with divinity and thus with the power and meaning of the world. The spirits descend to touch and illuminate human hearts, and without the spiritual center, life is—as Barcelos puts it—a deception and a shame. In *Umbanda,* the power to heal through spiritual connectedness is available to those who have the most to gain.[37]

My own conclusions begin in the social context, for it is undeniable that *Umbanda* emerged from a specific Brazilian society, with its many complexities, and the race and class relations and the upheavals accompanying twentieth-century social changes have shaped its formation. As Bastide implied, *Umbanda* could not have appeared elsewhere. *Umbanda* reflects and even participates in social change, but neither the religion as a whole nor any of its leaders has significantly affected their Brazilian situation. Through participation, *Umbanda* leaders secure a minimal income and limited prestige, while mediums gain independence, honor, and a broadened network of social contacts; none have yet changed economic or social relations in Brazil. Further, as *Umbanda* remains stigmatized as an inferior religion, little status enhancement is available except within its limited community. Currently *Umbanda* is increasingly drawing upper-class Euro-Brazilians to its *centros* and has, in effect, bleached its ethnic roots so that little living practice remains from its Brazilindian or African past; these trends may transform its social role to that of assimilation and stability rather than change.

The psychological benefit attributed to participation in *Umbanda* must also be reassessed in this perspective; my inclusion of the social context and the Umbandists' understanding of their religion precludes the reduction of the possession trance to a mere outlet or "safety valve" for the expression of frustrations felt by the participants. The existence and use of trance in religion require, first, an established history within the religious tradition and, second, religious content in the experience itself; both of these are present in this case. Imposition of such external analyses may serve as a basis for assessing the value of trance generally but cannot advance our study of this preeminently religious event.

From an internal perspective, the *Umbanda* possession trance is above all a healing ritual for both medium and consultant. Umbandists, as noted above, explain that one's spiritual self—soul or peri-soul—is sensitive to disruptions in the environment and may be restored by contact with a higher truth. This explanation may be understood to transmit their understanding of the impact of social change on the self. Sensitive to the disruptions around them which precipitate physical and mental illness, Umbandists gather to build a community of spiritual support. Mediums, through their almost daily contact with and mastery of overwhelming powers, learn to strengthen themselves and share their insights with others seeking such strength. In this analysis, I accept Bourguignon's theory on the adaptive value of trance in reorganizing the personality and Pressel's connection of each spirit category with a psychological or behavioral skill (Indians are courageous, blacks patient, *crianças* bold, and so on). But the situation for which this psychological development prepares Umbandists is not highly rigid but unstable and sometimes fluid. Umbandists often consider themselves to be upwardly mobile and through *Umbanda* seek to transform personal and social deficiencies into assets.

The healing that occurs in *Umbanda* has religious meaning, for it is also the spiritual self that is transformed. Confronting the disjuncture between their psychic development and their goals, between their physical environment and their material needs, between their physical and social limitations and their desires for fulfillment of their human potential, Umbandist mediums may experience empowerment by the very racial heritage that society denigrates. For the possessing spirits bring power to the *Umbanda* community, the power of the unspoken Brazilian past and its yet fomenting present. Brazilindian religion, African tribal rites, and even the structures of European beliefs combine to empower the community and challenge the restrictions set by the Eurocentric model. Through *Umbanda*, multiracial Brazilians can reclaim religions which encourage full participation by all members in an experience of communion with the centers of meaning. This empowerment through reclamation opens a depth of spirituality for the Umbandists inaccessible to them in the Eurocentric Christian religion of Catholicism, which remains formalistic.

I suggest that, in the face of the dominant monotheistic institution of Roman Catholicism, participation in *Umbanda* also represents a powerful political statement. As the voices of the Brazilian past speak through them, Umbandist mediums undercut the authority of priests, bishops, and cardinals. This increased sense of political power may also be found in the contemporary electoral scene as well, for at least two candidates for local office have announced themselves as providing an Umbandist platform.

The meaning of *Umbanda* in contemporary Brazil thus exceeds psychological and social reorganization and includes spiritual dimensions usually theoretically ignored. While discussion abounds concerning individual psychic states and social group formation, and the accustomed methods and analyses impart a scientific reality to them, the functions and meanings of religion and spirituality still elude objectivizing study. My studies suggest that this situation is not calamitous, but in fact opens scholarship to grounding in the reality of the events under consideration—as those involved see it. In the study of *Umbanda,* as with other religious communities, scholars must listen to and accept as significant data the description of religious experience from the participants themselves. From this perspective, one can reconstruct the definition of trance in the following manner: the term *trance* designates an altered psychophysiological state expressed in a set of learned behaviors, religiously understood as an experience of contact with an independently existing spirit resultant in the achievement of religious insight and deeper spiritual empowerment.

NOTES

1. Pedro McGregor, *Jesus of the Spirits* (New York, 1966), 167–68.
2. Erika Bourguignon, *Possession* (San Francisco, 1976); and "Introduction: A Framework for the Comparative Study of Altered States of Consciousness," *Religion, Altered States of Consciousness, and Social Change,* ed. Erika Bourguignon (Columbus, 1973).
3. Charles Wagley, *An Introduction to Brazil,* rev. ed. (New York, 1971), 91–121.
4. Heitor Furtado de Mendoça, *Primeira visitação do Santo Ofício às partes do Brasil: Confissões da Bahia, 1591–1592,* ed. João Capistrano de Abreu (Rio de Janeiro, 1935), 28–29, 78–79, 64–65, 87–89, 104–7, 121–23, 157, and 167–73.
5. See, for example, Eduardo Galvão, *Santos e visagens,* 2d ed. (São Paulo, 1976), 66–81.
6. Roger Bastide, *The African Religions of Brazil,* trans. Helen Sebba (Baltimore, 1978), 109–13.
7. Ibid., 119–21.
8. Ibid., 191–203; and McGregor, *Jesus of the Spirits,* 56–61, 73–75.
9. The term *encantos* literally means "enchanted ones" or "charms" but is the *Catimbó* term for spirit.
10. Bastide, *African Religions,* 174–83.
11. McGregor, *Jesus of the Spirits,* 86–18.
12. The "classic" studies of Afro-Brazilian religions, such as Arthur Ramos, *O Negro brasileiro* (Rio de Janeiro, 1934) or Edison Carneiro, *Candomblés da Bahia* (Bahia, 1948), do not include Umbandist groups; the first major treatment is by Bastide in *African Religions,* published in France in 1960.
13. Bastide, *African Religions,* 310–11.
14. Decelso [Rosa], *Umbanda de Caboclos* (Rio de Janeiro, 1967), 19–22.
15. McGregor, *Jesus of the Spirits,* 181.
16. Mario Barcelos, *Aruanda* (Rio de Janeiro, n.d.), 25.
17. This history was revealed by spirit guides to Barcelos, *Aruanda,* 25–27, and to W. W. da Matta e Silva, *Doutrina secreta da Umbanda* (Rio de Janeiro, 1967), 10–20.
18. Esther Pressel, "Negative Spirit Possession in Experienced Brazilian Umbanda Spirit Mediums," *Case Studies in Spirit Possession,* eds. Vincent Crapanzano and Vivian Garrison (New York, 1977), 335–38.
19. The summary is based on Esther Pressel, "Umbanda in São Paulo: Religious Innovations in a Developing Society," in *Religion,* 286, corrobated with reference to Aluizio Fontenele, *O Espiritismo no conceito das religiões e a lei da Umbanda,* 3d ed. (Rio de Janeiro, 1949), 15, 63–65; McGregor, *Jesus of the*

Spirits, 185–87; and Bastide, *African Religions*, 322–25. Decelso [Rosa] sharply criticized the use of these *Linhas* by his fellow Umbandists Fontenele and Matta e Silva, pointing out in *Umbanda de Caboclos*, 33–34, that the categories are shallow and confusing, and "define nothing."

20. Bastide, *African Religious*, 316, 340–41; and Pressel, "Umbanda in São Paulo," 313–15.

21. Fontenele, *O Espiritismo*, 17.

22. Pressel, "Negative Spirit Possession," 338–39.

23. Fontenele, *O Espiritismo*, 27, 28.

24. Pressel, "Negative Spirit Possession," 335–36, 341; and Pressel, "Umbanda in São Paulo," 279.

25. Pressel, "Negative Spirit Possession," 342–44; and Barcelos, *Aruanda*, 84–87.

26. Pressel, "Umbanda in São Paulo," 276–78.

27. Ibid., 309.

28. Ibid., 302–10.

29. Bourguignon, *Possession*, 3; and "Introduction," in Bourguignon, *Religion*, 3–7.

30. I. M. Lewis, *Ecstatic Religion* (Baltimore, 1971), 30–36.

31. Pressel, "Umbanda in São Paulo," 264–65, 295–300.

32. Bastide, *African Religions*, 326.

33. Ibid., 155–68, 320–26, 380–81.

34. Robert Wilson, *Prophecy in Ancient Israel* (Philadelphia, 1980), 3–5, 34, 52–63.

35. Bourguignon, *Possession*, 7–10, 23, 31–41.

36. Fontenele, *O Espiritismo*, 20–21; also Matta e Silva, *Doutrina Secreta*, 47–53.

37. Barcelos, *Aruanda*, 35–36; also Fontenele, *O Espiritismo*, 21–28, 53–65; and Decelso [Rosa], *Umbanda de Caboclos*, 176–77.

— 5 —

Ritual Trance and the Social Order: The Persistence of Taiwanese Shamanism

Donald S. Sutton

How has ritual trance[1] survived in China in spite of being deplored for centuries by political and social elites? While other ancient popular practices under Confucian attack died out—for example pre-Confucian saturnalian festivities, and most disapproved marriage and death customs—mediums continued to flouish. Southern Fujian, which for many centuries celebrated the work of the great Neo-Confucian Zhu Xi (1130–1200) as a reformer of local customs, continued to sustain one of the most vigorous spirit medium traditions. In and after the seventeenth-century, migrants from that region brought the custom of ritual trance to Taiwan, where it is widely practiced. Despite an attempt at suppression under the Japanese colonial occupation (1895–1945) and official disapproval under the Guomindang in the past forty-one years, there must be few village and suburban festivities where entranced mediums do not play an essential role. Even universal modern education has not shaken the custom.

The dominant Chinese elite have disliked spirit mediums, especially in recent centuries.[2] They find them vulgar and unlettered. They are uncomfortable with their claim to be possessed by a god while in trance, because good Confucians prefer to leave the gods out of direct sight and contact, and to treat them with decorum. They criticize their contribution to the people's wastefulness in ritual expenditure. Above all, however, they deplore the medium's chaotic ritual behavior. This is because Confucian moral codes, widely enforced by the Ming and Qing periods (1368–1644–1912), emphasized that outward conduct should both express inner beliefs and help to structure orderly social relationships. Chaotic, disorderly behavior could thus be considered to spring from dangerous thoughts and to lead to social disruption.

But was ritual trance actually chaotic behavior, and did it readily lead to social disruption? The elite's fears seem to be given credence by two great regional anti-dynastic movements of the nineteenth century, the Taipings and Boxers. Both, however, were *sui generis;* the Taiping leaders, monopolizing god-possession as a source of charismatic authority, grafted a set of egalitarian concepts borrowed from Christianity in building a revolutionary movement, and the Boxers half a century later merged possession with a variety of local martial arts cults. These were unique political elaborations of trance, each evolved in peculiar social and political circumstances. Neither movement supplies evidence that ritual trance by village mediums is akin to, or tends to promote, social disorder. But the position must be taken seriously, for it has been elaborated in several Western studies. A recent dissertation presents mediums in Taiwan as exceptions to the general rule that religion mirrors and by implication sustains social structure: "Trance gods rebel against the social structures upheld by the rest of the pantheon."[3] An unpublished study of Taiwan mediums attempts to link them with anti-Guomindang sentiment.[4]

If we were instead to hypothesize that mediums in some way supported local social interests, it would help to explain why unlike European Reformation leaders, Confucian, Japanese, and Guomindang elites failed to put an end to disturbing popular rituals. Such a hypothesis would also be more consistent with social anthropological presumptions of manifold interconnections between religion and society. This chapter focuses on procession behavior, which as the most disturbing and spectacular form of ritual trance was most disliked by reforming elites and ought to have been most easily suppressed. I propose that the temporary reversal of social values in trance is not dysfunctional; rather, in the approved ritual forms, it satisfies key individual and social needs. The first part of this chapter briefly outlines some of the ways in which mediums typically served to satisfy local needs and sustain the local order. The concluding section suggests that neurophysiology, as outlined in some recent discussions of ritual trance, may have abetted persistent cultural values in Taiwan to perpetuate mediumship as a vocation.

As for my general purpose, I cannot attempt here the full historical exploration that the topic deserves, nor shall I examine the adaptation of Taiwan mediums to recent urban and industrial change.[5] My purpose as a social historian is to make preliminary sense of ritual trance as observed in my brief periods of fieldwork over the past five years in

Tainan county,[6] by drawing eclectically on theory from anthropology and neurophysiology, in preparation for further historical work on ritual trance in Taiwan and the China mainland.

Ritual trance, it will be apparent by this point, is used in Taiwan to indicate the presence of a god.[7] Possession is most commonly termed "attachment [of the god] to the body *(fushen)*"[8] and there are two standard forms, which Jordan calls oracular and performative:

1. In seance: A spirit-medium (Taiwanese: *tang-ki,* Mandarin: *jitong*) speaks in tongues before an altar for the purpose of treating patients, and resolves nonmedical problems concerning the cult or individual members.[9]
2. In procession: A spirit-medium walks and dances and mortifies himself (herself) in a periodic god's parade.[10]

Taiwan mediums are possessed almost always by a god (less often by two or a series of gods) of their own gender, generally one of low rank in the celestial bureaucracy. They claim to have been chosen in spite of themselves, and come to this realization in many cases after an illness or involuntary trance experience. They have learned to control their trances (god-possessions) and perform and conduct seances without special training, but are recognized by most people to be full mediums only after an arduous period of seclusion. Some few receive ritual instruction from a Daoist priest at this time,[11] but usually only the god and themselves are responsible for the simple rituals they use. Mediums are found everywhere in Taiwan, but they are a larger percentage of village than of town population. They are traditionally not specialists, but pursue normal farming (and more recently factory) occupations. In the large towns some, instead of trancing at temples, have their own altars at home. These, generally women, may receive remuneration for their services. In the villages and smaller towns, advice is given free at a local temple or shrine, but a small contribution from patients is expected—if not at the time of the seance, then later when funds are being raised for a festival or for rebuilding.

It should be stressed that practicing mediums, by definition, do seances, and the great majority at some point also appear in procession, even if it is only once a year at a pilgrimage center like Beigang. To the extent that a spectacular performance helps to draw patients for oracular seances, and a successful healer makes a charismatic focus for procession ritual, it is clear that the dual function reinforces the practice of mediumship.

Entranced Mediums: Rebels or Eccentrics?

Some examples of medium behavior will serve to clarify why they irritate members of the social elite, even those who work closely with them. Once in trance, mediums are certainly unlike other people. This is not to say they are wild or chaotic in their behavior: uncontrolled gambolling and spasmodic sword-waving is a sign of an untrained medium, a bystander's spur-of-the-moment possession. But caught sight of in a procession, mediums look odd. Their movements are stylized and strange; head facing forward or slowly shaking, eyes closed or half closed, fingers pointed in the fashion prescribed for the god possessing them, feet moving zigzag two or three steps at a time. Second, normal social courtesies are abandoned. They do not greet or acknowledge those they know, or communicate directly to people at all except through gestures of impatience, for example to redirect the god's sedan. They do not speak in procession apart from an occasional *sotte voce* bird-like twitter in front of another entranced medium or a harsh cry as they leave trance. Third, their attire lessens customary distinctions of gender. Men and women alike are barefooted, and wear a red sash round their waists or the brightly colored apron that denotes they are in trance. Though female mediums wear a T-shirt with a window at the back or retain a bra if barebacked, still their appearance contrasts with the usual decorum and restraint expected from women. These ritual actions, taken as a whole, imply the reversal of usual social norms. Mediums are outside normal behavior, beyond social propriety, almost transcending gender.

To some extent, entranced mediums are freed from the constraints of time. The organizers of a temple festival may issue a program declaring that the last god's sedan will enter the home temple at exactly 10 P.M.— as they did for the 1988 Xigang *jiao* (grand festival)—but everyone knows that it will be well after midnight when the exhausted committeemen finally go home. It is the mediums who hold matters up, as two other cases illustrate. The first was at the 1987 *jiao* of Jiali, Tainan county. As usual, Daoists hired for the occasion managed the inner ritual, creating a special out-of-bounds sanctum within the temple for the duration of the *jiao;* and the temple committeemen ran the procession and its rituals in collaboration with other temples. In the *jiao* in question, a key informal role was played by a nearby temple dedicated to the Third Prince *(Taiziye)*. On the evening that the escorting paper generals and soldiers were taken to have their eyes ceremonially dotted at the site of the sacrificial boat burning, each temple group returned late at night to the temple; the Third Prince medium who led the procession arrived at the temple still in trance, entered the main space before the permanent altar, and lay motionless for about twenty minutes, spread-eagled on his back in an unrehearsed and idiosyncratic ritual pose. Naturally there could be no interference, and the temple officers did nothing to disturb him. The chief ritual advisor, an expert from another temple, told me later that it had been a complete surprise. But there had been no way of preventing this interruption.

The second case was the annual pilgrimage of a village temple to Wu Ben, the God of Medicine at Xuejia. The purpose was a ceremony at the edge of a river, the presumed site at which the first residents of the region landed three hundred years before with an image of the god. The high point was a series of rituals beside the river. It was conducted with the help of an officiating Red Head priest as the villagers and their guests watched, but the most active role was played by a group of mediums who had to be entranced before the rite began. Villagers and guests and the Red Head had to wait for twenty minutes until the main god's medium went into trance, the only hiatus in the all day ritual. By the time he was ready to lead the culminating part of the day's ritual, he had exploited the dramatic tension to the utmost. Like the medium spread-eagled on the temple floor, this one too had ignored the organizers and their schedule, setting his own (or his god's) ritual time.

This neglect of time (or one might say its inversion) suggests a certain wilfullness, an independence from the requirements of others. It is a god who calls the tune in trance, and there is no arguing with the gods. Temple officials keep out of their way; so do Daoist priests, except on the rare occasions of ritual collaboration between a medium and a Daoist of the Red Head vernacular tradition. Trance licenses them to treat the powerful bluntly, even rudely. Once I heard an aide of the Tainan mayor, both of them key supporters in the construction of a Wangye sacrificial boat, criticized for his fondness of liquor and sex *(jiuse)*, much to the amusement of ten or so spectators. Such independence can be a source of considerable irritation to temple leaders and Daoist priests, who may be dubious that the god is actually speaking through the medium's mouth.

The assumption of authority is particularly striking in that the medium is often a very ordinary member of the community. At the end of one day's festivities we met the old man who had been Third Prince at an immense village banquet and enjoyed the open air feast at the same table. No special place had been prepared for him among the hundreds of tables, and no special attention was paid to him when the organizers walked round toasting each table. He did not stand on ceremony, and liberally helped himself and us all to wine. In the traditional custom of ordinary villagers, he also filled a large bag he had brought with food, competing energetically with an old female villager of his acquaintance for some of the tastier morsels when his favorite dishes were placed on the table. This was entirely normal feast-day behavior; none of the god's dignity had rubbed off on this villager, once he was out of trance.

Since compulsory education has been in force from the 1950s, almost all but elderly people can read and write Chinese. But people who consult mediums (or as they would say their gods) do not necessarily prefer the better educated. A medium I once met was paid to come from Kaohsiung to Tainan by a woman who wanted to contact her dead husband at the Temple of the Eastern Peak (Dongyue dian). I discovered, when he answered some questions from me through my Taiwanese interpreter after the seance, that he was unable to remember his own telephone number, or when reminded to write it down for me without correction. The woman who had hired his services was not in the least surprised or disturbed by this, and for good reason. Education, I have heard it said by other clients, may make mediums cunning and corrupt. Better to choose one too ignorant or too innocent to be a charlatan.

Ritual trance, then, can be the vehicle whereby even illiterate members of society embody the authority of the god. For a brief time he or she is the focus of attention. His temple helpers gather round to minister to him. Skewers perhaps are stuck through his cheeks, smoking incense is held before his nostrils to renew trance; periodically his broken or burnt skin is sprayed with rice wine spittle, his sweat is wiped with a towel, and his blood is absorbed by paper money (This is saved for a later occasion, to be burnt and dissolved for medicine.). When he uses the instruments of mortification vigorously, he is restrained by onlookers, who shout "Alright! Alright!" or "Enough." When he rests he is supported by his helpers, and when he comes out of trance, falling or throwing himself backwards, arms in the air, he is caught by them. Thereafter the medium is unremarkable. Ignored by those who watched over him so solicitously moments before, he walks off slowly through the crowd. Soon he has washed and put his shirt on, now just an ordinary member of his temple group. But while in trance, his social position had been momentarily transformed. Ritual trance in this way can be said to invert social heirarchy.

In an extreme case, normal social values may for ritual purposes be entirely transgressed. One night in Tainan city I witnessed the funeral ceremony of a medium's father. To my surprise the medium—an only son—did not wear sackcloth mourning hat and cloak or sit in a son's place in the mourners' area. Instead while the rest of the Daoist service was being conducted by the priests, he squatted or stood on the sidelines chatting with the hired musicians, Daoist acrobats, and chairbearers. When the time came to rescue the dead man's soul from purgatory, he led the ritual as a bearer of the possessed chair. Obviously his status as a medium on this occasion overrode his responsibilities as a son, in spite of the fact that it was the most important filial ceremony of his life.

But this is not moral revolt; it is the permissible eccentricity for indicating a god's presence. The only conclusion possible from these various incidents is that ritual trance temporarily transforms social status. Trained mediums are understood to have an alternative personality along with their alternative social role as the god's mouthpiece; and ritual trance activates it.

Mediums' Uses in Local Society

People in charge of local ritual events put up with all these eccentricities either because they take them as the whimsical acts of the possessing god, or at least because they realize that the people rely upon mediums. Their role is too important to be dispensed with and too peculiar to them to be substituted. This is true both in their oracular and performative functions.

Mediums compete with priests as specialists of the *yin* world (the underworld). Most do simplified Daoist rituals of exorcism, and they have been described as mere puppets of the Daoist priests.[12] But seen at local level, their role is generally independent of any priest and is very different in nature. That is why they are indispensable.

Mediums are readily available, and much more common than Daoist priests, for most villages in the Tainan countryside, and many urban shrines, have one or more.[13] Since they are not paid, any village can afford one, and since they are not elaborately trained or (with few exceptions) heritors of a family tradition, almost any villager in principle can become one. They are available to serve a particular community regularly, whereas the priest and his assistants are hired for short periods on special occasions like *jiao* and funerals. They are *the* village practitioners, still the only consultants on the spot for a variety of family problems and physical ailments, and the only human manifestation of a local god at festivals and pilgrimages.

Even where priests are at hand, mediums often have the edge. This is evident, if one attempts to see the *yin* world as the villager does. Interaction with it is essential, in order to cure physical ills, change bad luck in agriculture and business, resolve family quarrelling, and settle the souls of those who have died unhappily. Priests also work to restore a balance between *yin* and *yang*, but they work at a more abstract and esoteric level.

For one thing, people believe that a particular god protects the community, serving like a lower bureaucrat in a celestial hierarchy. Such a god is without interest to Daoist priests; when they are hired for three to five days of rituals in a *jiao*, they will mutter the host temple god's names in the middle of a long list of divine figures; and if questioned on the god's identity they will deny the truth of current local legends. By contrast the medium represents the god's tangible material presence whether awesomely mortified in procession, or handling problems specific to the community or temple members while the god is "attached" to him in seance.

People also believe that the dead of the community may trouble the living as unhappy ghosts. A great amount of community ritual, especially the *pudu* universal salvation ghosts' banquets during the seventh or ghost month, is designed to make the ghosts (good brothers, as they are euphemistically called) happy and contented, but such festivals are meant without distinction to placate all the troublesome dead. These rites, and also funeral rites for specific families, are conducted by the Daoist priest. It is the medium, however, who diagnoses individual problems caused by specific ghosts, makes contact with them to ascertain the cause of their unhappiness, and proposes remedial action (a ghost marriage, or perhaps the rebuilding or resiting of a grave).

The utility of the medium, as a local practitioner, is therefore clear. In oracular seance, possessed by a god, his ministrations are personal while the priest's are impersonal; his concerns are specific and rooted in particular communities while the priest's are general and universal; and he facilitates direct contact with divine and ghostly forces while the priest usually allows them only to be imagined. He thus meets the need of ordinary people for oral and visual contact with those known dead who still weigh on their minds, and with the god that aids the community and promotes its unity. Through him the people can reestablish direct contact with the forces that affect them.

Mediums also compete with traditional herbal doctors and now modern physicians. Here their advantage, as in other societies, depends on a holistic and balancing approach to disease. Unsuitable behavior is responsible for disease and by changing behavior one can cure it. An indisposition is to be cured by a more moderate diet, the behavior of a daughter-in-law is to be tolerated, father is to be heeded, extravagance is to be put aside. This point could be argued at length.[14] What is to be underlined here is the personal acquaintance that the medium has with the members of his temple.[15] Only as a community member (or one thoroughly familiar with other members of the village or temple group) could he treat the whole person. He is the grass-roots practitioner par excellence.

Spirit mediums are usually attached to shrines, not to larger or long-established temples. When asked about their absence, some temple managers say "There used to be one, but he retired (or died) some years ago, and the god has not recently possessed anyone." But many others will frankly admit that such people are "mischievous" and "unreliable"; they "cheat" or are not genuine representatives of the god. When one considers the range of questions asked of the god, it is easy to see the mischief that could be done. At the start of biweekly seances, the god might be asked through him whether there should be a *jiao?* Will these dates be all right for it? How many ritual masts should be erected to attract the ghosts? Whether the interpreter controls some or all of the answers, together they plainly have a large impact on the temple's finances and its committeemen's time, for if a question is answered plainly by the god it is hard to ignore it. Some of the oddest-looking Taiwan temples owe their aspect to the advice of entranced mediums who demanded the construction of permanent poles of extraordinary height, or statues inside or outside the temple of novel design and coloring. This is consistent with Emily Ahern's theoretical remark that divination by medium is "less restricted" than other forms, with the result that: "The gods can order, direct, command, express displeasure or anger very dramatically, and thus quite effectively compel respect for their authority."[16] Unscrupulous mediums could use this latitude for personal advantage. Other methods of divination (moonblocks or divination sticks and slips or the divination chair) are safer for temple managers because they are more predictable and keep authority in their hands.

The situation of a small shrine is quite different. It needs a source of income, for it has little property. It needs to be able to raise money for building. Therefore it needs an active and enthusiastic following of believers. This is noticeable in town shrines which are rarely restricted to the inhabitants of a single neighborhood but (given modern two-wheeled motor transportation) can draw on a wide area. What attracts believers more than anything else is a spirit medium. If the medium is impressive in procession and effective in seance, it is a sign of the god's magical efficacy. When the time comes to celebrate the god's birthday, add to the god's statues or altar furnishings, or build a full-scale temple they will gladly volunteer money.[17]

In fact, the contrast between the gods of new and and old temples recalls Max Weber's distinction between charismatic and bureaucratic authority. The medium adds the dynamism of charisma which the growing temple needs. But, for the established temple which has property to manage and protect, fabric to repair or paint, rent to collect and invest, and charity and public services to dispense, the medium would be not only unhelpful, but with all his unpredictability, would be a liability. How then does the established temple attract excitement and worshipers? There are a few large temples that have retained their own charismatic appeal by becoming the focus of smaller, tributary shrines. Thus the religious centers for Wangye at Madou and Nankunshen, and those for Mazu at Beigang and Luermen, receive annual pilgrimages of gods' images and mediums from all over Taiwan; and the regional center of the Xigang Mazu temple celebrates triennial visits from Wangye during which its iconic papier mâché carps earlier sold to local people are brought back for ceremonial display, while the mediums of over seventy surrounding communities escort their gods' sedans in processions culminating at its steps. But these are all famous cases, and the option of attracting worshipers from a wide area is not generally available—though sometimes would-be pilgrim temples are not averse to adding concrete aprons and putting up signs of welcome in order to attract passing tour buses. More commonly, an established bureaucratically oriented temple will compensate for its lost charisma by setting up one or more small permanent shrines under its auspices to carry on regular evening sessions for mediums. The faithful want to consult the god, I was told in one such temple in Tainan city, but one cannot permit the hubbub of a seance until the early hours of the morning, and in such conditions the security of images and other valuables in the main temple could not be guaranteed. Old temples that do not possess such dependent shrines may, in the case of a *jiao* or god's birthday, invite a friendly shrine along with its gods and mediums to make up the van in the procession and add the requisite noise and bustle. Thus efforts to overcome routinization lead to various forms of interconnectedness among temples and shrines, demonstrating the continuing importance of mediumship, even to well established temples.

Important though mediums are in these various ways, their low out-of-trance status, in the majority of cases, should again be noted. Furthermore, temple communities control carefully whom they admit as the god's voice. Many mental illnesses take the cultural form of god possession, and at every festival people are possessed in the crowd who have never been possessed before, but no one is accepted unless he or she has undergone training. In principle this involves a seclusion and fasting in the shrine or an annex under the care of a priest, or more often lay temple people, for forty-nine days, the interval prescribed for mourning.

After this symbolic death, the medium is, as it were, reborn from the womblike space under an altar table, in a community rite of initiation resembling Gennep's rites of passage.[18] In some shrines there are those who do seances and perform without having done the full seclusion, but their "cultivation" is not regarded as complete. Clearly there is a process of socialization that gradually embeds the prospective medium in the local community.

Disorderly Performance and Ritual Order

The procession form of trance, to all appearances, signifies disorder. Yet by showing that ritual dance and mortification are a form of what anthropologists call ritual reversal, I shall argue that here too the medium serves local social interests. Two forms of medium are most common as god's sedan escorts, the trickster and the mortifier.[19]

The tricksters are all well known from popular fiction and drama. The Monkey King *(Sun Wukong)*, the beloved character of the *Journey to the West*, bounds to and fro, scratching at himself, making to steal fruit from the altar, a human being with the mannerisms of an animal. The Tipsy Monk *(Jigong)*, a comic figure who is the subject of a fictional biography, staggers from temple to temple with a gourd in the left hand and a fan in the right, dressed in a patched yellow or black gown, his drunkenness contradicting the precepts of his religious status. In trance both represent an inversion of commonly accepted social values.

Then there is the Third Prince, No Cha, a mischievous child, sent down to humanity from heaven, and possessing the capacity to transform his shape. Like the Monkey King and the Tipsy Monk he makes people smile, and does outrageous things. As a mortifier he wears the standard brightly colored chest-covering. Since he uses the mortifying instruments on himself (incidentally, like all the tricksters, it is invariably a male medium) he may be seen as an intermediary category between tricksters and mortifiers.

The tricksters are very popular in Taiwan today, especially in the center and north of the country, and deserve separate study. My impression is that they are almost always urban or suburban (village mediums are usually male mortifiers). Their popularity is undoubtedly due largely to their oracular role in gambling:[20] their gods are of low enough status to give advice on the lottery, and such consultations have increased as public concern with the lottery has become obsessive. Their unwillingness to take themselves seriously perhaps suits poorer city Taiwanese particularly well, and a god that makes fun of himself may be in a better position to disarm the rationalism and skepticism which the better educated tend to spread in the larger cities like Taipei and Taichung.

There are several ways of viewing the tricksters. Jean DeBernardi, who uses the term *trickster gods,* shows that those in Singapore are actually associated with an underworld of "black societies" in Penang, but emphasizes that inversions of values are temporary and do not alter the marginality of the cult and its supporters.[21] Tim Lane, in a recent dissertation on Taiwan mediums,[22] sees them as "unruly gods" who he claims are antisocial, even socially destructive in meaning. I would prefer to see them as an effort to let off steam, not necessarily a social threat—a temporary paradox that reinforces regularity, momentary forbidden behavior with a cathartic effect.[23] When the men who on two evenings a week give moralistic and largely conventional advice in seance are the same ones who give frenetic or drunken procession performances on feast days, it is hard to see the latter as a force of social disruption.[24] In short, status reversal appears as rather conservative.[25]

Actually, in spite of the irreverence and humor, comic reversal may have a patently moral edge,[26] as a personal experience suggested to me at the start of my field research. At a break in the annual election of an incense-keeper *(luzhu),* the performers and ritualists went to one side of the temple to eat, I accepted an offer to join them, not realizing that temple members were not partaking at that point. Some time after the meal, which was both substantial and delicious, one of the temple's mediums was possessed (in his usual way) by a series of gods. When the Monkey King appeared and pretended to steal fruit from the altar, a bystander who had watched me eat without himself eating, volunteered an interpretation for my notebook: this was to show that if people were invited to a banquet it was not necessarily appropriate to accept the offer! Evidently people are aware that what tricksters do is not just play, with the purpose of simple amusement.

The mortifiers occupy almost the same ritual space as the tricksters, just leading the sedan, sometimes preceding a mortifier if they are part of the same temple group. Observers watch stony-faced, some betraying a sense of awe, as mediums arriving before a temple are handed their weapons of punishment one by one: the thin sword, the swordfish bill, or metal saw; the nail-stick (used on the front scalp, arms or the back); the axe (beaten rapidly on the front scalp); and the prick-ball (which may be swung on its string, or thrown into the air and caught, or allowed to bounce onto the head, or which may be affixed to the scalp or back for a time). Some mediums instead extinguish lighted incense sticks on their chests, even chins; or have themselves impaled with metal skewers. It is a spectacle of excess, in which dance and gesture are almost always rudimentary: the most appreciated performances tend to be the bloodier and more violent ones.

There is no standard interpretation by participants to explain self-mortification: like so much else it is "just an old custom." But the link with martial power is obvious. Self-mortifying mediums are those of military not civil gods, notably such territorial gods of relatively low rank like Wangye, originally the plague god. Thus the instruments of self-mortification underline the god's awesomeness by conveying martial authority. Informants often confirm the military associations. Several mediums described their ritual self-beating as "taking the roll of the soldiers *(dianbing).*" Others use the standard term "five camps *(wuying)*" to describe the flags stuck through the skin of Wangye's mediums, the five camps being those of generals protecting the community's sacred space.[27] Divine power is released by mortification, for it happens at a sacred moment, when the god is indubitably present. The god's power expressed in the male *yang* force inheres in the blood spilled in self-mortification. That blood is dangerous if seen by a woman within a month after childbirth, yet medically beneficial if absorbed in paper money, and later burned and taken as a potion.

It is certainly clear that the intention is not, as it is in the European medieval confraternities, to atone for personal or communal sins by self-punishment. Mediums do not suffer: they mortify themselves with a kind of joy, because, they will say, they itch to do it. Before the temple, they reach out impatiently, eyes closed or half closed, for their weapons. They do not admit to feeling any pain, unless they are not in trance when they strike themselves. Even if heavily scarred, they insist there are no long-term physical effects—because of the god's protection. Older practitioners even attribute their longevity to it.

Self-mortification to foreign observers may seem an affront to normal behavior, but it is still more so in the context of rural and small-town Taiwan, which is still under the influence of recognizably Confucian ideas. As David Jordan pointed out, citing the *Classic of Filial Piety,* in traditional China one was obliged to keep intact the "body and limbs, hair and skin . . . given us by our parents." Bloodying the body and risking injury is an offense against them. How to explain the discordance? The medium, Jordan suggests, is "deliberately flouting the rules[,] . . . cut off from the world of ordinary mortals and their responsibilities and becoming (while he is in trance) *entirely* the instrument of the god."[28] This is consistent with the discussion above. Self-mortification is thus a mark not of rebelliousness but of authentic possession, a sign that the god is unmistakably present. By making visible the intensity of what the medium feels and perceives, self-mortification gives what Geertz would perhaps call an "aura of factuality" to those sensations and to divine presence itself.[29] It is through this extraordinary upside-down behavior that individual trance is converted to social use.

Like the costumed tricksters, the self-mortifiers are thus seen as a variety of deliberate reversal for ritual purposes, not as a challenge to social morality. To see them as immoral would be to see the god himself as an immoral force, which is contrary to Chinese belief. What, then, does the presence of reversal behavior add to a typical performance? Anthropologists have written of the period of sacred time or non-time at a ritual high point and have noted that dramatic reversal often signals that moment. Leach suggests that the contrasting moods of formality and masquerade precede and follow ritual role reversal.[30] In Taiwan processions, the entranced medium normally advances immediately before the sedan that bears the image of the god possessing him.[31] The following ritual acts succeed each other at every temple and shrine along the line of march. At the head of each temple's group (if it is a full complement) right after standard bearers, there are: (1) masked players and musicians who simply bow or do their act if time and space permit—the "masquerade" part of the temple group; (2) fireworks greet the visiting sedan as it approaches the temple, preparing the extraordinary moment of divine encounter; (3) the visiting mediums mortify themselves rhythmically, greeted by the temple's medium who is expected to follow suit—signifying the full entry into the sacred period of "reversal"; (4) the sedan makes three rushes toward the temple in greeting; and (5) gifts are exchanged by committeemen representing the visiting and receiving temples, while the temple bell and drum sound solemnly—the element of "formality"; (6) the sedan leaves, led by the mediums, to another burst of firecrackers, returning to the ordinary, or in Leach's formulation to secular time.

Much the same occurs at a pilgrimage visit, with several hours or an overnight stay separating arrival and departure from the shrine. Either the self-mortifier or trickster performs immediately before the arrival and departure of the god's sedan. In this case two periods of sacred time are entered and left, but in both, ritual trance performance marks the climax.

Put differently, these temple rituals bring participants to a stage of liminality, creating what Turner calls communitas, the sense, that is, the barriers and inequalities of everyday society have dissolved, and that its members are momentarily bound in mystical union.[32] The medium has the focal role here because he (or she) represents the god's presence— not any god, but that of the local temple, who more than anything else signifies the undifferentiated community—the abstracted essence of all they have in common. By virtue of his training and the community's acceptance, sometimes hard-won, that he really represents the god, the medium has a special status outside the social structure, and with the help of ritual trance is uniquely fitted to bring about the moment of communitas.

Recent suggestions drawn from neurophysiology link this sense of ritual unity with interactive workings of the brain hemispheres.[33] Repetitive stimuli, visual or aural, can produce a collective "high"—technically a "high discharge of both autonomous subsystems." This may be achieved, at least by some participants, in the procession approach to the temple, when a sort of crescendo of repetitive sights and sounds occurs. The entranced medium slowly shakes his head, the god's sedan rocks from side to side, the strings of firecrackers are set off, the instruments of mortification beat rhythmically, the sedan makes its three rushes, and the temple's bell and drum sound, again and again, several drum beats to one longer clang of the bell. Intensifying the rhythmic stimuli, the visiting temple group may have its own light drums. At the moment of greeting, the customary structural separations disappear. The protective exclusiveness of the communities and their gods is replaced by a sense of union among all participants, whether actors or spectators.

Personal Uses of Mediumship

The ability to go into trance is universally human, according to some psychologists, but it is much more usual in some societies than others. It is likely that cultural predispositions combine with innate human capacities in a particular social setting in cases like southern Taiwan to make ritual trance common.

A personal predicament in the family setting can contribute to a trance illness and its resolution in the adoption of medium status. I found this in a number of interviews with women mediums in Tainan. In one case, harsh treatment by the father had led to bouts of unconsciousness and visions of a god. He married her off quickly against her will, fearing that such visions might obstruct marriage. But the visions reappeared during the marriage, which was unhappy. After giving birth to two sons, the relationship worsened. She informed her husband that the god wanted her for her service, and that she must undergo seclusion. He had no alternative but to agree, and indeed helped her through it. When she emerged seven weeks later, local people flocked to her shrine for seance consultation. At the time of my interviews, the husband was long absent, and she was self-supporting. Similar life histories are given by Lane, and examples could be multiplied. Family problems are not always settled so neatly by possession, nor are mediums always recruited in this way, but the example suggests that psychosomatic responses to difficulties unsolvable by other means can bring about resolution through mediumship.

Recent research confirms the neurological authenticity of trance and spells out some of its special circumstances and effects.[34] If one is trying to account for the persistence of mediumship, this is striking evidence. More striking still is the parallel support of "emic" Taiwanese cultural interpretations in the following examples.

Training: (a) Possession brought under control. A Taiwanese first learns involuntarily of his or her ability to go into trance; later it is gradually brought under control through the instruction of the god. Experienced mediums can trance on demand with little or no stimulus. The ability to learn trance control is partly substantiated in the literature;[35] (b) the Forty-Nine Day seclusion *(xiujin).* As noted, this is the accepted method of induction. Mediums eat only altar fruit or perhaps vegetables, or in some cases nothing at all. Those willing to discuss the experience speak of visions brought by the god who possesses and instructs them. It is known that sensory deprivation leads to hallucination, "the result of impaired right hemisphere function" appearing *[inter alia]* under the effects of nutritional deprivation.[36]

Entering Trance: (a) Retching. This precedes the trance on some occasions. Mediums often explain this as a effort to rid themselves of impurity, since they are generally not vegetarian. Lex notes that emetics (and presumably vomiting or retching) stimulate the vagus nerve of the parasympathetic system, which is linked with trance states;[37] (b) offering incense. At the beginning of the medium's routine trance, and intermittently in the course of it, sticks of incense are held before him, and he inhales deeply. The cultural interpretation is that this presenting of incense *(jinxiang)* is showing respect to the god. Inhaling smoke vapors is a widely practiced means of facilitating trance.[38]

During Trance: (a) Glossolalia in seance. The cultural interpretation is speaking in the voice of the god; some mediums cannot be understood at all, others require an interpreter, yet others intersperse the god's language with Mandarin, the dialect of schools and officialdom in Taiwan. The use of glossolalia, a "rhythmic pattern of meaningless sounds and stereotyped utterances"[39] is thought to reflect temporary right-side dominance in the brain (that is of the usually nondominant side); (b) speechlessness in performance. In procession or before the home temple, mediums never speak, though some twitter in a high pitched birdlike fashion. This is explained in terms of a taboo; that is also the explana-

tion if the skewer is stuck through the cheeks at the time trance begins.
Though keeping silence in procession is in seeming contradiction to the
glossolalia in seance, the two types of trance can be explained by the
fact that there appear to be several types of autonomic balance;[40] (c)
painlessness. The absence of pain is noted in studies of excitation by
"driving mechanisms" (rhythmic stimuli) leading to "tuning" between
the two hemispheric brain systems.[41]

After Trance: (a) Inability to remember what one said or did while
the god was "attached." Amnesia about trance experience is noted in
research done in the 1960s.[42]

Thus the neurophysiological basis of trance gives a further explanation, alongside cultural and social factors already discussed, of persisting
spirit mediumship. Trance is partly spontaneous: mediums are themselves bemused by the experience, and it is reasonable to believe that
when they feel and see their own bodies behaving in otherwise unac-
countable ways, their confidence in the prevailing Chinese cultural interpretation (possession by a god) must be strengthened. On the other hand
the ritual aspect of trance is trained and consciously executed, containing
an element of acting and artifice. By drumming or head shaking the
medium learns to produce the reality of trance: what Lex and others call
driving mechanisms can deliberately tune the trophotropic/ergotropic
systems, achieve right hemisphere dominance, and achieve an ecstatic
inexpressible state. So there are ever new recruits to the ranks of mediums. In short, the neurophysiological reality of trance convinces those
who experience trance episodes of their destiny. And of course being
convinced, mediums are able to convince others, who for their part
accept trance as both familiar in itself and resonant with other cultural
beliefs and behavior.

So mediums do indeed present an image of disorder, but it is disorder
in the service of order and community. This has never been understood
by dyed-in-the-wool Confucians or latter-day reformers, hence the efforts to extirpate them. Reforming zealots turned away when the pa-
rades went past, and failed to experience the psychic moment when the
community was as one. But the uses of mediums must always have been
partly grasped by those humbler, less educated or at least less intolerant
leaders who themselves took on the responsibility to see that the god's
periodic rituals—on which the welfare of the community depended—
were properly performed and whose family members regularly consulted
the village medium.

NOTES

Field research for this paper was partially supported by the American Philosophical Society (Summer 1984), by the Inter-University Program for Research and Language Training in Taipei under the sponsorship of the Committee for Scientific and Scholarly Cooperation of the Academia Sinica, Republic of China (1986–87), and by Carnegie Mellon University through its faculty development fund (1986). I wish to thank these organizations, and also Chen Mei-li and Su Mei-yu for their interpretive assistance.

1. I use the term *trance* for physiological states of dissociation, as distinct from *possession,* which I use for the particular interpretation that explains trance by the presence of a spiritual entity. *Ritual trance* is the use of this state in established ways during recurrent public ceremonies. See also n. 7.

2. Donald S. Sutton, "Elite Attitudes Toward Shamanism in Late Imperial China," in *Orthodoxy in Late Imperial China,* ed. Kwang-Ching Liu (Berkeley, forthcoming).

3. Timothy Lane, "In the Presence of Gods: Bicameral Minds in Taiwan," (Ph.D. diss., University of Pittsburgh, 1987), chap. 9, p. 11.

4. Richard C. Kagan and Anna Wasescha, "The Taiwanese Tang-ki: The Shaman as Community Healer and Protector," unpublished manuscript, 1981.

5. I have met hardly anyone who thinks they are declining in number, and their resilience obviously adds force to my central question: Why have they held such a secure place in popular practice and belief?

6. In the summer of 1984, the spring of 1985, during many visits in the course of eighteen months in Taipei (1986–87), and in the early summer of 1988. I used a Taiwanese-Mandarin interpreter where necessary. Younger and middle-aged people have learned to speak Mandarin, but are often more comfortable speaking Taiwanese.

7. It should be added that the presence of a god (even with ritual) does not necessarily involve trance: chair bearers, two or four men who rock rhythmically and from time to time throw themselves about violently, are not considered to be in trance themselves; rather the chair itself is considered to be liable to be possessed. But the directing role is generally taken by the man on the left (left front in the case of a four-man chair) and his air of severe concentration combined with ritual rocking is not very far from trance behavior.

Conversely trance does not necessarily involve the presence of a god. In a parade one of the bearers of a god's sedan may go glassy-eyed, often in the excitement in front of the temple, and be replaced by someone else. Or a person in the crowd may go into a trance, without being recognized by others as genuinely possessed by the god, and even dance around with eyes half closed, and eventually be subdued (usually gently) by temple representatives.

8. See David K. Jordan's standard work on Taiwan spirit mediums (*Gods, Ghosts, and Ancestors: Folk Religion in a Taiwanese Village* [Berkeley, 1972], 82–84).

9. Or the medium of a spirit writing cult, before an altar, tracing in sand the answers to a variety of questions; see David K. Jordan and Daniel Overmyer, *The Flying Phoenix* (Princeton, 1986).

10. There are troupes of god's generals (known as Bajiajiang) entranced one by one in a god's parade; there are also spur-of-the-moment trances by bystanders, who (if disruptive of the proceedings) may be physically overpowered and removed to the sidelines.

11. Compare Bernard Gallin, *Hsin Hsing, Taiwan* (Berkeley, 1966).

12. Kristofer Schipper, *Le corps Taoiste* (Paris, 1982).

13. Some villages in southern Taiwan have at least three active ones and other men and women who are occasionally possessed.

14. But for the purpose of this paper I shall simply refer to Jordan, *Gods, Ghosts, and Ancestors,* and Arthur Kleinman, *Patients and Healers in the Context of Culture* (Berkeley, 1980) who make similar arguments.

15. Along with their assistant who may be a (more or less) equal partner in diagnosis.

16. Emily M. Ahern, *Ritual and Chinese Politics* (Cambridge, 1981), 89–90.

17. These conclusions are based largely on my intermittent five-year observation of the relationship of an established temple and a growing shrine in Tainan city, as well as interviews at other temples and shrines of the Wangye and Wufudadi cults.

18. In Arnold van Gennep, *The Rites of Passage* (London, 1909).

19. For a detailed consideration of mortification, see my unpublished paper "Taiwanese Self-Mortification in Its Ritual Context" (1989).

20. Hu Tai-li, "Shen, Gui yu Dutu: Dajiale duxi fanying zhi minsu xinyang" (Gods, ghosts, and gamblers: Popular customs and beliefs reflected in the "everyone happy" gambling game), unpublished paper, Academia Sinica, Nankang, 1987.

21. Jean DeBernardi, "The God of War and the Vagabond Buddha," *Modern China* 13, no. 3 (1987): 310–32.

22. Lane, "Presence of Gods," chap. 9.

23. Compare Victor Turner on upside-down rites of status reversal in *The Ritual Process: Structure and Anti-Structure* (Chicago, 1969), 176.

24. Such a view is broadly consistent, in the African case, with Norbeck's careful revision of Gluckman's discussion of rituals of rebellion. Max Gluckman, *Rituals of Rebellion in South-East Africa* (Manchester, 1954). Norbeck names these rituals of conflict, places them in a larger category of temporary suspensions of usual behavior for ritual purposes, and follows Gennep in seeing their function as "making memorable and enhancing the importance of the social occasions upon which they are observed." Edward Norbeck, "African Rituals of Conflict," in *Gods and Rituals: Readings in Religious Beliefs and Practices,* ed. John Middleton (New York, 1967), 218.

25. Turner and others note that evolution into real protest may take place in the proper circumstances. See also Natalie Davis, *Society and Culture in Early Modern France* (Stanford, 1975).

26. This is true of a common category of (nontrancing) procession troupes

in which female forwardness is lampooned, as I have argued elsewhere. Similar reversal phenomena have also been noted by Piet van der Loon, "Les origines rituelles du théâtre chinois," *Journal Asiatique* 265, nos. 1 and 2 (1977) for historical China as well as Taiwan.

27. See Schipper, *Corps Taoiste*, 287.

28. Jordan, *Gods, Ghosts, and Ancestors*, 82–84.

29. Clifford Geertz, "Religion as a Cultural System," in *Anthropological Approaches to the Study of Religion*, ed. Michael Banton (London, 1966).

30. Edmund Leach, "Time and False Noses," *Rethinking Anthropology* (London, 1961).

31. The nonmortifying trickster-god mediums (Monkey King and the Tipsy Monk) occupy the same ritual space and fulfill the same ritual function in procession as the self-mortifiers.

32. Turner, *Ritual Process*, 172–79.

33. Eugene G. d'Aquili, "Human Ceremonial Ritual and the Modulation of Aggression," *Zygon* 20 (1985).

34. Lane, in "Presence of Gods," has applied some of this research in an interesting dissertation on a variety of Taiwan trance behavior, but in my opinion has not been able to prove right-side dominance in EEG or eye-movement tests, or to establish a clear distinction between two types of trance.

35. E.g., Kamiya 1969 on controlling Alpha brain waves, cited in Barbara W. Lex, "The Neurobiology of Ritual Trance," in *The Spectrum of Ritual: A Biogenetic Structural Analysis*, ed. Eugene G. d'Aquili, Charles D. Laughlin, Jr., and John McManus (New York, 1979).

36. Lex, "Trance," 127, citing Baldwin 1970, 3–8.

37. Lex, "Trance," 119.

38. Ioan M. Lewis, *Ecstatic Religion* (London, 1971), 39.

39. Lex, "Trance," 128.

40. Ibid., 133.

41. One might add the physiological quirk of rapid healing. The wounds caused by self-mortification are said to heal quickly owing to the god's help. Athletes and others in times of high metabolic activity have noticed that capacity, but I have not traced research on this topic.

42. Lex, "Trance," 126.

— 6 —

Social Historians Entranced; or, The Medium Is the Message

Eugene G. d'Aquili

The preceding chapters are excellent examples of social scientists' finally coming to believe native accounts when they maintain that something mysterious or mystical is going on as a part of their cultural institutions. My message, to drive this point home, is what it has been to anthropologists since Charles Laughlin, Jr., and I first published *Biogenetic Structuralism* in 1974, namely, that when native informants tell us that something weird to Western ears is happening, believe them. At least believe them until you can prove conclusively otherwise. Many generations of social scientists, for example, believed that trances were, to put it bluntly, frauds. To be sure there were many qualifications. From Malinowski on we have all been well aware that cultural institutions have been maintained in societies to perform many functions, often of a complex nature. British structural functionalism has raised such functional analyses to a high art. But, in the last analysis, our social scientist ancestors looked upon *possession* or trance states such as those induced by the *Umbanda* or Taiwanese mediums as obvious dissimulations, although undoubtedly these frauds were fraught with considerable social importance. I am very happy today to see how far we have come. Social historians, anthropologists, and even some sociologists have begun to understand that many changes in psychophysiologic baseline functioning, many altered states of consciousness, many transitory changes of cognitive-affective alignment to reality form the foci on which powerful cultural institutions develop. Furthermore it is becoming increasingly clear that such powerful neuropsychological changes usually have intense intrinsic value for the persons in whom they occur. Thus they have intense personal value as well as often becoming the foci for the development of socio-cultural institutions which, once formed, then promote powerful ends in themselves. I must emphasize that the causes which bring a sociocultural phenomenon into existence are not necessarily the same forces which maintain it in a society.

An adequate biogenetic structural analysis of what Murdock calls a universal sociocultural institution must take into account first and foremost the possible neuropsychological mechanisms which account for any unusual states or behaviors around which a cultural institution may form. I might add parenthetically that a complete biogenetic structural analysis must consider the evolution of the brain mechanisms generating abstract thought, language, and the other prerequisites which permit culture to be formed at all. Specifically it must consider those mechanisms which permit the envelopment of altered or unusual behaviors by a belief system and cultural elaboration, giving birth to what we call a cultural institution such as the Brazilian *Umbanda,* Taiwanese mediums, or medieval flagellant sects.

In principle a biogenetic structural analysis can be applied to any cultural institution which can be called universal in Murdock's sense. In actual practice my colleagues and I have tended to focus on cultural institutions organized around altered states of consciousness or altered behaviors which may properly be called religious in the broadest sense of that word. Hence my interest in commenting on the chapters in this section, all of which involve trance states in one way or another. So let us turn our focus on a neuropsychological analysis of trance states.

In a number of works my colleagues and I have proposed that rhythmicity in the environment, be it visual, auditory, tactile, or proprioceptive drives the sympathetic-ergotropic system to maximal capacity with intermittent spillover and simultaneous activation of the parasympathetic-trophotropic system creating unusual subjective states.[1] One of the things that happens, is progressive activation of certain parts of the nondominant parieto-occipital region of the brain (which I have called the "holistic operator")[2] creating an increasing sense of wholeness, progressively more and more dominant over the sense of multiplicity of baseline reality. Because of alterations in prefrontal cortical functioning, the baseline sense of ordinary time can be altered in a number of ways. We have discussed the complex effects of rhythmicity and entrainment of brain waves elsewhere (d'Aquili and Laughlin, 1975).[3] A couple of minor points however ought to be noted here. Activation of the holistic operator and the attainment of certain ecstatic and blissful states can be strongly reinforced if not totally achieved via other mechanisms. The use of incense and other powerful fragrances directly affects the limbic system which, in fact, in the old neurological terminology used to be called the rhinencephalon or the nose brain. There are a number of connections both direct and indirect between the olfactory bulb and various mid-brain-limbic structures including the median forebrain bundle. This latter structure is generally considered a major "pleasure center," and it has been shown that rats would much rather stimulate it than eat. In fact rats can die of starvation by overstimulating their median forebrain bundles and not taking enough time out for nourishment. The stimulation of the olfactory bulbs and adjacent structures by the use of incense represents a powerful synergistic mechanism to the rhythmicity noted above in the production of ecstatic unitary states.

And "unitary states" is the operative phrase here. The bottom line in understanding the phenomenology of subjective religious experience is to understand that every religious experience involves a sense of the unity of reality at least somewhat greater than the baseline perception of unity in day-to-day life.[4] This is another way of saying that a more intense application of the holistic operator to incoming stimuli, over and above its base line function, coupled with the limbic or emotional stimulation that accompanies such increased functioning, always results in experiences which are described as religious or spiritual in varying degrees. Whatever the mechanisms for the increased functioning of the holistic operator may be—whether they be rhythmicity and entrainment of brain waves, olfactory stimulation in certain contexts, extreme fasting, electrolyte imbalance, or meditation—the final outcome is stimulation of the holistic operator with accompanying experiences of increased unity over multiplicity.

In a previous paper I described eight primary epistemic or knowing states, and particularly contrasted our base line epistemic state with a rare mystical state which I called Absolute Unitary Being.[5] AUB is a state described in the mystical literature of all the world's great religions. When a person is in that state he loses all sense of discrete being, and even the difference between self and other is obliterated. There is no sense of the passing of time, and all that remains is a perfect timeless undifferentiated consciousness. When such a state is suffused with positive affect there is a tendency to describe the experience after the fact as personal. Hence, such experiences are often described as a perfect union with God (the *Unio mystica* of the Christian tradition) or else the perfect manifestation of God in the Hindu tradition. When such experiences are accompanied by neutral affect they tend to be described after the fact as impersonal, generating concepts such as the abyss of Jakob Boehme, the void or nirvana of Buddhism or the Absolute of a number of philosophical traditions. There is no question that, whether the experience is interpreted personally as God or impersonally as the Absolute, it nevertheless possesses a quality of transcendent wholeness without any temporal or spatial division whatsoever. We have postulated that these rare states of AUB are attained through the "absolute" functioning of the holistic operator.[6] In all likelihood the neurological substrate for the holistic operator involves the function of a part of the parietal lobe on the non-dominant side.

In 1975[7] my coworkers and I first presented a model, since considerably elaborated, which attempted to explain the attainment of Absolute Unitary Being by integrating W. R. Hess's ergotropic-trophotropic model with the then relatively new split-brain research which was coming out of Professor R. W. Sperry's laboratory[8] and was elaborated by Bogen, Trevarthen,[9] and others.

In this model we proposed that the ergotropic system be extended upwards to include the dominant hemisphere and that the trophotropic system be extended upwards to include the non-dominant hemisphere. By driving either one or the other system to a state of saturation we postulated that the opposite system would be stimulated as we know occurs in third state autonomic stimulation such that, for a brief period, there would be firing of both systems. Thus during Absolute Unitary Being not only would there be maximum discharge from the holistic operator and other neural structures on the nondominant side generating a sense of absolute wholeness, but there would be an intense firing of structures on the left or dominant hemisphere associating with that wholeness the intense consciousness of the reflexive ego associated with normal left hemispheric functioning.

Consequently the experience of Absolute Unitary Being is not a vague sense of undifferentiated wholeness but one of intense consciousness since both systems are maximally firing. If this model is correct it should be obvious that AUB involves an extreme state of functioning of the holistic operator. More usual or ordinary perceptions reflect some sort of balance between analytic and synthetic or gestalt perception. We propose, however, that even in more normal perceptions, whenever the sense of wholeness exceeds the sense of parts or discrete elements, there is an affective discharge via the right brain-limbic connections that Schwartz and his colleagues[10] have shown to be of such importance. This tilting of the balance towards an increased perception of wholeness, depending on its intensity, can be experienced as beauty, numinosity (religious awe), or religious exaltation merging into trance states. We are proposing that there is an aesthetic-relgious spectrum, and that the point on this spectrum that any perception has depends on how far tilted it is in the direction of wholeness.[11]

The more the holistic operator functions in excess of a state of balance with the analytic functions of the left hemisphere the stronger the associated emotional charge will be. Thus in any aesthetic perception, whether it is a piece of music, a painting, a sculpture, or the perception of a sunset, there is a sense of meaning and wholeness which transcends the constituent parts. In aesthetic perceptions, however, this transcendence is slight to moderate.

In the next stage along this aesthetic-religious continuum the holistic operator functions with a degree of intensity which generates a very marked sense of meaning and wholeness expanding well beyond the parts perceived or well beyond the image generated. This experience Jung characterized as numinosity or religious awe. It is often experienced when an archetypal symbol is perceived or when certain archetypal elements are constellated in a myth. It is an experience during which the connotation of what is perceived vastly exceeds the denotation.

As we move from numinosity along the spectrum, that is as the function of the holistic operator more and more overwhelms analytic perception, we reach the state of religious exaltation which Bucke has called Cosmic Consciousness. This state is characterized by a sense of meaning and wholeness extending to all discrete beings whether subjective and objective. The essential unity and purposefulness of the universe is perceived as a primary datum in spite of knowledge of, and the perception of, evil in the world. During this state there is nothing whatever that escapes the mantle of wholeness and purposefulness. But this state does not obliterate discrete being, and it certainly exists within a temporal matrix.

As we move beyond the state of religious exaltation and cosmic consciousness we move into the realm of trance states where the increased sense of unity begins to obliterate the boundaries between perceived entities both in the external environment and especially the boundaries between self and other. This is the area on the aesthetic-religious continuum that the preceding chapters have been considering with their examples of medieval religious practices assaulted by the Counter-Reformation, Taiwanese mediums, and Brazilian *Umbanda*. Certainly trance states can exist in varying degrees of intensity involving a mild blurring of boundaries at one end all the way to merging into the state of absolute unitary being at the other. This represents the extreme of the aesthetic-religious continuum and the absolute functioning of the holistic operator. During this final state there is nothing but a timeless and perfect sense of meaning and wholeness without any perception of discrete entities. One might call AUB the ultimate trance.

Before closing this chapter I would like to discuss briefly the place of pain in the reinforcement of trance states especially since it plays a prominent part in both Taiwanese medium trances and in medieval penitential practices.

There are two physiologic mechanisms that have evolved in *Homo sapiens* to deal with severe pain. One is the production of vocalization, either moans or screams, which have been shown to decrease to some extent the perception of pain. The other is a change of focus from the perception of discrete linear sequential reality which is certainly subserved by the perception of pain to a more holistic perception of reality which is compatible with, and may even at times be constitutive of, what we call trance states. It has been noted that those suffering torture often go into trancelike states. Furthermore there is an extensive medical literature on the use of hypnosis and autohypnosis for anesthesia. I must point out here, however, that the belief system of the sufferer himself reinforces the effectiveness of the underlying neuropsychological mechanisms. Thus it was noted in the concentration camps that those who believed in God or who had some transcendent belief system bore suffering much better than committed atheists. Belief in God, it seems, or in some transcendent absolute is compatible with and strongly reinforces the sense of transcendent unity obtained through trancelike states. The atheist seems to have his belief system running contrary to the psychophysiology naturally built-in to help him bear pain. All this is a long way of pointing out that inflicting pain, like the use of incense, strongly reinforces trancelike conditions via the activation of the holistic operator. Of course the mythic meaning of inflicting pain or of the use of incense may be, and usually is, quite different within a specific mythic system from what is actually happening neuropsychologically. But that involves the question of incorporating myth into ritual, or vice versa, which is a whole topic in itself.

Let me conclude with a brief summary statement. An adequate analysis of any cultural institution which is formed around behaviors or states which deviate from normal baseline maintenance activities is vastly more complex than a simple functional analysis of what those behaviors, once institutionalized, may do for a society. A neuropsychological analysis of such behaviors or states is absolutely essential to any fundamental understanding of a cultural institution formed around them.

NOTES

1. E. G. d'Aquili, C. Laughlin, Jr., and J. McManus, *The Spectrum of Ritual: A Biogenetic Structural Analysis* (New York, 1979); E. G. d'Aquili and C. Laughlin, Jr., "The Biopsychological Determinants of Religious Ritual Behavior," *Zygon* 10 (1975); E. G. d'Aquili, "The Myth-Ritual Complex: A Biogenetic Structural Analysis," *Zygon* 18 (1983): 247–69.

2. E. G. d'Aquili, "The Neurobiological Bases of Myth and Concepts of Deity," *Zygon* 13 (1978): 257.

3. D'Aquili and Laughlin, Jr., "Biopsychological Determinants."

4. E. G. d'Aquili, "Myth, Ritual, and the Archetypal Hypothesis: Does the Dance Generate the Word?" *Zygon* 21 (1986): 141–60.

5. E. G. d'Aquili, "Senses of Reality in Science and Religion: A Neuroepistemological Perspective," *Zygon* 17 (1982): 361.

6. Ibid., 361.

7. D'Aquili and Laughlin, Jr., "Biopsychological Determinants."

8. R. W. Sperry, "Lateral Specialization in Surgically Separated Hemispheres," in *The Neurosciences: Third Study Program,* ed. P. J. Vinkin and G. W. Bruyn (Cambridge, 1974).

9. J. E. Bogen, "The Other Side of the Brain," part 2, "An Appositional Mind," *Bulletin of Los Angeles Neurological Society* 34 (1969): 135–62; C. Travarthan, "Brain Bisymmetry and the Role of the Corpus Callosum in Behavior and Conscious Experience," paper presented at the International Colloquium on Interhemispheric Relations, Czechoslovakia, 10–13 June 1969.

10. G. G. Schwartz, R. J. Davidson, and F. Maer, "Right Hemisphere Lateralization for Emotion in the Human Brain: Interactions with Cognitions," *Science* 190 (1975) 286–88.

11. D'Aquili, "Myth, Ritual, and the Archetypal Hypothesis."

PART III

LITERACY, COGNITION, AND HISTORICAL CHANGE

Literacy and the Origins of Inquisitorial Christianity: The Exegetical Battle Between Hierarchy and Community in the Christian Empire (300–500 C.E.)

Richard Landes

Translating the Religious Message

The story is told of a PTA meeting in the South in the 1960s where one man complained: "I don't know why my children need a foreign language; why if English was good enough for Jesus, it's good enough for my boy." Given how hard it was for this man's religious progenitors to even get Jesus' words into English, his remark carries an appreciable irony. In fact, by incorporating both an embrace of the English Bible with a militant assertion of the originality of this translated text, this statement embodies the kinds of contradictions that first led the Latin church to claim for its vernacular, the Vulgate, a privileged status precluding any further translations, including this man's English one.

The ironies involved in such developments go deep, because as with no other revealed faith Christianity originates in an act of translation. The movement's principal spiritual drive—communicating the experience of conversion—entailed, among other matters, constant transla-

This chapter is in the fullest sense an "essay," an attempt to sort out some difficult issues that, inevitably, bring up topics with which I have limited familiarity. As a result, some of the elements of my presentation may be less informed or nuanced than they should be, and will need reformulation. The central problem remains, however, and it is toward its closer examination that I present the following reflections. I thank those who have already helped me with their criticism, in particular Geoffrey Koziol and Philippe Buc for their close readings of a previous draft; I hope I have done well by their suggestions.

tion:[1] from the crucified Jesus to the Risen Christ, from the Jewish world to the Oecumene, from Aramaic (Yiddish of the day) to Koine Greek (Esperanto). As a result, the eventual fourth century Christian canon consists almost entirely of translation from Hebrew and Aramaic.[2] Further missionizing entailed further translations (at least partial), into Syriac, Coptic, Latin, Ethiopic, Armenian, Georgian, Gothic, Punic: any of the seventy-two tongues among the nations.[3] This tradition of translation has continued throughout Christian history to the present.[4]

And yet, in the Latin West from the eleventh to the sixteenth century, the Catholic Church developed one of the most violently anti-translation campaigns in religious history:

> Lay people shall not have books of scripture, except the psalter and the divine office: and they shall not have these books in the vulgar tongue. Moreover we prohibit that lay people should be permitted to have books of the Old or New Testament, except perchance any should wish from devotion to have a psalter, or a breviary for the divine office, or the hours of the blessed Virgin: but we most strictly prohibit their having even the aforesaid books translated into the vulgar tongue. (Dominican Council of Toulouse, 1229)[5]

This urgent prohibition comes from some of the earliest representatives of the medieval Inquisition, men treading a slippery slope toward the development of the most psychologically and socially intrusive bureaucratic movement before modern times.[6] Subsequent hostility from medieval ecclesiastics toward the later translators of the Bible in the West—Wycliffe, Luther, et al.—derived from the set of attitudes first established in this early thirteenth century. Only with the invention of the printing press did the tide turn decisively back in favor of the early Christian attitude favoring translation,[7] at which point that strain within the Catholic church which had countenanced translations all along once again came to the fore.

Despite the obvious historical connections between certain vernacular translations and "heresy," historians have paid little attention to the converse of this correlation—the Latin church's opposition to translation and the development of the Inquisition as a method for supressing heresy. On the contrary, the perception of the link as a minor factor in the Inquisition,[8] and the tendency to play down the significance of opposition to biblical translation in the medieval Church,[9] have all but placed the two discussions on separate tracks.[10] In any case, the conjunction of the two forces is generally seen as a late development dating from the end of the twelfth century at the earliest.

Recent work on the impact of literacy on a culture, and particularly of alphabetic literacy, suggests that the connection between opposition to vernacular translations and what might be called an "inquisitorial attitude" may run considerably deeper than would seem. The purpose of this chapter is to trace the origins of ecclesiastical efforts to control access to and interpretation of the Bible to the early history of the church (1-500 C.E.), and place these developments within the wider framework of literacy's place in society during this same period.[11] By highlighting the role of alphabetic literacy in this process, I hope to suggest a particular dynamic that causally links resistance to translations and inquisitorial persecutions.

I will start with some general remarks about the implications of religious texts for the structure of the communities that embrace them as sacred. From those observations I will identify a series of texts in the Christian Bible which strongly imply egalitarian if not more radical community structures, forming what one might call a revolutionary biblical corpus. Following these texts as they pass from community to community, from Aramaic Jewish, to Greek Mediterranean, to Latin imperial, we see the emergence within Christianity of hierarchical social and political structures that explicitly contradict the egalitarian messages of these texts with an hierarchical counter-exegesis. In the polarization between various readings of this radical corpus, the phenomenon of "heresy" and its inquisitorial repression take on a different configuration from that generally accepted by modern historians, and obey a dynamic at once ironic and revealing.

The Alphabet and Social Structure

The most fruitful work on literacy's impact on social development has come from conceiving the act of writing down as a translation—from the heard to be seen, from the evanescent to the permanent, from the interpersonal to the impersonal.[12] The kinds of intellectual developments such an act of translation encourage—e.g., splitting off historical or scientific from mythical thought, enhanced abstract and mathematical thought, allegorical interpretation—then play major roles in the shaping or reshaping of society.[13] Writing, unlike all other tools for social and economic activity, transforms not only the capacities of he who wields it, but also his psychology, his perceptions, his relationship to the past, the present, and the future.

Of all forms of writing, the alphabet seems to have an exceptionally dynamic role in encouraging and disseminating ongoing intellectual, psychological, and social changes. While traditionally the alphabet has been assigned the role of "democratic" script, more recent studies have indicated that the kinds of abstract utopian thought alphabetic literacy encourages, and the power it affords bureaucratic structures can also produce profoundly authoritarian social movements.[14] The very word *hierarchy* is the product of an alphabetic intellectual tradition.[15] At the two extremes of these dynamics we find democracy and totalitariansim, apparently both distinctive contributions to world history from alphabetic cultures.[16]

The *"Democratic" Dimension of Alphabetic Literacy: Textual Communities and Isonomia*

In pursuing the *Implications of Literacy* in the eleventh and twelfth centuries, Brian Stock has argued that the "textual community" constitutes a crucial unit wherein literacy and social change intersect.[17] The constituent element of such a community is the presence of a text—possibly very brief—whose moral and spiritual demands form the goal of those members who join. Members, even leaders, may be incapable of reading, but their lives are transformed and shaped by their texts, and they therefore acquire many of the traits normally associated with literacy.[18] These communities are voluntary societies, very often representing a radical break with previous and contemporary patterns of social organization, stating by their very existence a critique of the status quo. In the eleventh and twelfth centuries, Stock argues, they were the "laboratories of social organization" which provided a significant measure of the remarkable dynamism that characterize European society from the eleventh century onward.[19]

In most cases of a textual community, the crucial texts serve as laws, a phenomenon that explains how the text necessarily translates into actions.[20] In a number of cases—cases of particular concern in this inquiry—the law applies equally to all, thereby providing a powerful source of commitment and solidarity. The Greek term for a society ruled by the idea of equality before the law is *isonomia,* and it constitutes a notion whose "boldness and rarity cannot be overstressed."[21] Taken as a basic element in the formation of more or less egalitarian literate societies, based on freedom of speech, rights of individuals, and impartial law courts,[22] isonomia appears most often in discussions of early phases of democracy.[23] This, however, is somewhat misleading, and has relegated the term to a minor place in political theory. In fact isonomia can exist as a founding principle in a wide variety of governmental structures: monarchy, oligarchy, republicanism, and so on; but in every case it severely limits the actions of the ruling classes. As a result it can be adopted by the United Nations as a principle to be adhered to by all nations in the twentieth century, and, as the shaky history of the *Declaration of the Rights of Man* shows, it continues to have revolutionary implications.

Moreover, isonomia involves literacy at two crucial junctures: as the activities of Solon (sixth c. B.C.E.) and Kleisthenes (5th c.) indicate, isonomic reforms publish written laws as part of their program. This publication of the laws played a crucial role in the institution of any constitutional system in the ancient world, as the numerous cases of law codes engraved in stone attest.[24] But publication is especially important for a society based on equality before the law, since only an informed citizenry, aware of the law, could hope to protect its legal rights against the constant encroachments of those in power.[25] To have a sense of the importance of "permanent laws, permanently exhibited where all can see them" (Livy), one has only to consider the reaction of the fifth century B.C.E. Roman patriciate to the Ten Tables of the Law. Their ferocious resistance even to a law that privileged them, underlines how threatening artistocratic groups find such measures.[26] The fate of the laws in Orwell's parable *Animal Farm* provides another example of the relationship between isonomia and textual community on the one hand, and the incapacity for authoritarian elites to tolerate such public law-codes on the other.

Contents of Christian Texts I: Hebrew Bible and Isonomia

Historians tend to ignore ancient Israel as a source of political thought, and despite acknowledging an ancillary role to some elements of biblical thought, seek the origins of modern democratic institutions in ancient Greece.[27] This is partly due to the lack of explicitly political thought among the Hebrews; partly to the role of apparently anti-democratic theocracy in both Jewish and Christian traditions.[28] The principle of *isonomia* rather than democracy, however, brings into focus another perspective; for despite a lack of democratic institutions, no polity in the ancient world so systematically pursued the principles of isonomia as ancient Hebrew society.[29] Whether one takes the Decalogue as the founding document of the twelfth century B.C.E. Hebrew religious community, or a later (post-exilic) reformulation of a founding event, these commandments published on stone tablets, and applicable to all the members of the community regardless of status or wealth, constitute one of the earliest and most remarkable cases of an isonomic textual community in history.[30]

The Bible (really *Biblia:* "these books," "this collection"), is the eventual product of this textual community, and the subsequent texts bear every mark of adhering to this isonomia regardless of the form of government practiced in Israel.[31] The practice of public readings of the Pentateuch, and the development of translations for the common folk *(targumim)*, attest to the isonomic commitment not only of the texts, but the community which shaped and transmitted them.[32] It is in this context, then, that the most "dangerous" passages of the Hebrew Bible are to be understood. Some of the elements in this tradition are:

1. *Classlessness.* The cry of the 1381 Peasant Rebellion in England, "When Adam delved and Eve span, who was then the gentleman" expresses a characteristic reading of this passage by the Christian lower classes, and dates back several centuries at least.[33] It is linked to the uniquely biblical, monotheistic notion of a Creator making a generic dyad of man/woman, progenitors of all mankind, rather than genesis myths in which the mixing of gods and men produce demigods who found racially distinct ruling dynasties. The fact that Adam and Eve worked, even in Paradise, represents another anti-aristocratic element of the tale. The subsequent role of manual labor and the cyclical redistribution of property in Mosaic law underscores all these political elements found in the creation myth.[34]

2. *Liberation from tyrannical oppression.* The Exodus, as both Michael Walzer and Adam Wildavsky have recently shown, contains fundamental teachings on how to pass from oppressive hierarchies to autonomous self-regulating societies.[35] The revolutionary potential of the Exodus tale has inspired generations of political activists, and continues to do so today.[36] Most particularly the elements of collective liberation, the passage from a slave class with a slave mentality to a free people capable of the rewards and responsibilities of freedom, the notion of a covenant uniting the entire people, has made this text politically dangerous over time.

3. *Anti-monarchism.* Samuel's reaction when the children of Israel demanded a king (1 Sam. 8:7–8) reveals a basic stance of Hebraic political thought: monarchies and courts are breeding grounds for the abuse of power characteristic of the other nations; God's chosen should be capable of regulating their own communities without the need for centralized institutions of rule. The failure, therefore, of the charismatic system of circuit judges represented a moral failure on the part of the children of Israel and a rejection of God as king. "No king but God" expresses most accurately the Hebrew political interpretation of monotheism;[37] and monarchy, even when accepted, at no point envisages a king above the law (Deut. 17:16–20). These principles stood at variance with other, more promonarchical passages in the Hebrew Bible,[38] from

which almost all royal ideologies in the Middle Ages drew their imagery, but the redeployment of the anti-monarchical reading by the Calvinists in the sixteenth century contributed to the development of constitutional theory in the early modern period.[39]

4. *Social justice.* The call to care for the poor, the helpless, the stranger in your midst, which forms one of the main themes of the social legislation in the Mosaic code,[40] reaches a climax of emotional and rhetorical insistence in the prophets. Their denunciations of both political and economic forms of oppression provide the most potent texts for the rejection of inequities in society.[41] Amidst all the voices of the ancient world, the Prophets stand among the few who denounced the "idolatry of power" with such fervor and impartial consistency.[42]

5. *Revolutionary upheaval.* All of these radical tendencies in Hebraic moral thought contrasting God's will for a just society with the abuses of those in power culminated during the period of domination by external empires (Babylonian, Greek, and Roman) with the emergence of millenarian expectations of a violent, total upheaval that would produce a reversal in the nature of power: the meek and oppressed would enjoy peace and prosperity while the oppressors burn in Hell.[43] The millenarian "reign of the saints" which this apocalyptic tradition invoked highlighted classic revolutionary themes of liberty, equality, and fraternity,[44] thereby guaranteeing popularity for those who articulated them.[45] Its blanket condemnation of imperial authority made Jewish millenarianism particularly dangerous to the ruling authorities; and from as early as the Maccabees, such beliefs repeatedly fostered nationalist guerrilla uprisings against imperial rule.

This revolutionary tradition reached a fever pitch in Palestine around the turn of the Common Era. The cry of the Zealots (ca. 3–70 C.E.) so often crucified by Rome for these guerrilla tactics, was the anti-monarchical "No king but God."[46] This slogan encapsulates the political implications of the Bible as some Jews read it:[47] the hostility to foreign domination to be sure, but even to native authoritarian rulers.[48] It may be taken as the motto of egalitarian monotheism: God's rule over all men, precludes the rule of man over man.[49] Such a view underlies the reading of the classlessness of the time of Adam and Eve.

If I have emphasized the politically radical elements in the biblical texts it is because they play such an important role in the subsequent development of Christianity. This in no way suggests that there are not other, more conservative and hierarchical elements in both Hebrew scriptures and Judaism.[50] In fact, because of the emphasis of Christian tradition on the hierarchical elements in the Old Testament, this aspect of Jewish thought is best known to modern readers in terms of that "theocracy" which Josephus said Moses had instituted. As noted, however, isonomia can subsume both democratic and monarchic forms of government, and when Josephus coined the phrase, *theocracy,* which to modern ears implies a priestly hierarchy and its oppressive authority, he did so to illustrate how Moses' law preserves "one law for all" and avoids the tyrannous excesses of the other nations' forms of governments, be they monarchies, oligarchies, or democracies.[51] My present concern, in any case, is these still more radical passages, which have received relatively little attention from scholars concerned with political issues,[52] and which, if anything, received still more radical interpretation in the hands of the early Christians.

Contents of Christian Texts II: New Testament and Millenarianism

In the time of Jesus, this apocalyptic millenarianism so hostile to Rome had reached a fever pitch in Judaism;[53] and if later writers tried repeatedly to underplay this element of Christian origins, historians can still see the basic role in the early movement played by both the apocalyptic announcement of an imminent end to this unjust world and the millenarian hope of a kingdom of peace and plenty to follow.[54] Indeed, this future kingdom was the good tidings, the gospel, in its earliest form. The rustic language of the movement—its Koine Greek—highlights the immediate and popular appeal of its message which, as its opponents often noted, made great headway among the less educated elements of the population.[55]

Passages from the New Testament repeatedly encourage radical breaks with the past,[56] with tradition,[57] with contemporary society. Pointing to the emphasis in the *New* Testament on calls for a "new man" to replace the old, for a faith in unseen and anticipated things over the assurances founded in a sacred past, on the imminent destruction of the present order of things and its replacement with a new heaven and a new earth, Denis de Rougemont has argued that both the modern and the revolutionary world views stem directly from Christianity.[58] In their attitude toward their parent religion, Christians are avowedly antinomian.

Directly linked to this message, was an equally fervent commitment to communicate it to as many people as possible. It is in this context of urgent prostletization that we should understand the rendering of Jesus' Aramaic sayings in Greek, and the ultimate composition of a religious canon in a language the founder of the movement could not have read or understood. This translation for the sake of preaching to the gentiles, moreover, permitted a major new form of creating "textual communities." The model of these new communities, with its radical egalitarian ethic and communist organization, is the community of the first apostles in Jerusalem (Acts 2:44–47; 4:32–37).

It is important to keep in mind the inevitably anti-Roman element of any egalitarian or millenarian message at this time in Jewish history, no matter how "passive" or pacifistic one might wish to present Jesus' message;[59] and it is above all for this that the Romans crucified Jesus between two Zealots (that is, religious guerrillas), whatever his personal position on armed rebellion. Even though, by the early third century, this original (anti) political message had virtually disappeared in certain Christian circles, the dangers of these new textual communities continued to strike traditional authorities as radically subversive of the social order.[60]

Both the apocalyptic predictions of an imminent End to the World, and the millenarian promise of a kingdom of Peace and Plenty so offensive to Rome also became problematic to the gentile followers of Jesus. Eventually Christian leaders found it necessary to play down these issues, and in so doing they shifted the focus from a temporal, Jewish sense of collective salvation to come in this world, to a spatial Hellenistic one of individual salvation both within and above.[61] The resultant contrast between Jesus' timeless and inclusive message of love and the exclusive Jewish apocalyptic hope in vengeance and salvation became a stock topos in the Christian polemical arsenal, an intentionally misleading one which has survived the fall of Christian cultural hegemony with remarkable tenacity.[62]

To better understand the role that apocalyptic millenarianism played in early Christianity, let us consider the Book of Revelation, politically the most explosive of all the New Testament texts. From the times of the Fathers, this text has been the black sheep of the New Testament,[63] and modern commentators still question whether it is in fact really "Christian."[64] Recent historical studies, however, have given this text great prominence in the early development of Christianity:[65] no other book in the New Testament has the mythical intensity and dramatic power; the ironically, despite its terrible reputation among ecclesiastics, few books had a more widespread appeal to the rank and file of Christendom. John Gager has explained its strength from an ability to create a proleptic experience of the coming reign of the Saints.[66] The clearly oral context ("Blessed is he who reads and blessed are those who hear" [1:3]), and the cathartic emotional drama, serve to make this text on the Kingdom-to-come one of the major sources of textual community in a movement whose sense of imminent closure was incessantly frustrated.

The Church and Rome: Conversion of Christianity

Not surprisingly a text in which Rome appears as the Whore of Babylon at whose spectacular collapse the saints in Heaven shout "Halleluliah!" (Rev. 19:1–8), proved a major source of embarrassment for subsequent churchmen. In fact the intensifying hostility to the Book of Revelation among the church fathers of the second and third centuries corresponds in many cases with the development of apologetic literature. Here they tried to phrase the Gospel in a meaningful way for intellectuals of a Hellenistic milieu whose apoliticism (at best) served well in the face of imperial exigencies.[67] The cultural rapprochement between Christian theologians and Hellenistic intellectual circles intensified the language of hierarchy within the Church, both spiritually and organizationally. Without this development, the subsequent political union between a hierarchical Christianity and a reforming imperial Rome could never have occurred.[68]

In the early fourth century the Emperor Constantine himself converted to Christianity, and in the course of his long reign set the Roman Empire on the way to becoming the "Christian Empire." His conversion, however, had little impact on his continuation of Diocletian's reforms; on the contrary they were, if anything, more hierarchical, coercive, demanding, and confining than those of his predecessor.[69] In other words, just as the emperor converted to Christianity, the Roman Empire's role as taxer and oppressor of the poor and the powerless reached new heights. And yet the ecclesiastical hierarchy had little difficulty with this organization of society:[70] indeed it contributed important new elements to the divinization of imperial authority, one of the most authoritarian aspects of Diocletian's innovations.[71]

As Peter Brown has pointed out, then, the real conversion may have been Christianity's;[72] and among the vital elements of the older Christianity to meet with blanket condemnation from the imperial episcopacy was millenarianism.[73] Eusebius, the great propagandist for the conversion of the Roman Empire to Christianity at once praised Constantine as a virtual messianic emperor, and denounced millenarianism as a dangerous superstition. By the later fourth century no significant theologian, East or West, embraced any but the palest allegories of millenarianism. Even modern scholars who acknowledge the millenarian roots of Christianity, believe it no longer played much of a role by the fourth century, thus underestimating the significance of this revision.[74]

For our investigation this "disappearance" of millenarian themes from the texts, once so vital in Christian spirituality, plays a crucial role in the political problems of the medieval Church. One might best describe the kind of "cognitive dissonance"[75] that Imperial Christianity posed for a millenarian Christian in the fourth century by examining the rapprochement in patristic thought between Isaiah's Messianic Peace and the Pax Romana. That no two things could be farther apart is underlined by the fact that crucifixion was the standard means of dealing with dissidents who resisted Roman imperium, the punishment for so many thousands of Jewish Zealots and messianic pretenders. It symbolized, as it were, the way the Romans nailed down their "Pax Romana." Now Eusebius would have Christians believe this Pax was homologous with the Kingdom of God Jesus had announced. And yet by the fourth century Christian theologians had so convinced themselves that the Jews and not the Romans had killed Christ that the irony had apparently escaped them.

Exegesis and Cognitive Dissonance

These systematic inversions of the original meaning of the text characterize numerous pronouncements of political import that the Fathers publish. Only two need retain us here: the kingship texts in the Hebrew Bible and the millenarian texts in the New Testament.

Kingship texts. The essential revision concerns the view of monotheism toward monarchy. As we saw, the motto "No King but God" provides the isonomic exegesis of Samuel. In order to reread the texts highlighting the hierarchical elements, Eusebius introduced the hellenistic form of monotheism founded in a (neo)platonic conception of a hierarchical universe: "One God in Heaven, One ruler on Earth."[76] Such a principle permits the reader to defend monarchy not only by focusing on different passages (divine selection of monarch, annointing, popular acclamation) as did Jewish monarchists, but to actually reverse the meaning of the most troublesome passages. Thus the "manner" of a king in Samuel's list of royal abuses-to-come becomes the divinely appointed "rights" of the king.[77]

The complete exegetical reversal this principle permitted enables us to distinguish between two kinds of hierarchical thinking. In even the promonarchical versions of Jewish thought, no king stood above the law; no king could revoke the rights of his subjects to suit his will. As a religious corollary to this situation, Jews distinguished radically between divine and human nature, denying any kind of human theophany.[78] To argue that a human ruler's powers were comparable to God's, therefore, would therefore constitute an idolatrous blasphemy. So if "We have no king but God" represents the radical end of the political spectrum, "no earthly king can be as God" represents the limits of monarchical Jewish thought.[79] The hellenistic principle, however, breaks the restraints on monarchical power, and by equating the emperor with the messianic king, Eusebius effectively took Christian "political" thought into a sphere completely alien to most Jewish and most early Christian attitudes. One can interpret Augustine's teachings on the Two Cities as an attempt to undo such an impossible exegesis;[80] and the continued prominence of the parallel earthly/divine-ruler in early medieval Latin thought of as a sign of how tenacious it had become.

Millenarian texts. Since the beginning, millenarian Christians believed Babylon meant Rome (Rev. 14:6 *ff,* 17, 18)—purveyor of the worst social and political oppression in human history, a reign of injustice that, from the point of view of the plebs, had only increased with Diocletian and Constantinian taxation and legislation. For millenarians, the New Heaven and New Earth meant the overthrow of this idolatrous Roman order (Rev. 18–19), the punishment of the proud and cruel: for this was the faith and the patience of saints (Rev. 13:10).[81] All this talk of obedience to the powers that be (Rom. 13:1–10) was only predicated on the imminent end of that order (11–13), certainly not as a fulfillment of the messianic promise. And any Christian that became the handmaiden of the Empire could only be among those who adored the image of the Beast (Rev. 13:11–18). From this hermeneutic then the apostate (i.e., Catholic) church was now a servant of Antichrist: indeed was not Eusebius' deification of Constantine a worshipping of the image of the Beast (Rev. 13:15)? Little wonder the Fathers disliked the expectation of a carnal Kingdom of Heaven.

The Catholics' subsequent use of the "secular arm" of the Empire to persecute dissidents (e.g., the Donatists)[82] would have only served to confirm this interpretation.[83] Indeed, from a purely political standpoint, the Church's persecution of the Donatists closely parallels the pattern of Roman persecution of Christianity,[84] and from a religious one, it approaches the scenario of deicide which ecclesiastics levelled at the Jews: a politically compromised priesthood, jealously guarding its power, killed its own dissidents. Regardless of how the theologians in the "Patristic Golden Age" might have interpreted scripture to justify the imperialization of the Church, how many Christians, in addition to the Donatists, were scandalized by what they would, with full scriptural support, above all in the ethical demands of Jesus himself (e.g., Matt. 5:11–12, 21–26, 43–48, etc.) perceive as a devastating moral capitulation?[85]

The reference to millenarians as "Judaizers" points up one final aspect of the imperial revolution in Christianity: the intensification of hostility to the Jews. With the power official recognition granted, the bishops rapidly sought to limit Judaism's freedoms, and with the intensification of ecclesiastical intolerance for deviance and diversity in the later fourth century, attacks on Judaism and Jews reached a peak which, at least for invective, few subsequent periods have excelled.[86] At the same time as the Church took on more and more of the characteristics of those who crucified Jesus—imperium, coercion, oppressive class stratification— Churchmen found it increasingly necessary to repress heretics with force, and to flay Jews and Judaism for the blind hypocrisy with which they had betrayed (and by refusing to convert, continued to betray) Christ.

To encourage anti-Judaism among the population resolved a host of problems: in the now irreconcilable exegetical battle, the Jews and the millenarians lined up on one side against the teachings of the apostolic (hierarchical) Church. Frustration, confusion, anguished oppression among laymen loyal to the Church, thus had an outlet in righteous anger.[87] This pattern of guilty projection, and the concommitant hatred of Jews it fostered, became a permanent feature of the High Middle Ages.[88]

Prudent Historiography and the Textual Communities of History

Historians have been reluctant to discuss the moral stake in these issues in detail, perhaps from a reluctance to pass judgments,[89] or from a reluctance to argue *ex silentio* about what commoners were saying or thinking,[90] but also because they do not perceive the problem in a sustained fashion.[91] The consequent tendency to tell the story from the point of view of the theologians who constitute our prime source of information, exaggerates the ease with which Christians at all levels of the society experienced the moral contradictions of a Christian Empire, *a fortiori* one that executed dissidents. Among other things, such an approach can lead the historian to replicate the distortions of the theologians supposedly objects of study: thus one historian has presented the idea of monotheistic monarchy as coming from Judaism,[92] and another has argued that "the form of government overwhelmingly practised in the Middle Ages, that is the descending [i.e. hierarchical] form, had roots deep in the Bible [and especially O.T.], rather than in the Roman constitution of the late Roman empire." And yet so many of the proffered proofs are torn from context and literally stood on their heads, exactly as medieval political exegetes had already done.[93]

A still more important result of such scholarship is to underestimate the importance of a readership whose documentation does not reach us. Here the notion of textual communities becomes a particularly valuable concept: the isonomic exegesis of these texts carried its greatest weight not in textual commentaries preserved by hierarchical institutions and hence accessible to us historians by virtue of their orthodoxy, but in lived communities. By shifting focus from the logistical complications of Roman Christianity as experienced by those committed to the marriage of the two traditions, to its moral contradictions as experienced by less powerful but equally committed Christians of the day, genuinely anguished by the politicization of their communities, the hermeneutic battle for the meaning of the Bible takes on greater meaning.

At this point, the reading of the texts, particularly those in the "revolutionary" corpus I mentioned above, became a matter of central political importance. No longer could the isonomic and millenarian interpretations exist side by side with the hierarchical ones, as they had in the high period of apologetics (ca. 200–320). The unification of the Church under imperial auspices could not tolerate the older tradition.

This perspective sheds important light on the issue of the imperial Church's anti-Judaism. Jews did not merely represent a convenient (because defenseless) scapegoat. They represented an alternative textual community whose hermeneutic was now in many ways closer to the original Christian one than was that of the Fathers. Not only did they sustain their isonomic interpretations,[94] but also their political and cultural corollaries: rejection of idol worship,[95] non-hierarchical community structures,[96] millenarian expectation in a fall of Rome.[97] Constantinian Christianity, on the other hand, began a campaign of monumental sculpture, relic worship, and cultic images, all of which promoted the cause of the peace and the emperor, the icon of God.[98] It is interesting to note that Chrysostom's most violent tirades against Jews and Judaizers come in his series of sermons in the wake of anti-tax riots during which the statues of the emperor and his wife had been torn down. Such a popular rebellion corresponds precisely to the millenarian Jewish profile.[99] If anything, then, with the conversion of the Empire/Christianity, Jews posed a still more serious exegetical threat.

The checkered career of the Book of Revelation also makes sense in this light. It belongs to a category of texts modern scholars call *apocalyptic* (i.e., "revelations" specifically about the End of Time) which, despite early favor in Christian circles (three in canonical contention), became the object of violent attack in the wake of the millenarian activities of the Montanists (ca. 150–70). By the early fourth century, Revelation alone and despite violent attacks, remained in contention for inclusion in the canon. In his ecclesiastical history Eusebius speaks of it with undisguised hostility, and draws back from condemning it only because so many brethren view it with favor. Predictably, with the coming of the Empire Eusebius' hostility to millenarianism only intensified; and when Constantine ordered fifty copies of the Bible to use throughout the Empire, Eusebius may well have left Revelation out.[100] The Eastern

Church subsequently did leave it out for centuries.[101] Since *canonical* means a text one "read, or published in church to the people," the exclusion of Revelation functions to remove it from public discourse and hence robs it of its power to bond textual communities. Its absence from Eastern liturgical texts underlines this point.

But if such a solution were viable in the East, the Latin Church had no such possibilities: at no time was the exclusion of Revelation even suggested; it held a prominent role in the liturgy, and allegorical readings found little support.[102] It fell to Augustine, then, to domesticate this infinitely troublesome text, a task he accomplished with prodigious subtlety and energy by analyzing all of human history in terms of the coexistent visible earthly city, and the invisible heavenly one. No institution was coterminus with the Heavenly City; even the Church was a mixed body. On the other hand the Heavenly City existed and penetrated earthly life, and with the ascension of Christ, the Millennial Reign of the Saints, which literal, carnal-minded simpletons had awaited as a future event on earth, has in fact been in progress in the Heavenly City. The reinterpretation is a tour-de-force; and it involves some complete inversions of the text's meaning in order to work.[103] It dominated ecclesiastical exegesis until the twelfth century; and hence, scholars believe, Augustine "eliminated" millenarianism from Christianity for over eight hundred years.[104]

Augustine also championed the notion of the "Three Sacred Languages"—Hebrew, Greek, and Latin—a concept which looked anxiously at the apparent link between vernacular translations and heresy (e.g., Gothic and Arian);[105] and would legitimate the prohibition by High Medieval theologians of further vernacular translations. He based this idea of the "Three Sacred Languages," which could only have appeared in the region of the last and least of them, on the passage in John where Pilate wrote "Jesus Christ King of the Jews" in these three tongues. The claim of Latin, therefore, was based on the Romans holding sway over almost all peoples, and particularly appropriate to imperial Christianity.[106] It was a language with its own particular characteristics, and well-suited—particularly in the capable hands of Jerome—to shaping the biblical texts in the hierarchical direction now so necessary.[107] In light of the above analysis, it is little wonder that this "anodyne speculation" became the main justification for closing the book on further translations.

Conclusion: Alphabetic Literacy and Exegetical Polarization

The thesis presented here argues that it was in the fourth to fifth centuries, at the point when the Church fully allied with, and adopted, the political structures of imperial Rome, that we first find the constellation of traits which, reappearing in the eleventh century, would produce the Inquisition by the thirteenth: alliance with monarchic secular authority, use of coercion against Christian dissidents, inciting popular violence against Jews, and attempts to control access to biblical texts. This configuration, which one might label inquisitorial, is best understood as one side of a social and exegetical battle against a variety of isonomic textual communities grounded in a radical reading of the Bible, for which the reigning hierarchical institution had an intensely negative value.

If such a situation exists by the mere presence of the contradiction, any hierarchically organized and politically powerful Christian Church will develop repressive institutions. (This seems to be the assumption behind the principle of the "division of Church and State.") But there are more specific social and political conditions that activate the tension between these contradictions, moments when the isonomic reading and its radical variants strike home with more force,[108] in turn driving ecclesiastics to ever-more repressive measures. And among these conditions, I think alphabetic literacy constitutes a significant factor.

This investigation began with the role of literacy in contributing to both conceptual and social transformations, suggesting that the particularly penetrating influence of alphabetic literacy had implications at both extremes of the spectrum: political order conceived hierarchically and enforced bureaucratically and social organization conceived laterally and enforced by the community. I have argued that in Christianity both traditions found exegetical support in the Bible, but by the nature of those texts, the two points could reach a virtually absolute polarization: each side saw the other as Antichrist.

But not all Christian societies display the kinds of tensions and violence I argue derive from this exegetical antagonism. So under what circumstances does this battle for meaning polarize?

According to the present hypothesis, two conditions are essential, one from above, the other from below, neither necessarily taking precedence: (1) the hierarchical authorities intensify their demands on the population (e.g., taxes and other forms of property transfer to officials, legal or political devaluation of status), thus increasing their resemblance to the villains in the biblical texts; (2) the biblical text becomes available—

through preaching or reading—to people who have a natural interest in interpreting it as a critique of the present order. Significantly, the hierarchical Church, as keeper of the sacred Scriptures and mother of Christian spirituality, will always produce figures of great ecclesiastical influence who read the text in remarkably radical ways, thus guaranteeing some degree of diffusion of the more anti-authoritarian views to the laity.[109]

In this exegetical battle, alphabetic literacy injects a double impulse: (1) on the one hand it encourages the hierarchical thinking of ecclesiastical literates, offering both intellectual (philosophy, theology), and practical (bureaucracy, law) tools for articulating and extending claims to authority. A period of advancing literacy in a Church structured on the principle of hierarchical monotheism will encourage clerical distinction from laity, dogmatic uniformity and expansionism; and if that Church supplies the secular powers with administrators, government will also take on these traits; (2) on the other hand, the spread and the uses of literacy in a society, permitting the development of a wide variety of social and economic activities, makes the concept and practice of voluntary associations more common. In such circumstances the biblical texts particularly conducive to isonomic textual communities take on greater meaning.

Nothing in this analysis seems inevitable: hierarchies and bureaucracies can assert claims to power without viciously oppressing those under them; and such socially valuable voluntary associations as guilds, confraternities, corporations, and partnerships need not lead to radical egalitarianism and complete renunciation of society. This is where the singular nature of the Christian biblical corpus comes into play. As the Angel told John to tell the church of Laodicea: Because you are lukewarm—neither hot nor cold—I will spit you out" (3:16). Literacy interacts with the biblical texts and polarizes positions.

Sixth-century developments bear out point one above (top-down) as a determining variable. In the East, where both literacy and imperial political structures remained relatively high, the persecution of heretics became a basic element of political culture, particularly in periods of expanding pretensions to power (e.g., Justinian).[110] In the West, the rules of the game changed drastically: literary activity dropped conspicuously; populations lost large numbers in an endemic struggle merely to survive; and rulers had difficulty just staying in power.[111] Political efforts looked to ways of reconciling various religious and ethnic communities rather than of rendering them uniformly subject to a single will.[112]

For reasons that are not clear, however, at the beginning of the eleventh century, the tensions reemerged in European society with remarkable force. Although I cannot trace out the details here, it seems to me that four major elements already discussed above play a crucial role in making the polarities of eleventh- to fourteenth-century Western Christendom greater than at any previous time in Christian history, and therefore the potential threat of the texts all the more serious.

1. *Clerical monopoly of literacy.* For the intervening half a millennium, Latin Christendom moved north of the Alps and converted tribes with neither literacy nor Latin. As a result, by the year 1000, literate meant a clerical writer of Latin—a language laymen no longer spoke,[113] thus creating, ipso facto a cultural split between lay and cleric that had never existed in the East where lay literacy remained a constant feature of society. The resulting self-definitions of the clergy, and their attempt to impose them on the laity, take on a more central role in the West. With the advent of lay literacy this technological prop to clerical distinction was threatened, and ecclesiastics responded emphatically with new and more absolute distinctions between their *ordo clericalis* and the laity.

2. *Most revolutionary biblical corpus.* Revelation and its accompanying millenarianism, remained vital (if not actually central) elements of Latin Christendom.[114] In other words the most polarizing of all texts in the Bible retained an active place in the exegetical battle. As a result, it could support the radical reading of other passages which, on their own, posed fewer problems (e.g., Genesis and classlessness, Exodus and peoplehood, Acts and communal life).

3. *Internalization of polarities by Church.* In part because of the prominent place of Revelation in the Western canon, the polarities of exegesis penetrated the very core of the Latin church. As noted above, any Christian church, no matter how dedicated to the exercise of power in this world, will produce holy men and women who reach and preach a radical and anti-hierarchical gospel. But in the Latin church this reading went still further, to the core of the institution. By the mid-eleventh century, the papacy began a reform program that produced the extraordinary phenomenon of a Church restructuring itself along virtually Donatist lines,[115] and opposing secular authorities that disagreed in apocalyptic terms—even the Emperor was called Antichrist.[116]

4. *Popular participation.* The ferment accompanying such developments had the unintended effect of encouraging radical religiosity at every level of the lay population, contributing to the development of "popular religion" in the West, which with its isonomic textual communities (apostolic life, confraternities, communes) and mass movements (pilgrimage, peace movements, flagellants, crusades), ranks among the most explosive and protean expressions of religious culture in history.[117]

But this lay religiosity did not derive exclusively from the clerical (indeed that was the problem), for its first significant appearance preceded, and in many ways contributed to the ecclesiastical reform movement.[118]

5. *Lay literacy.* One of the phenomena accompanying and amplifying this lay religious ferment was the increase in the use of literacy in every sense: from religious textual communities imitating the apostles, to business contracts, to international communication.[119] In this sense, lay Europe's period without literacy created a fallow soil. Rather than the situation in the Roman Empire where the educational system had existed for centuries, and largely mirrored the elitist structure of society, eleventh-century Europe saw a spread of literacy through a wide variety of media: monastic schools for laymen, textual communities, but especially in the new and flourishing urban agglomerations.[120] This situation buttresses the argument that the ease of acquiring alphabetic literacy makes its influence all the more potent: it was possible for individuals to acquire the rudiments of writing outside of institutional structures, and hence to have self-taught literates appear in places where the traditional literate elites had little control.

The results could be mutually reinforcing hostility, as we can see in an example from the year 1025: the bishop of Arras, a region of northeastern France, discovered the existence of a community of local commoners led to the apostolic life by a wandering Italian holy man. It was a classic textual community in its combination of oral and literate modes and members, in its intimate connection between understanding and radical action, in its insistence on the salvific efficacy of the lived community and utter rejection of the Church and the aristocratic hierarchy it embodied.[121] Among the principles of life embraced by this community ("*lex et disciplina nostra*"), we find the notion that "all should live by the labor of their own hands." No more serious blow could be delivered to the claims of a priestly caste who, with an ideology of "three orders" claimed to live justly off the labor of others.

In the process of denigrating and ultimately condemning these lay commoners' attempts to understand the biblical texts, the bishop accentuated all those literate elements which set aside the priests as the sole and full-time, professional interpreters of the sacred text. In the course of an interminable sermon to the heretics (which they could not understand), the attention shifted away from their beliefs to "a complex defence of the church's control of religious literacy."[122] Asad has underlined the role of literate attitudes and skills in defining (i.e., creating) heresy, a way of targeting those "social and ideological dangers encountered and dealt with by a developing, empire-building Church."[123]

From the eleventh century onwards, European literacy rates climb almost constantly until the present: this was an enormous source of power. The multiple uses of literacy that both lay and ecclesiastical culture developed showed virtually limitless creativity and variety in its uses, and apostolic communities that were naive and largely oral in the early eleventh century gained in both textual knowledge and mistrust of the Church over the succeeding centuries. It is in this context of the implications of literacy for both groups that the inherently dangerous conflict between popular egalitarian religiosity and ecclesiastical religion in Christianity reached the violent proportions of an inquisitorial Church willing to risk anything to control access to and interpretation of their sacred scriptures. Thus, indeed, where they burned books, they also burned people.

NOTES

1. Acts 2:1–12, where the apostles speak in tongues that men from all nations can understand. As my colleague Lionel Rothkrug emphasized to me, this is the first "cultural" miracle of the New Testament, and undoes the work of Babel. For a recent treatment of the origins of Christianity which privileges the significance of "translating" Jesus' message from Jewish to Hellenistic cultures, see Paula L. Fredriksen, *From Jesus to Christ* (New Haven, 1988).

2. The Aramaic passages in the Hebrew Bible (the Old Testament) are found in the latter, apocalyptic portion of Daniel. This language, a mixture of Hebrew and Babylonian which dated from the first exile (589 B.C.E.), was the spoken Jewish tongue throughout the period of Jesus' teachings and the formation of Rabbinic Judaism (Mishnah ca. 200 C.E., Talmud ca. 450).

3. For a discussion see, J. N. Birdsall, "The New Testament Text," *Cambridge History of the Bible, Volume I: From the Beginnings to Jerome* (Cambridge, 1970), 245–77; and Bruce M. Metzger, *The Early Versions of the New Testament: Their Origin, Transmission and Limitations* (Oxford, 1975).

4. "There is a verse in the Bible that has been translated into over 1100 languages [Jn 3:16] ... here recorded in twenty-five of the important world languages." *New Testament, Psalms, Proverbs*, Gideon's pocket Bible (Nashville, 1968, 1982), vi–xv.

5. Canons of 1229 Council of Toulouse, no. 14; J. D. Mansi, *Sacrorum conciliorum nova et amplissima collectio*, vol. 23 (Venice, 1768), 197; C. J. Hefele and H. Leclercq, *Histoire des conciles d'après les documents originaux*, vol. 2 (Paris, 1913), 1494–1501.

6. Recently historians have argued that to speak of an Inquisition in medieval Europe reflects not the historical record, but the mythical monster created out of Protestant and later liberal polemic (e.g., Richard Kieckhefer, *Repression of Heresy in Medieval Germany* [Philadelphia, 1979], 4–7; Edward Peters, *Inquisition* [New York, 1988], 1–10). And granted, any medieval inquisitorial activity we find in the sources pales before this proto-totalitarian monster. But from the

point of view of previous history, this medieval Inquisition far surpasses any earlier efforts to surpress religious dissent in its systematic intrusion into the lowest levels and farthest reaches of society (e.g., twelve-year-old peasant girls, mountain villagers). At its height, the Roman persecutions (Pagan and Christian) were no match for any of the developments of the thirteenth century. If the medieval Inquisition was no modern totalitarian state, it nevertheless pioneered some of the latter's fundamental techniques of psychological and social intimidation.

7. Margaret Deanesly, *The Lombard Bible* (London, 1923); Elizabeth Eisenstein, *The Printing Press as an Agent of Change: Communications and Cultural Transformations in Early-Modern Europe,* vol. 1 (Cambridge, 1979), 303–450.

8. Histories of heresy are more likely to discuss the issue of vernacular Bibles (e.g., Herbert Grundmann *Religiöse Bewegungen im Mittelalter* [Hildesheim, 1961], 97–100, 442–52) than histories of the Inquisition (e.g., Richard Kieckhefer, *Repression*).

9. Since the treatment of M. Deanesly, *Lombard Bible,* 18–88, historians have come to emphasize the limited degree and circumstantial nature of ecclesiastical opposition to vernacular Bibles, e.g., L. Boyle's defense of Innocent III from Deanesly's widely accepted misreading ("Innocent III and Vernacular Versions of Scripture," *The Bible in the Medieval World: Essays in Memory of Beryl Smalley,* Studies in Church History, subsidia 4 [Oxford, 1985], 109–30). A major history of the Church typically makes no mention of the issue (*Handbook of Church History,* eds. Hubert Jedin and John Dolan, vol. 4 [London, 1970], 104–13); and few mentions of heresy appear in the essays on translations in *The Cambridge History of the Bible,* vol. 2, ed. G. W. H. Lampe (Cambridge, 1969), England, 391–94; Germany, 427ff.; France, 441; Italy, 462. Emphasizing the number of translations throughout the Middle Ages, has led some historians to dismiss clerical opposition to biblical translation as a momentary aberration of the Inquisition rather than an abiding ecclesiastical position (e.g., C. R. Sneddon, "The 'Bible du XIIIe siècle': Its Medieval Public in the Light of Its Manuscript Tradition," *The Bible and Medieval Culture,* Medievalia Lovaniensia, ser. 1, studia 7 [Leuven, 1979], 127–40). Such a trend, however, cannot justify comments like: "The facts are coherent and their significance is clear. In the Middle Ages the Church never forbade the reading of the Bible; but very few of the laity had the ability to do it. The Church cannot be reproached with not having done all she could to instruct people, but . . ." Yves Congar, *Lay People in the Church* (Westminster, 1967), 314–15.

10. As J. Leclerq has noted, most studies of vernacular translations study not the social context, but the philological issues. His own study, although intended to address this lacuna, mentions heresies only in passing; and focuses primarily on the internal, meditative texts (Psalms, Song of Songs) licitly translated ("Les traductions de la Bible et la spiritualité médiévale," *Bible and Medieval Culture,* 263–78).

11. The role would be defined in terms of literacy's distribution, its uses, its educational structures.

12. Harold Innis, *The Bias of Communication* (Toronto, 1951); Marshall

McLuhan, *The Gutenberg Galaxy: The Making of Typographic Man* (Toronto, 1962); Walter Ong, *The Presence of the Word: Some Prolegomena for Cultural and Religious History* (New Haven, 1967) and *Literacy and Orality* (New York, 1983); Jack Goody and Ian Watt, "The Consequences of Literacy," *Comparative Studies in Society and History,* 5 (1963): 304–45, reprinted in *Literacy in Traditional Societies,* ed. Jack Goody (Cambridge, 1978), 27–68; and J. Goody, *The Logic of Writing and the Organization of Society* (Cambridge, 1986).

13. In addition to works cited in previous note, see the variety of work on the impact of the alphabet on classical Greece by Eric Havelock: *Preface to Plato* (Cambridge, Mass., 1963); *The Greek Concept of Justice* (Cambridge, Mass., 1978); *The Literate Revolution in Greece and Its Cultural Consequences* (Princeton, 1982).

14. Goody, *Logic,* 87–125; Karl Popper, *The Open Society and Its Enemies: The Spell of Plato* (Princeton, 1962), 86–119, 169–201, for the antidemocratic reaction in Platonic Athens; Sheldon Wolin, *The Politics of Vision* (New York, 1965), chap. 3, on the shift from citizenship in the city-state to subjection in the Empire.

15. Coined by Dionysus the Areopagite, a sixth-century pseudonymous mystic, whose correlation of celestial and earthly hierarchies shaped much of medieval theocratic thought.

16. See the study of the relationship between these two in the eighteenth and nineteenth century, J. L. Talmon, *The Origins of Totalitarian Democracy* (London, 1952, 1970).

17. Brian Stock, *The Implications of Literacy: Written Language and Models of Interpretation in the Eleventh and Twelfth Centuries* (Princeton, 1983), 88–240.

18. "If it happened that any ignorant, tongue-tied persons were enrolled among the partisans of this error, it was stoutly asserted that at once they became more eloquent than even the most learned Catholics, so that it almost seemed as if the really true eloquence of the wise could be overcome by their garrulity." Letter of Bishop Wazo of Liège to Bishop Roger of Chalons (1043–48), *Heresies of the High Middle Ages,* eds. W. L. Wakefield and A. P. Evans (New York, 1969), 90.

19. Given the difficulties inherent in using Troeltsch's dichotomy "sect" and "church" (see Bryan R. Wilson, *Religious Sects: A Sociological Study* [London, 1970], 14–35), and the advantage that "textual communities" pinpoints a crucial dynamic in the formation of these groups, Stock's term seems more encompassing. One might then call a sect an egalitarian textual community.

20. This is not a point brought out by Stock in his theoretical discussion, but every example he then gives indicates that whether explicitly as a law, or implicitly as a moral imperative, the texts serve this function.

21. Moses I. Finley, *Economy and Society in Ancient Greece* (Penguin, 1953, 1981) 84–94. Herodotus has a Persian spokesman for democracy declaim:

Contrast this [the tyrannical excesses of monarchy] with the rule of the people [democratia]: first it has the finest of all names to describe it—

equality under law [isonomia]; and secondly, the people in power do none of the things that monarchs do. Under a government of the people a magistrate is appointed by lot and is held responsible for his conduct in office, and all questions are put up for open debate. *The Histories* 3.80.6 (trans. de Selincourt [New York, 1973], 239).

Popper argues that isonomia is the one definition of justice that Plato cannot refute but also cannot tolerate, and he therefore passes over it in silence when discussing either justice or democracy (*Open Society,* 93–119).

22. Note that on 29 September 1988, a Swedish Governmental agency denied the king special parking privileges on the principle that as a citizen he should be treated like all other citizens.

23. Victor Ehrenberg, *From Solon to Socrates* (London, 1967); W. G. Forrest, *The Emergence of Greek Democracy* (New York, 1966).

24. E.g., Hammurabi's Code (ca. 1970 B.C.E.); Mosaic Commandments (ca. 1200 B.C.E.); the Gortyn code in Crete (ca. 450 B.C.E.), the Twelve Tables of the Law in Rome (ca. 450 B.C.E.).

25. Here we see one of the peculiar capacities of script at play: by objectifying the law, by setting it in stone, writing permitted a whole new level of public scrutiny and the accountability of judges and rulers.

26. For a translation of the (eventually) Twelve Tables of the Law engraved in bronze, see *Roman Civilization: Sourcebook I, The Republic,* eds. Naphtali Lewis and M. Reinhold (New York, 1966), 101–9, with bibliography. For Livy's lurid account of the difficulties in establishing and publishing these tables see *The Early History of Rome* 3.32–60 (trans. de Selincourt [New York, 1971], 216–50), quotation is from 3.58, pp. 247–48. For commentary, see Alan Watson (*Rome of the XII Tables: Persons and Property* [Princeton, 1975], 177–86), who does not feel that the class distinctions were effectively so great.

27. Like most works of political science, Wolin (note 14) does not consider the Hebraic tradition in his coverage of antiquity; e.g., John Bowle, *Western Political Thought: An Historical Introduction from the Origins to Rousseau* (New York, 1949); Mario A. Levi, *Political Power in the Ancient World* (New York, 1968); L. Strauss and J. Cropsey, eds., *History of Political Philosophy* (Chicago, 1963, 1972, 1987); Moses I. Finley, *Democracy Ancient and Modern* (London, 1973); Larry Arnhart, *Political Questions: Political Philosophy from Plato to Rawls* (New York, 1987). The examples could be multiplied at will, as could, with considerably greater difficulty, the exceptions: e.g., William A. Irwin, "The Hebrews," *The Intellectual Adventure of Ancient Man: An Essay on Speculative Thought in the Ancient Near East* (Chicago, 1946, 1977), 327–59 (note the absence of any bibliography on the political dimension); Leo Strauss, "Jerusalem and Athens: Some Preliminary Reflections," *Studies in Platonic Political Philosophy* (Chicago, 1983), 147–73; and the brilliant but idiosyncratic study of Paul Eidelberg, *Jerusalem vs. Athens: In Quest of a General Theory of Existence* (Washington, 1983).

28. See later discussion in this chapter.

29. Josephus considered isonomia ("one law for all") as the highest achieve-

ment of civilization, and attributed its first and best articulation to Moses; *Against Apion* 2.15–16 (ed. and trans. H. J. Thackery [Loeb Classical Library Cambridge, 1926], 353–69, esp. 354–55).

30. This is true whether one places them in the context of the original Mosaic covenant (twelfth c. B.C.E.) or in a later period of Jewish history (down to sixth c.); see discussion and references in John Bright, *The History of Israel* (London, 1972), 141–45, esp. 142 n. 5. The insistence with which the presentation of the Ten Commandments forbids idol worship may be an element of this isonomic reading (e.g., Deut. 5–7): idol worship is spiritual slavery.

31. For a number of examples see below. On the specific subject of isonomia see the prescriptions to judges on impartial justice (Exod. 23:1–9; Deut. 16:18–20); the privilege of Sabbath rest to all, including non-Jews, servants, slaves, even animals (Exod. 20:8–11; Deut. 5:12–15); the rights of the individual against the incursion of ruling authority (Samuel's claim of never abusing his position for personal advantage [1 Sam. 12:3], the king's incapacity to expropriate property without the consent of its owner [1 Kings 21]). Also worth noting, the Sabbatical and Jubilee years institute a cyclical repetition of the kind of material enfranchisement that Solon found a necessary adjunct to isonomic reforms (cf. Exod. 21, Lev. 25, Deut. 15, with Solon's poem on the Abolition of Debts, Aristotle *The Constitution of Athens* 12.4 (trans. in *Ancient Greece: Documentary Perspectives* [Dubuque, 1985], 6–7). Note that by freeing Hebrew slaves every seven years, the ability of all to have free status was guaranteed over time.

32. Josephus insists on the importance of these public readings (*Against Apion* [Loeb Classical Library, pp. 362–65]).

33. Class here should not be understood in purely economic terms. The objection to gentlemen at this point was not their wealth, but their privileged status before the law. For early examples, see the not entirely clear reference to the "song of our first ancestor as he followed the plough," Adalbero of Laon, "Carmen ad Rotbertum regem" (1028), *Adalberon de Laon. Poème au roi Robert*, ed. C. Carozzi (Paris, 1979), 4, l. 42; and the explicit case of the peace movement called the Capuciati (1180s), which "strove to acquire liberty, saying that it belonged to them from the time of Adam and Eve," described in A. Luchaire, *Social France at the Time of Phillip Augustus,* trans. J. Baldwin (New York, 1967), 11–19; citation, p. 19, translated from the chronicle of Robert, monk of Saint-Marien of Auxerre.

34. The commitment to manual labor is a continual element in all forms of Judiasm until modern times (rabbis must have their own profession); man's Sabbath as a recapitulation of God's emphasizes the significance of work as a divine as well as human activity; and the Sabbath applying to all underlines the principle (wholly foreign to both Greek and Roman aristocrats) that all work and all rest.

35. Adam Wildavsky, *The Nurturing Father: Moses as Political Leader* (Birmingham, 1984); Michael Walzer, *Exodus and Revolution* (New York, 1984); see also the classic homiletic expression of this perspective, M. Buber, *Moses* (New York, 1946).

36. Roland Robertson, "Liberation Theology in Latin America: Sociological Problems of Interpretation and Explanation," *Prophetic Religions and Politics: Religion and the Political Order*, eds. J. K. Hadden and A. Shupe (New York, 1986), 103–22.

37. See, e.g., Gideon's refusal of the monarchy: "the Lord will rule over you" (Judg. 8:23); Samuel's reaction to the request for a king: "The Lord is your King" (1 Sam. 12:12); God's response to the same request: "They have rejected Me, that I not rule over them" (ibid., 19–20); "Then will God rule the kingdom." Obad. 21. Also, below n. 47. On the work of Erik Peterson, *Der Monotheismus as politisches Problem* (Leipzig, 1935), see below, n. 92.

38. There is an immense literature on the biblical attitude toward kingship, with one school attributing the antimonarchical sentiments to a redactional strand added later, after the failure of the kingship had become apparent; whereas the other views these sentiments as representing the original layer of the texts. An interesting variant is proposed by Shemaryahu Talmon, who argues that the passages are original, but not antimonarchical (*King Cult and Calendar in Ancient Israel* [Leiden, 1987], 9–67, with references to further literature). His thesis lays heavy emphasis on the promonarchical reading, while ignoring or dismissing any counter evidence (e.g., 18 n. 29). For my argument, the presence of the diametrically opposed interpretations among the rabbis (Talmud, Tractate Sanhedrin 20b) suffices. See also nn. 37, 47.

39. The key issue was: did the Bible positively command the Jews to a monarchy? Those who said no pointed to Samuel's warning against the tyrannical behavior of kings (he will take your daughters and sons for slaves, and so forth; echoed in the restrictions on kingly prerogative to be found in Deut.). Those who argued yes tended to reinterpret Samuel's speech as the divinely ordained "right of kings." See John of Salisbury (mid-twelfth century) for a particularly subtle combination of these two readings (*Policraticus* 4, on the king subject to the law; 8 on the "right of kings" [trans. M. F. Markland, New York, 1979]). Although no medieval Jewish commentator on these passages published the antimonarchical reading (an understandable reluctance), it resurfaced in full complexity and thoroughness with Abravanel in the late fifteenth century (see translation in *Medieval Political philosophy*, eds. and trans. Ralph Lerner and Muhsin Mahdi [New York, 1963], 254–70). The battle over the meaning of Samuel reaches a climax in the sixteenth and seventeenth centuries among Calvinist thinkers: see Jules Franklin, *Constitutionalism and Resistance in the Sixteenth Century* (New York, 1969); Quentin Skinner, *The Foundations of Modern Political Thought* (Cambridge, 1978). Note Hobbes's analysis of the passage, which synthesizes covenant and divine right of kings in *Leviathan* 2.20 (ed. C. B. MacPherson, New York, 1968, 258–61).

40. See the injunctions against oppressing the disadvantaged in such key texts as the "holiness code" (Lev. 19–21), and the two covenant commentaries (Exod. 22:21–8; and Deut. 15:7–11; 24:17–22).

41. See the analysis in Maria L. Arduini, "Biblische Kategorien und mittelalterliche Gesellschaft: *potens* und *pauper* bei Rupert von Deutz und Hildegard von Bingen (XI. bzw. XII. Jh.)," *Soziale Ordnungen im Selbstverständnis des*

Mittelalters, vol. 2, ed. Albert Zimmermann, Miscellanea Medievalia 12/2, (Cologne, 1980), 471–79.

42. Abraham Heschel, *The Prophets: An Introduction,* vol. 1 (New York, 1955), 159–86.

43. Paul Hanson, *The Dawn of Apocalyptic,* 2d ed.; (Philadelphia, 1979) more recently on the atmosphere at the time of Jesus, David E. Aune, *Prophecy in Early Christianity and the Ancient Mediterranean World* (Grand Rapids, 1983).

44. I use the term *millennialism* (also *millenarism, millenarianism, chiliasm*) in the extended sense developed by social scientists: movements that expect the radical transformation of *this world* by the overthrow of the present order and its replacement with a new order of justice, peace and plenty. See Y. Talmon, "Millenarism," *International Encyclopedia of the Social Sciences,* vol. 10 (New York, 1968), 349–65. These scholars include in the definition a sense of the imminence of the transformation; but my own research has indicated that this dramatic (and what I term *apocalyptic*) millennialism has a more long-range, less visible, but equally significant counterpart, R. Landes, "Lest the Millenium be Fulfilled: Apocalyptic Expectations and the Pattern of Western Chronography 100–800 c.e.," *The Use and Abuse of Eschatology in the Middle Ages,* eds. W. Verbeke, D. Verhelst, and A Welkenhysen, Medievalia Lovaniensia ser. 1, studia 15, (Leuven, 1988), 141–211, esp. Appendix on Definitions, 205–8. It is worth noting that the modern sociological definition comes close to the Patristic one.

45. E.g., Josephus' comment that their position on the resurrection of the dead and a Last Judgment assured the Pharisees of enormous popularity among the commonfolk (*Antiquities of the Jews,* trans. L. H. Feldman [Loeb Classical Library, 1981] 18.1.4).

46. Josephus, *Antiquities of the Jews* 18.1.6, vol. 9, pp. 12–23. Note that he describes this revolutionary doctrine, that originates around the beginning of the Common Era, infecting the nation "to an incredible degree" (18.1.1). See also S. G. F. Brandon, *The Fall of Jerusalem and the Christian Church* (London, 1968).

47. "We have no King besides You," remains a part of the Jewish liturgy to this day, in a prayer dating from at least Talmudic times (Nishmat, mentioned in Talmud, Tractate Pesachim, 118a).

48. See above, note 38. The role of the prophets was essentially to keep the kings in check (Nathan and David; Elijah and Ahab). The Essenes rejected the Temple of the second commonwealth as impure both because of Saduceic corruption and the building program of Herod who built the presently standing Western wall with his customary slave labor.

49. "They have a passion for liberty that is almost unconquerable, since they are convinced that God alone is their leader and master. They think little of submitting to death in unusual forms . . . if only they may avoid calling any man master" Josephus on the Zealots, *Antiquities* 18.1.6, vol. 9, pp. 20–21.

50. Almost every passage lends itself to a possible opposite reading (e.g., the incident in Eden ends the with subordination of woman to man; the flood ends with the subjugation of the Hamites to the Shemites; etc.). And in fact this aspect of the Hebrew canon has received the lion's share of the attention from medieval

scholars who tend to orient their investigations around an Old Testament steeped in theocratic hierarchical notions which eventually informed the rise of the early medieval royal theocracies of converted tribes, and a New Testament focused on a supremely significant "individual" who transcends social limitations. See e.g., W. Ullmann, *Principles of Government and Politics in the Middle Ages* (London, 1961), 19–25, and "The Bible and Principles of Government in the Middle Ages," *La bibbia nel alto medioevo*, Settimane di Studio del Centro Italiano di Studi sull'Alto Medioevo, 10 (Spoleto, 1963), 181–227.

51. Josephus, *Against Apion* 2.15–16 (Loeb Classical Library, 352–69); see above, nn. 29, 32.

52. See above, n. 27.

53. Aune, *Prophecy*, 121–37; and Richard Horsley, *Jesus and the Spiral of Violence* (New York, 1987).

54. John Gager, *Kingdom and Community: The Social World of Early Christianity* (Englewood Cliffs, N.J., 1975); Edward P. Sanders, *Jesus and Judaism* (Philadelphia, 1979); Paul Fredriksen, *From Jesus to Christ* (New Haven, 1988).

55. The present direction of scholarship has emphasized the wide range of Christianity's appeal, see discussion, nuances and literature cited in Wayne Meeks, *The First Urban Christians: The Social World of the Apostle Paul* (New Haven, 1983), 51–73, esp. the works of Edwin A. Judge. Such corrections in the image of a proletarian movement should not, however, disguise the unusual degree to which the Christian movement strove to integrate members from the lowest levels of an extremely stratefied and status conscious society. The openness to men and women from all levels of the culture has remained a distinctive quality of Christianity throughout its history: Peter Brown, *The World of Late Antiquity* (New York, 1971), 88–89; Erich Auerbach, *Mimesis: The Representation of Reality in Western Literature* (New York, 1957), 73–83.

56. On the renunciations necessary for discipleship: Matt. 8:18–22, 10:34–39; Luke 9:57–60, 12:51–3, and most extremely stated: "He who does not hate his own father and mother and wife and children and brothers and sisters, yes and even his own life, he cannot be my disciple," 14:26–7.

57. Whatever Jesus' attitude toward the Torah, under the influence of Paul and the gentile churches, the violent rejection of all past tradition concerning the Scriptures in Judaism became a defining characteristic of the movement (Fredriksen, *From Jesus to Christ*; Marcel Simon, *Verus Israel: Etude sur les relations entre chrétiens et juifs dans l'empire romain (135–425)* [Paris, 1964]).

58. Denis de Rougement, "Role de la Modernité dans les relations Europe-Monde," *L'Europe et le monde* (Paris, 1976), 3–16.

59. See A. Y. Collins, "The Political Perspective of the Revelation of John," *Journal of Biblical Literature* 96, no. 2 (1977): 241–56.

60. See Sheldon Wolin's analysis of the threat to Rome posed by Christian communities as alternate societies, *Politics of Vision*, ch. 4, esp. p. 102.

61. Note that this is precisely how J. P. M. Sweet characterizes the distinction between "authentic Christianity" and the millenarian views found in Revelations that are in spirit "unchristian, even anti-christian" (*Commentary on the Book of Revelation*, Westminster Pelican Commentaries [Philadelphia, 1979], 48–49).

62. On these anti-Jewish polemics which Parkes called the "Original Sin of Christianity" see J. Isaac, *L'enseignement du mépris* (Paris, 1952); more recently R. Reuther, *Faith and Fratricide* (New York, 1974) and J. Gager, *The Origins of Antisemitism* (New York, 1986). On their *nachleben* in the scholarly world, see Edward P. Sanders, *Jesus and Judaism* (Philadelphia, 1979), 23–58. The importance of eliminating Revelation from "true" Christian literature becomes clear in the context of the polemical contrast between the "Jewish God of vengeance" versus the "Christian God of love" (e.g., the Jews crucified Christ because he taught a God of love which they could not tolerate; Carmody and Carmody, *Introduction to Christianity*, 2d ed., [Belmont, Calif., 1988], 16). In fact the Jewish God is one who combines love and mercy with justice and punishment over time, while the Christian God splits these into a first Incarnation of mercy and love, and a Parousia of vengeful justice. The former incarnation makes no sense without the latter (e.g., Romans 12:19–20). See below, n. 81.

63. See below, n. 100.

64. D. H. Lawrence called it the "Judas" of the New Testament (*Apocalypse* [London, 1931]); and J. P. M. Sweet finds it contradicts the teachings of "authentic Christianity" and compares its study to that of a visitor to a tropical isle, revolted by what he sees but unable to understand anything if he does not overcome his repugnance (*Commentary*, 48–52). Note also how such sentiments seem more Jewish than Christian to him. Cf. Nietzsche on the climax of such a tradition in Christian thought in *Genealogy of Morals*, trans. W. Kaufmann (New York, 1967), essay 1, pp. 48–54.

65. H. Bietenhard, "The Millennial Hope in the Early Church," *Scottish Journal of Theology* 6 (1953): 12–30.

66. John Gager, *Kingdom and Community: The Social World of Early Christianity* (Englewood Cliffs, N.J., 1975), 19–65, esp. 49–57.

67. See Wolin, *Politics of Vision*, chaps. 3–4 on the ways in which Greek philosophy accommodated imperial necessities.

68. Brown, *World*, 49–82; Carl Morrison, *Tradition and Authority in the Western Church, 300–1140* (Princeton, 1962), 8–33.

69. Rostovtzeff called the post-Diocletian empire "one big prison cell," and if he was wrong about reality, the theory certainly envisaged such high levels of control of population, prices, movement, career choices, and so on. See e.g., William C. Bark, *Origins of the Medieval World* (Stanford, 1958), 29–66.

70. It is noteworthy that the social problems of the Empire solicited little concern at the councils of the imperial Church: trinitarian doctrines overshadowed any such discussion.

71. See the brief but candid discussion in Karl Baus, *History of the Church*, vol. 2, ed. Hubert Jedin (New York, 1980), 401–11. Note that diocese was originally a division created by the Diocletian reform.

72. Brown, *World*, 82–94.

73. With the interesting exception of Lactantius. On all of these issues, see Landes, "Lest the Millennium."

74. "The old millenarian dreams were again being redreamt [e.g., by Hilari-

anus in the late fourth century] . . . , but hardly a live force in Augustine's day."
Robert Markus, *Saeculum: History and Theology in the Age of Augustine*
(Cambridge, 1970), 20.

75. The term was first coined by Leon Festinger as a result of his studies of
how groups who predicted the end of the world dealt with the objective disconfirmation of a central tenet of their belief system (L. Festinger, H. W. Reicken,
and S. Schachter, *When Prophecy Fails: A Social and Psychological Study of a
Modern Group That Predicted the Destruction of the World* [New York, 1956],
25–30; and L. Festinger, *A Theory of Cognitive Dissonance* [Stanford, 1957];
criticized by Roger Brown, *Social Psychology* [New York, 1969], 601–8). The
term identifies a contradiction between two elements in an individual or group's
view of the world. In our case the dissonance appears in the contradiction
between the traditional reading of the New Testament (God's chosen are persecuted by the powerful and oppressive, in particular by Rome), and the new
status of the Church (allied with Rome, weilding earthly power in spiritual
matters, supporting an oppressive hierarchy).

76. For the intellectual history of this idea, see above, n. 37 (Peterson) and
below, n. 92; and Wolin, *Politics of Vision*, 69–94, esp. 92–94. Eusebius used
this idea to make the emperor into an "icon" of God (see on isonomia and
iconoclasm above, n. 30). *Praise of Constantine, Select Library of Nicene and
Post-Nicene Fathers of the Christian Church*, eds. P. Schal and H. Wace, 2d ser.,
vol. 1 (New York, 1890), 581–610; and a discussion of the larger issues in Baus,
History, 78–81; Edward Cranz, "Kingdom and Polity in Eusebius of Caesaria,"
Harvard Theological Review 44 (1950): 47–66.

77. See later discussion in this chapter.

78. For a survey of Rabbinic views of man and his relationship to the divine,
see Ephraim E. Urbach, *The Sages: Their Concepts and Beliefs* (Jerusalem,
1975), chap. 10. The political contrast traced in the present text has a philosophical parallel in the manner (and limits) of Jewish borrowing of platonic and
gnostic ideas of the relationship of the soul to God (ibid., 235–54, esp. 248–
51). See also the provocative essay of Paul Eidelberg, *Jerusalem vs. Athens*, 47–
68, contrasting Greek and Hebrew notions of pride and humility.

79. See above, n. 31.

80. Edward F. Cranz, "*De civitate Dei* 15.2 and Augustine's Idea of the
Christian Society," *Speculum* 25 (1950): 215–25.

81. See the discussion of the importance for heavenly bliss of seeing the
damned tormented in hell among Christian writers in Neitzsche, for whom it
represents the height of "*ressentiment*" (*Genealogy of Morals*, essay 1, p. 15),
and G. G. Coulton, who links it to the doctrine that a tiny portion of mankind
will be saved at the Last Judgment (*Inquisition and Liberty* [Boston, 1959], 16–
21).

82. On the development of Imperial Christian persecution of Christians,
culminating in the Western Church under the auspices of Augustine, "the theoretical architect of the medieval Inquisition," see Charles Cochrane, *Christianity
and Classical Culture* (London, 1944), 328–47, 346–57; Herbert Deane, *The
Political and Social Ideas of St. Augustine* (New York, 1963), 172–220; Peter

Brown, "St. Augustine's Attitude Toward Religious Coercion," *Religion and Society in the Age of Augustine* (New York, 1972), 260–78.

83. On the self-conception of the Donatists as the True Church persecuted by Antichrist, see W. H. C. Frend, *Martyrdom and Persecution in the Early Church* (Oxford, 1965), 536–69; Pierre Courcelle, *Histoire littéraire des grandes invasions germaniques* (Paris, 1964), 319–37; Jean-Paul Brisson, *Autonomisme et christianisme dans l'Afrique romaine* (Paris, 1958), 325–410. See also below, n. 84.

84. This is clearly the Donatist's position; and Augustine himself hesitated to use the death penalty for fear that the Donatists would use it to paint themselves as martyrs (Ep. 100, cited Deane, 210, 329 n. 129); which they did (*Liber Genealogus* continuatio ad A.D. 455, *Monumenta Germaniae Historica, Auctores Antiquissimi*, vol. 9, ed. T. Mommsen, 154–96). But outside this polemical war, what would a concerned but undecided outsider think? (See below, n. 85 on students.)

85. If one presents the Donatist controversy to students today without identifying which party argued which position, they will consistently identify the Donatist position with the Catholic Church.

86. The most virulent anti-Semitic preacher, John the "Golden Mouth" (Chrysostom), bishop of Antioch (386) and later Constantinople (398) seems particularly concerned about the possible influence Jews might exert on the Christian co-citizens. See Malcolm Hay, *Thy Brother's Blood: The Roots of Christian Anti-Semitism* (New York, 1950) for a value-laden appraisal; more recent and more scholarly treatment, Robert Wilken, *John Chrysostom and the Jews* (New York, 1986).

87. For an analysis of this development, using the concept of "religiosity supportive of authority" to define the situation of Christianity in the late empire, see Gavin Langmuir, "From Ambrose of Milan to Emicho of Leiningen: The Transformation of Hostility Against Jews in Northern Christendom," *Gli Ebrei nell'alto medioevo*, Settimane di Studio del Centro Italiano di Studi sull'alto Medioevo, 26 (Spoleto, 1980), 321–35. See also Simon, *Verus Israel*.

88. Among the manifold analyses of this dilemma of projected guilt, see, Lester Little, *Religious Poverty and the Profit Economy in Medieval Europe* (Ithaca, 1978), 42–59, esp. 232 n. 69; and Jeremy Cohen, *The Friars and the Jews: The Evolution of Medieval Anti-Judaism* (Ithaca, 1982).

89. E.g., Cranz comments on the use of the Kingdom of God in imperial propaganda: "Catholic or Protestant may disagree, for example, about the Kingdom of God; each, however, will probably feel that Eusebius is arbitrary or perverse in his use of the concept to explain the imperial power of Constantine. But Eusebius, all in all, appears to have been an honest writer and to have been guided in his thought by a form of the Christian experience." Cranz, *"De civitate,"* 48. Whatever Eusebius thought, it would seem important to address what contemporaries thought of his arguments.

90. This not only tends to preclude the attitudes of the nonliterate who leave no documents but also nonorthodox whose writings are either burned or distorted. The discussion of millenarianism in the period after Constantine has

suffered precisely from this methodological prudence (Landes, "Lest the Millennium," esp. 158–60, 181–91, 203–5).

91. A. H. M. Jones, *Constantine and the Conversion of Europe* (New York, 1948; reprint, Toronto, 1978) esp. 201–8; and more recently, E. G. Weltin, *Athens and Jerusalem: An Interpretative Essay on Christianity and Classical Culture*, American Academy of Religion Studies in Religion, 49 (Atlanta, 1987), 49–58; Arthur P. Monihan, *Consent, Coercion, and Limit: The Medieval Origins of Paliamentary Democracy* (Montreal, 1987), 28–56 (despite his reading of Samuel, 21–27); Peters, *Inquisition*, 214–39. On the failure of outsiders to the field of Church History to appreciate what is at stake, see the reflections of Mann, *Sources of Social Power* (Cambridge, 1986), 303 in which the changes in the Christian message as it moved out of Palestine and through various constituencies in and beyond the Roman Empire are "subtle," and the message "remained recognizably the same." Cf., however, Wolin's appreciation of "a process that began in paradox and ended in irony" (*Politics*, 96, also 97, 103, 111, 117–23). On the place of Judaism in the discussions of mainstream historiography, see Gavin Langmuir, "Majority History and Post-Biblical Jews," *Journal of the History of Ideas* 27, no. 3 (1966): 343–64.

92. Peterson, *Monotheismus* takes as his starting point the thoroughly hellenized Philo of Alexandria while making no mention of the evidence to be found in his younger contemporary, Josephus. A recent reevaluation of Peterson's life and work does not address the issue: *Monotheismus as politisches Problem? Erik Peterson und die Kritik der politischen Theologie*, ed. Alfred Schnidler (Gutersloh, 1978).

93. Ullmann, "The Bible," 224. Let one example suffice: Charlemagne adopted the biblical *imperium*-idea when he spoke of the two empires (East and West) in terms of the passage "Faceres imperium bipartitum" (Eccles. 47:23). But in context, that line refers to the disastrous division of the kingdoms in Israel due to Solomon's deplorable weakness for women. The Bible here served not as inspiration but as proof-text for a venture conceived of along profoundly different lines. Note that the author contradicts himself immediately after stating his conclusion (224–25). In addition to the scepticism among other scholars that greeted this presentation (331–36), see also the next article in the collection, in which P. E. Schramm argues that a book on the meaning of the Bible for medieval political thought is impossible precisely because the meaning of any given passage is too multivalent to assign it any clear causal role in inspiring a given position ("Der alte und das neue Testament in der Staatslehre und Staatssymbolik des Mittelalters," *La bibbia nel alto medioevo* [Spoleto, 1963], 231–55); and the still more remarkable effort to deal with the problem in a nuanced fashion by M. Arduini, "Biblische Kategorien."

94. The earliest reference to the Nishmat (containing the line "We have no king besides You") dates from this period, see n. 47.

95. See above, nn. 30, 76.

96. Salo Baron, *The Jewish Community: Its History and Structure to the American Revolution* (Philadelphia, 1942).

97. Scholars generally consider Rabbinic Judaism as an "anti-apocalyptic"

tradition (i.e., against the imminent expectation of the end), particularly since the failure of the millenarian revolts of 66–70 C.E. and 135 C.E. Jewish messianic expectations, however, remained fundamental to Rabbinic belief no matter how they were delayed or extenuated, and hence, by the definition used here, the Jews of the later Roman empire are millenarian (above, n. 44). See discussion of apocalyptic vs. nonapocalyptic millenarianism in Landes, "Lest the Millennium," 137 n. 2; 144–49, esp. 147; 205–8.

98. See generally, Baus, *History of the Church,* 289–336; on the problem of Christian art and the second commandment, see Walter Lowrie, *Art in the Early Church* (New York, 1901, 1969), 9–19, and Constantine's effect on the artistic development of the Church, 88–131. On the role of relics in supporting then replacing the systems of patronage at work in the late imperial period, Peter Brown, *The Cult of the Saints in Late Antiquity: Its Rise and Its Function* (Chicago, 1981).

99. Chrysostom's corpus has been translated, including the series of sermons preached after the riot (Homilies on the Statues) in the *Select Library of Nicene and Post-Nicene Fathers of the Christian Church* 1st ser., vol. 9, reprint (Grand Rapids, 1975), 317–489. See also Robert L. Wilken *(John Chrysostom),* who does not deal specifically with these tax riots, but details the kinds of attractions Judaism held for Christians and the threats it therefore posed to the Church of Antioch (esp. 66–94).

100. See discussion in Bruce M. Metzger, *Canon of the New Testament* (Oxford, 1987), 206–7. Discussing the only surviving manuscript that appears to be directly descended from Eusebius' prototype, but breaks off in the middle of Hebrews, he comments that it "doubtless contained the Book of Revelation as well (207). But we know both: 1. that Eusebius' antipathy to the book and to millenarianism only increased over time, leading him to expunge discussions in his *History of the Church* that might give it any validity (R. M. Grant, "Papias in Eusebius' Church History," *Mélanges d'histoire des religions dédiés à Henri-Charles Puesch* [Paris, 1974], 209–13; Landes, "Lest the Millennium," 150 and n. 47); and 2. that the subsequent major theologians associated with Constantinople in the fourth century do not cite it at all (Metzger, 210–17).

101. Metzger, *Canon of the New Testament.* The Armenian Church did not consider the book canonical until the twelfth century (*Cambridge History of the Bible,* vol. 1, 366–67).

102. For more details on these points see Landes "Lest the Millennium," 156–60; for bibliography, n. 77.

103. The most striking example comes when Augustine explains how the peace of the millennial age actually means increased war both on earth and within individual humans (*De civitate Dei* 20.7–11 [trans. David Knowles, London, 1972, 906–20]).

104. Cf. Landes, "Lest the Millennium," 158–65, 203–5.

105. Based on the fact that Pilate wrote, "Jesus Christ King of the Jews" in those three languages according to John (19:20); see J. Schwering, "Die Idee der drei heiligen Sprachen im Mittelalter," in *Festschrift A. Sauer zum 70. Geburtstag* (Stuttgart, 1925), 3–11; R. E. McNally, "The 'Tres Linguae Sacrae' in Early

Irish Bible Exegesis," *Theological Studies* 19 (1958): 395–403; and E. Dekkers, who suggests that the initially anodyne speculation gained substance in conflicts with heretical groups, "L'église devant la Bible en langue vernaculaire," *The Bible and Medieval Culture,* eds. P. Riché and G. Lobrichon (Louvain, 1979), 7–9.

106. Underlining the suspect origins of this authority, their opponents called them Pilatians.

107. "It was Rome that shaped the Bible in its Vulgate form; it was not Jerusalem or Judaism or Hellenistic Christianity which the Bible conveyed to the Middle Ages . . . the tenor, language and orientation of the Bible came to show, if not affinity, at least no substantial difference with the themes of government exercised in the late Roman empire. . . . One might almost be tempted to speak . . . of a divinization of Roman law and the Roman constitution." Ullmann, "The Bible," 224–25.

108. E.g., the topos of a conversion experience at the hearing or reading of a text has great authority in Christianity (Thomas and the Eunich, Augustine in the garden). But not all periods abound in it: see also, the conversion of Peter Waldo, wealthy merchant, upon hearing first the song of St. Alexis, then on being read the passage "take all that thou hast."

109. Martin Luther is obviously the classic expression of this internally generated dissent which spills out into society. The eleventh century, particularly in the wake of the Reform, produces a significant number of such priest-heretics (Moore, *Origins of European Dissent* [New York, 1977], 46–82).

110. Hans Georg Beck, "The Early Byzantine Church," *History of the Church,* 433–56.

111. Patrick Geary, *Before France and Germany: The Creation and Transformation of the Merovingian World* (New York, 1988), 3–39.

112. For a discussion of Theodoric's policies at the turn of the fifth to sixth centuries, see Thomas Burns, *A History of the Ostrogoths* (Bloomington, Ind., 1984), 80–107.

113. Michael Clanchy, *From Memory to Written Record: 1066–1307* (Cambridge, Mass., 1979), 175–91.

114. Landes, "Lest the Millennium," 161–205, esp. 161–65.

115. The Donatist position—that only morally pure priests could effectively perform the sacraments—defines the attitude of the "sect" (Ernst Troeltsch, *The Social Teachings of the Christian Churches* [New York: 1931]), whereas Augustine's response—that the sacraments could not depend on the moral purity of the necessarily impure (human) priests—defines that of the "church." The fact that at a key moment the Gregorian papacy advanced a functionally Donatist position is a surprisingly little discussed aspect of the Reform, particularly since it was just those policies (ordering laymen not to attend the masses of impure priests) which caused the most social unrest ("revolution" if we follow its imperial opponents). See, however, Moore, *Origins of European Dissent,* 52–63.

116. On the radical nature of the "Reform," see Morrison, *Tradition and Authority,* 269–317; on the reformers' attitudes towards secular government,

see ibid., 390–408; and Claude Carozzi, "D'Adalbéron de Laon à Humbert de Moyenmoutier: La désacralization de la royauté," *La cristianità dei secoli XI e XII in Occidente: Coscienza e strutture di una società* (Miscellanea del Centro di Studi Medioevali, 10 (Milan, 1983), 67–85.

117. See R. I. Moore, *The Formation of a Persecuting Society: Europe in the Twelfth Century* (Oxford, 1986), and J.-P. Poly and Eric Bournazel, *La mutation féodale: Europe Xe–XIIe siècles* (Paris, 1981), chaps. 9–10. An English translation is in preparation at the University of Chicago Press.

118. On the role of popular spiritual demands in shaping the Reform movement, see R. I. Moore, "Family, Cult and Community on the Eve of the Gregorian Reform," *Transactions of the Royal Historical Society*, 5th ser., 30 (1979); on the Peace of God, the "first popular religious movement of the Middle Ages," see *Historical Reflections/Réflexions historiques* 14, no. 3 (1987). See also the hypotheses of Janet Nelson, "Society, Theodicy and the Origins of Heresy: Towards a Reassessment of the Medieval Evidence," *Schism Heresy and Religious Protest*, ed. D. Baker, Studies in Church History, vol. 8 (Oxford, 1972), 65–77; and a response from Talal Asad, "Medieval Heresy: An Anthropological View," *Social History* 11, no. 3 (1986): 345–62. On a new document concerning an early eleventh-century textual community, see Guy Lobrichon, "Le clair-obscur de l'hérésie au début du XIe siècle en Aquitaine. Une lettre d'Auxerre," *Historical Reflections/Réflexions historiques* 14, no. 3 (1987): 424–44.

119. In addition to Brian Stock, *[Implications]*, see Alexander Murray, (*Reason and Society in the Middle Ages* [Oxford, 1978]), who does not discuss literacy so much as various endeavors which build upon it, and considers the turn of the millennium as the starting point for his tale.

120. Murray's chapter on numeracy points to some of the new, unschooled, and potent uses of writing that the new urban dwellers began to use (*Reason*, 162–212).

121. Most of the subsequent discussion draws from Stock, *Implications*, 120–39; Moore, *Origins*, 10–28; Georges Duby, *Les trois ordres ou l'imaginaire du féodalisme* (Paris, 1978), 35–61.

122. Stock, *Implications*, 137.

123. Asad, "Medieval Heresy," 356.

— 8 —

Varieties of Literacy

Daniel P. Resnick and Lauren B. Resnick

Historical research has begun to focus on the development of mass literacy in the West, a process that has taken form over the past five hundred years. The printing press, Protestantism, publishing houses, national literacy movements, texts, public school systems, newspapers, and magazines have all been the subject of investigation.[1] For the first time in world history, access to relatively inexpensive alphabetic text was assured for large portions of the population. Much has been written about the kinds of materials that were published and the variety of public and private institutions in which they played a sustaining role. Yet, we still have great difficulty describing, from the standpoint of social history, the meaning of participation in the kinds of communities mediated by the printed word.

During the same half-millennium, Western societies, some more directly and rapidly than others, also accelerated the process of economic, social, and political development that, in the model offered by Max Weber, we have come to associate with modernization. Self-sufficient economic growth, rationalization of institutions, technological change, urbanization, mobility of populations, participant polities, and secularization all have been the focus of social research. Attention given to these processes overshadowed the remarkable growth of literacy, the increased participation of an ever-larger portion of Western populations in the exchanges mediated by reading and writing.

Treatment of the ability to read and write primarily as an indicator of modernization rather than as a significant aspect of personal and social experience was encouraged, in part, by the silence of the evidence. Until

171

the introduction of widespread public schooling in the latter part of the nineteenth century, the signature was considered the strongest and most direct evidence of participation in actions that demonstrated the ability to read and write by much of the population.[2] Although the signature was the product of a social situation in which the signer was serving as witness, contractee, or in some other participant role, the signature itself gave no clue to the attitude or role of the signer. If there were differences in the capacities, knowledge, or intentions of the signers, the signature was difficult to interrogate on these matters.[3] As a leading historian of literacy in the Tudor and Stuart period put it: "Only one type of literacy is directly measurable—the ability or inability to write a signature; and that by itself may be the least interesting and least significant."[4]

Treated as a cultural product of uncertain significance, signature literacy was assigned meaning in relationship to the larger processes of economic development, urbanization, and growth of the state. Through research on this larger process of modernization, we have learned that the ability to read and to write at even a minimal level was first the property of small elites; that people in cities were among the first to be literate and those who tilled the land in isolation from outside markets were among the last; that the distribution of wealth and status was, by the latter part of the nineteenth century when public education was introduced, a good predictor of years of schooling; that the state, by its use of records and written materials, and long before the introduction of public schooling, played a role in the promotion of literacy; that literacy played a role in some but not all stages of economic development; and that religious orders and religious texts were closely bound up with the spread of reading and writing capability.

These results constitute what is essentially a historical demography of literacy. However, they tell us little about the meaning of reading and writing for the actors most directly involved, a question of direct concern to social history. Nor do they respond to the public policy interest in how individual nations, drawing on the past history of the literacy process, might now accelerate literacy development in their populations. To respond to these questions requires reconstruction of the social, cognitive, and perhaps emotional environment in which reading and writing have been practiced. This act of reconstruction will have to proceed with some social theory of the nature of the reading and writing experience, a vigorous interrogation of available evidence, and examination of historical cases that are likely to reveal representative kinds of literacy transactions.

Our contribution to this volume on consciousness, cognition, and emotion attempts to reconstruct central elements in the modern experience of literacy in the West that have been neglected in the historical literature. In our view, literacy must be considered as a social rather than an individual experience. In that sense, as Sylvia Scribner has argued, "The single most compelling fact about literacy is that it is a *social* achievement; individuals in societies without writing systems do not become literate."[5] We go even further to claim that each literate act is in fact a social act. As such, it involves a transaction between a writer and reader, through the medium of a text. To understand the meaning of literacy for its participants, therefore, we must analyze both the nature of texts and the activities and expectations associated with the roles of reader and writer in different literacy transactions.

In this chapter, we explore six types of engagements, each establishing somewhat different relations among the reader, the writer, and the text. Within each of the types of literacy transactions, demands on the knowledge and skills of the reader can range widely, and will be greatly affected by the kind of purposes that the literacy performance of the reader is expected to serve.

Our argument may contribute to legitimating and broadening the notion of texts as a useful source for social history, a direction in which Peter Burke, among others, has encouraged social history to move as it deepens its study of mentalities.[6] This would help to link social history with the efforts of certain intellectual historians to extend concern with texts to a variety of informal and non-elite communications, and to treat more explicitly the relationship of readers to writers.[7] Of particular interest has been the pioneering effort of Robert Darnton in developing a new history of reading, sensitive to the concerns of both social and intellectual history. His excursion into the letters of Rousseau provides illustrative material for one of the types of literacy transaction that we examine (see section 8.2).

Our treatment of literacy as a transaction has also been encouraged indirectly by the Nobel laureate Joseph Brodsky's use of the metaphor of conversation to describe what transpires between the writer and reader of novels and poetry.

> A novel of a poem is not a monologue, but a conversation of a writer with a reader, a conversation, I repeat, that is very private, excluding all others—if you will, mutually misanthropic. And in the moment of this conversation a writer is equal to a reader, as the other way around, regardless of whether the writer is a great one or not. This equality is the equality of consciousness. It remains with a person for the rest of his life in the form of memory, foggy or distinct; and, sooner or later, appropriately or not, it conditions a person's conduct.[8]

8.1. *Literacy Transactions*

We begin with a simple definition of literacy as a social transaction mediated by text. In this definition, literacy is not a unitary descriptor of an individual's or a society's capacity to use the written language. We can understand texts, and therefore literacy, only by understanding the social exchanges that they mediate.

In cognitive psychology today, reading is understood as a process in which an individual uses a text, along with several kinds of prior knowledge, to construct a mental representation of the situation described, analyzed, or evoked by the author. The representation constructed by the reader does not exactly match the words of the text, but rather aims for coherence in the reader's mind, along with fidelity to the situation to which the text refers.[9] Reading is thus an interpretive act. This view of reading recognizes the transactive nature of the process: the reader *uses* the test to construct meaning; he or she does not *take* the meaning from the text or copy the text into memory.

It is not uncommon in cognitive analyses of reading to take into account readers' purposes in reading, their interests, and other characteristics of individuals that may affect the way in which they use the text to construct meaning. Yet there is little concern in the typical cognitive analysis for the origin of the text. The text in these analyses is a given. It is reified. The nature of its author, and the possible relationship of reader to author are not examined. For this reason, while the dominant cognitive theories of text comprehension are consonant with the point of view we wish to explore in this paper, they do not constitute socially situated analyses.

We want here to press further, to imagine an author-reader exchange that is not an isolated event, but rather is part of a particular social situation that constrains the kinds of texts that are written and read and the kinds of interpretations made. The fact that text-mediated social exchange can take place at great distances of place and time, and that the same text may serve in many different particular exchanges distinguishes written from conversational forms of linguistic interaction. A text may be used in different ways by different individuals and by different interpretive communities. Yet each time it is used it must be considered as a new social episode; to understand the episode, we will have to understand the relationship between author and reader *as construed by the reader* in the particular cultural and social space in which the reading takes place.

To understand literacy, then, we must ask not just what the text is (its content or its form), but what the relationship is between writer and reader. More specifically, for any occasion of literate behavior—i.e., any occasion on which a text is used—we want to know how the reader views the author in relation to herself or himself and what effects on behavior, cognition, or emotion are expected as a result of reading. In some cases (it is not possible, we think, for all), we may wish to enter the writer's perspective, to consider how he or she views the relationship with the reader and what actions or responses he or she hopes to produce in the reader.

Using this triple analysis of writer, reader, and text, we can identify a small number of paradigmatic types of literacy transactions. Each is an ideal type, in the Weberian sense, with certain heuristic and clarifying properties. These ideal types do not appear in their pure form in the real historical world. They nonetheless describe strongly defining features of these transactions that allow us to recognize them in their varying, imperfect and real historical forms. In our discussion, we identify six types of literacy transaction: the sacred, the useful, the informational, the persuasive, the pleasure-giving, and the personal-familial. For the first two we offer historical examples that illustrate the relationship between the ideal type and the historical case.

8.2. Sacred Literacy

Sacred literacy transactions are those in which reader and writer are in contact with powers and forces thought to overrule those in the natural world. Those forces may guide or inspire human behavior, demand certain kinds of sacrifices, intervene in the workings of the natural world, predict apocalyptic futures, and promise rewards and punishment in an afterlife. Although the realm of the sacred has been in retreat during the last five centuries, it has not followed its predicted Weberian course to extinction. Indeed, the dimensions of the sacred have been sustained not only within religious communities, as we argue, but also within nation states that have created their own civil religions.

Sacred texts play an important role in maintaining religious communities. The reader of a sacred text gains access through reading and proper interpretation to participation in a particular marked community that accepts the text as sacred. The author of a sacred text may not be known, may in fact not be a single individual. Indeed these "unknowable" aspects of sacred text may be part of what makes them sacred. They must be accepted in their traditional form. Ordinary "authors" do not have the wisdom or power to change them.

The expected behavior of the sacred text user is to learn the texts

themselves (perhaps by heart) and to acquire a body of standard interpretations of the text. These interpretations may be discovered through
independent reasoning (as in classical Talmudic study), but in prototyp-
ical sacred text functions, they must conform to an already established
range of acceptable interpretations. Only rarely do new interpretations
enter the sacred text corpus, and then such new interpretations may be
the cause of schisms and other community divisions.

Luther's *Little Catechism,* "the great textbook of instruction in the
Lutheran Church"[10] is an example of a sacred text, as we have defined
it. Within its covers, portions of the divinely authored Bible—the Ten
Commandments, the Apostles' Creed, and the Lord's Prayer—were presented in brief summaries, with guiding questions. Readers were
expected to be able to recall and repeat the summary statements
in response to the expected questions. They were not expected to
be able to put the text into their own words, or identify passages elsewhere in the Bible with similar themes. Nor were they asked to pick
out inconsistencies of argument, or extemporize on the meanings of
words.[11]

This analysis does not argue that all sacred literacy transactions discourage questioning and critical analysis from the reader, but that fixed
boundaries are placed on such expectations, especially for the reader
who wishes to remain within the social community confirmed by the
text. Sometimes the reader is led, as in the case of a powerful sacred text
like *Exodus,* examined in this volume by Richard Landes, to join others
in resisting the oppression of a host community, and to seek liberation
from bondage. That text has to be understood, in Michael Walzer's
words, as "a paradigm of revolutionary politics."[12] More often, however, the sacred transaction looks inward, seeking to bond the community of believers through common beliefs and rituals. It imposes certain
constraints on the reader, who is expected to participate in the reading
as a believer. Unorthodox interpretations are a threat to the faithful. The
novelist Haim Potok offers an example of this in his novel, *Davita's
Harp:*[13]

> In Mr. Helfman's class we completed studying the Book of Num-
> bers. The next day there was a siyum, the traditional party that follows
> when a group completes the study of a sacred Jewish text. We brought
> candies and cookies and chocolates to school, and Mr. Helfman gave
> a little talk about how the study of Torah had kept the Jewish people
> alive all through the centuries.
> The siyum lasted about half an hour. Then Mr. Helfman called the
> class to order and stood behind his desk and began to talk to us about

the Book of Deuteronomy, its first-person style, its lofty poetry, its ethical and moral themes. I listened and at the same time read quickly through the first verses. Names and dates. In the fifth verse I read two words that I remembered having read before, and I went back to the beginning of the book and found the words in the first verse: *b'ever ha-Yarden*. I glanced at the Rashi on the verse and found that Rashi had not bothered to explain the words—which meant that they were very easy to understand. Mr. Helfman went on with his introduction to the book, and a moment or so after he was done, the bell rang for the morning recess.

In the school library I found an English translation of the Bible and turned to Deuteronomy. The Hebrew words *b'ever ha-Yarden* were translated as "beyond the Jordan." The text read, "These are the words which Moses spoke to all Israel beyond the Jordan . . ."

What did those words mean? Beyond the Jordan.

It was snowing when school let out. I walked home with Ruthie in a wind that blew the snow in a steep slant across the parkway and was piling it in drifts against fences and homes.

Inside the apartment I found the verse in my father's copy of the Hertz commentary. There the words were explained as meaning at the crossing of the Jordan or on the banks of the Jordan or as referring to a fixed geographical name.

But what if there was another explanation? I thought of Jakob Daw writing this as a story. What would "beyond the Jordan" then mean? What if Jakob Daw were living on this, the Israelite, side of the Jordan? And what if he were writing this story? Wouldn't he simply write "beyond the Jordan" to indicate where the action of the story was taking place?

And wouldn't that mean that the writer of the story in the Bible had lived *after* the story had taken place, because he was on the Israelite side of the river and in the story the Israelites had not yet crossed the river? I thought that made sense. You didn't have to change the simple meaning of the words. I liked the idea that a human being had thought to write those words; it made the text seem more real to me.

The next day, when we came to that verse, I raised my hand. Mr. Helfman called on me. I recounted my explanation of the words *b'ever ha-Yarden*. I talked for what seemed to me to be a long time. Mr. Helfman let me go on. He kept looking at me and nodding. Behind me the class was very still.

Then I was done and sat back in my seat, listening to the drumming of my heart.

Mr. Helfman quickly cleared his throat. "Where did you read this explanation?" he asked.

I told him I hadn't read it anywhere, I made it up.

"You made it up," he echoed.

There was a silence. An airplane went by high overhead. The windows rattled faintly.

"It is the explanation given by Ibn Ezra," Mr. Helfman said. "Do you know who Ibn Ezra was?"

"Yes."

"It is not an acceptable explanation. It creates more problems that it solves. What problems does it create?"

I looked at him and did not know what to say.

Two rows to my right a boy raised his hand. This was Reuven Malter, the son of a Talmud teacher in a nearby Jewish parochial high school, a dark-haired, good-looking boy who was very popular and very smart.

"Reuven," Mr. Helfman said.

"If this verse was written by a person and not given by God, then how do we know other verses weren't written by a person, including verses that deal with the law?"

"Yes, indeed," said Mr. Helfman. "And what does that do to the Bible, Ilana? You understand, don't you? That is why the explanation of Ibn Ezra is unacceptable. Now, let's go on with the text."

In the sacred tradition of Talmud study and discussion, captured in the course work of the Jewish parochial school, this young Jewish student of secular and Marxist parents is very taken with the joyous celebrations surrounding discussion of sacred text and the apparent openness to participation and critical comment which the teacher invites in the classroom. She compares passages, uses reference works, imagines possibles meanings, and raises her hand. For the first time, she is led to challenge the hypothesis of single, divine authorship of the text, little realizing that by so doing she had exceeded the permitted liberties of the reader in this classroom environment. Her teacher immediately tries to establish the source of the error. He appears somewhat relieved, though puzzled, that it is the result of individual and independent thought, and not reading dissenting texts. He then underscores the danger to the Jewish community of Davita'a unorthodox interpretation—human authorship brings the divine authority of the laws into question—by calling on a young competitor in the classroom, the son of a Talmud teacher, to indicate why her views are socially unacceptable. Potok calls to mind all the features of the sacred literacy transaction: divine or transcendent authorship; text of unchallengeable authority, a social community that imposes accepted interpretations; and a reader whose understanding of the text must be developed within the framework of those social expectations.

8.3. Useful Literacy

A very different kind of literacy transaction, a functional one, develops when a reader uses a text to negotiate a particular, practical, here-and-now situation. Such situations can range from using printed directions (or even just signs) to find one's way, following assembly or operating instructions, reading timetables and schedules, using conversion tables, following diets, recipes, or investment advice, and any others of a myriad of very practical uses of the written word.

In the ideal type of this kind of functional literacy, relations between writer and reader are quite clearly defined. The writer is an "expert," knowledgeable in the specific domain to which the text applies, while the reader is acknowledged to be inexpert, someone needing guidance (or at the very least reminding) in how to perform. The reader presumably comes to the text with the purpose of negotiating a rather specific and practical task.

Functional literacy of the kind we have in mind may well be the dominant form of literacy in which adults who are not part of an intellectual community engage. The how-to-do-it book market represents a major segment of current American publishing, for example, with books of this type being marketed in stores such as K-Mart, according to the recent Sunday newspaper advertisements. Book sales analyses view this as one of the major markets.[14]

The rise of useful knowledge literacy seems to occur whenever personal and face-to-face relationships are no longer adequate to convey cultural information of a practical kind. This happens when people begin to be separated from their family and traditional communities—as for example when they move to the cities. It also happens as bureaucracies begin to develop and to control various aspects of individuals' behavior. Functional literacy transactions can be traced historically in applications as different as wood and metal trades, child rearing, and home health care.

Let us examine some sixteenth-and seventeenth-century examples of useful literacy as they come to us from the studies reported by Roger Chartier on the history of printed works and readership in early modern France. During this period, as exposure to printed text in the form of hawked pamphlets, flysheets, and displayed posters became common in cities, books entered the workplace and the home. A few master craftsmen, at this time, began to write for others in their trade. The existence of such readers in specialized crafts presupposes developed artisanal sectors geographically separated but sharing in common understandings, experiences with material and labor, and working vocabulary. This type of literacy transaction would not have been possible without such common elements in the artisanal experience.

Drawing on estate inventories from Amiens in the sixteenth century, a city of about 20,000, Albert Labarre has established that of the eight hundred or so estate inventories for the years 1503-1576 that mention books (20 percent of the total), about 100 were those of artisans. Metalworkers, leatherworkers, and those in the textile trades lead the list, generally with just a few items each. A recurring item in these inventories were the so-called books of "pourtraicture." These offered patterns, illustrations for procedure, models of both tools and products, written for artisans. The works produced might be anonymous, as in *Ung livre ou sont plusieurs pourtraictz servant au mestier de menuisier* (A book with several patterns useful to the craft of the cabinetmaker) but more often they would indicate the name and position of the artisan, likely to be a master craftsman. Thus, the author of *La fidelle ouverture de l'art de serrurier* (The reliable guide to the art of the locksmith) Mathurin Jousse, is described on the flyleaf as "master locksmith in the city of La Flèche."[15] Clearly, the author's qualifications were thought to be critical in attracting readers.

Craft secrets were a valuable commodity, generally passed from master to apprentice. We can only speculate about the reasons that some master artisans in seventeenth-century France chose to disclose their secrets or "mystery" to readers. Capital needs, perhaps for the purchase of new machinery, or the vanity of a literary reputation may have been among the motives. Relatively few chose to publish, even at the end of the eighteenth century, when the crafts had become weaker elements in the national economy.[16]

The American case was quite different. At the end of the eighteenth century in America, craftsmen entered the book market with zeal, writing for other tradesmen. Rorabaugh, who has traced the virtual disappearance of apprenticeship in American crafts between the Revolutionary and Civil Wars, found the traditional craft structures at the end of the century weakened by the Revolution. Respect for masters in the crafts had become more difficult to maintain during the economic trials, conscription, and unpredictability of the Revolutionary period. It was also true that within the crafts themselves, in the latter part of the century, some new technologies had gained more value than the craft knowledge of masters. Coal tar, for example, available on an open market, was better as a means of preventing wood from rotting in sailing ships than any closely held secrets about the treatment of wood that ship carpenters possessed.[17] These developments encouraged craftsmen to share trade secrets with their readers.

John Hargrove, in the preface to *The Weavers Draft Book and Clothiers Assistant,* published in Baltimore in 1792, directed his work to those already members of the trade. It was, above all, to be useful—a "public Assistant."

> I am the first Mechanic, who has ever favored the American Weaver and Manufacturer, with a public Assistant of this kind. Long! too long! has the Weaving trade remained a mystery (at least in the figured line) to hundreds, and thousands, who have served a regular Apprenticeship to that business, & followed it afterwards for many years: Selfish motives have prevented those, who *were* capable of giving instructions, from revealing the art, lest it might operate against their own personal interest (having no desire to promote the Prosperity of their Country at the risk of their own) but the secret has (in a good measure) lately fallen into the hands of one, who is willing that all concerned share the benefit.[18]

Others followed, in carpentry, mill building, dyeing, printing and engraving. Amanda Jones, who published a study of tailoring in 1822, made strong promises to the reader: "In a few hours, a person may acquire such a knowledge of the art, as will enable him to cut all sizes and fashions, with the greatest accuracy."[19]

Books could provide, by the early nineteenth century, a substitute for the knowledge brought by apprenticeship, even though the portion of those who tried to substitute that book-based knowledge for the mixture of knowledge and *praxis* brought by actual apprenticeship was quite small. The career of Alexander Anderson, who at the age of twelve in 1787 taught himself engraving from an encyclopedia article, and left us an autobiographical memoir, remains exemplary:

> Anderson found in a friend's encyclopedia an article on engraving, and he decided to try learning this art. He obtained a few copper pennies, visited a friendly silversmith, and had the smith flatten the pennies in his mill. Using a graver made from the back spring of an old pocketknife, Sandy, as the boy was called, etched a head on a flattened copper. Then he built a crude rolling press and printed copies of his engraving in red oil paint. Later he persuaded a blacksmith to make some engraving tools. Engraving on copper, pewter, or soft type

metal, Sandy found that small ships cut into type metal could be sold to the newspapers for use in advertising. Although Anderson later was apprenticed to a surgeon, he was so obsessed with engraving that the abandoned a medical practice to pursue his self-taught trade and eventually took a number of apprentices. He produced more than ten thousand engravings—not bad for a career that began with the perusal of an encyclopedia article.[20]

The home was also the target of certain useful knowledge tests. Authors sought to bring the parent into a literacy transaction that involved respected authorities on matters such as the care of the sick and the education of the young. Books of both kinds can be found in the *Bibliothèque bleue,* the term used to describe a low-cost series of volumes published in Troyes, beginning at the very start of the seventeenth century (the first one inventoried dates from 1603) and continuing for some 250 years. The slim volumes, bound in blue, have become the familiar designation for mass audience publishing in early modern France.

Medical advice for the household appears in the *Médecin charitable enseignant la manière de faire et préparer en sa maison avec facilité et peu de frais les remèdes propres à toutes maladies* and the *Opérateur des pauvres, ou la fleur d'opération nécessaire aux pauvres pour conserver leur santé et soy guérir à peu de frais.*[21] The reference to treatment "in one's own house," "easily" and "at low cost" indicates the author has directed the work to a reader prepared to create her/his own remedies, and eager for useful advice at low cost. The author assumes the reader will accept expert advice that comes from the text, and that herbs, roots and other material for home remedies are available for either purchase or gathering. The author indicates the choices, but cannot make them. Responsibility for the treatment outcome is thus shared with the reader.

Instruction of the young also appears as an important category of book production, including how-to-do-it books on teaching reading and treatises on moral and religious instruction. In the Troyes publisher's inventory, for example, in the mid-seventeenth century, we find *Civilité puérile et honnête pour l'éducation des enfants,* and models of conversation like the *Cabinet de l'éloquence française,* intended for an older user, perhaps ill at ease in urban, commercial, and court environments.

To enter the literacy transaction of parents seeking instruction on their relations with one another and with their children, we turn to Robert Darnton's examination of Rousseau and his readers in the 1770s and 1780s. We enter a French provincial and urban world of readers of Jean-Jacques Rouseau's *La Nouvelle Héloise* and *Emile.*[22] The source of knowledge of this literacy transaction comes from the published correspondance of Rousseau and his readers, and the unpublished correspondance of one of those readers with Rousseau's Neuchatel publisher.

After reading the six-volume sentimental novel of human relationships, *La Nouvelle Héloise,* an unhappy housewife, Constant de Rebecque, wrote to Rousseau that the novel had saved her marriage. She was now able to love her husband by picturing him as Saint-Preux, the hero, and herself as Julie, the heroine. And a young father of four writes, "Sincerely committed to a young wife, I have learned from you, and she has, too, that what had seemed to us to be a mere attachment based on the habit of living together is in fact a most tender love." And a La Rochelle Protestant merchant, entering marriage at the age of thirty, writes about Rousseau to his publisher: "Everything that l'Ami Jean-Jacques has written about the duties of husbands and wives, of mothers and fathers, has had a profound effect on me; and I confess to you that it will serve me as a rule in any of those estates that I should occupy."

When paternity approached, the same client wrote to his bookseller: "Please procure for me, if possible, an excellent dissertation on the physical education of children published by M. Balexerde of Geneva. I am about to become a father, and am thinking of how I can best fulfill my duties." The same reader also encouraged his wife to follow Rousseau's injunctions on breastfeeding and maternal love, purchased at least two copies of *Emile,* Rousseau's essay on child-rearing, and broke with familial patterns of naming children to call his second-born *Emile,* a name that does not appear in the family's lexicon of largely Old Testament choices. If the reader sought and received guidance, the author also expected to give it. In one of the two prefaces to *La Nouvelle Héloise,* Rousseau announces that this novel has been directed only to those most likely to be susceptible to its message. He seeks his dialogue with those who already reject the canons of sophisticated (and therefore corrupt) French society:

> Whoever resolves to read these letters [in *La Nouvelle Héloise*] must arm himself with patience about the incorrectness of their language, the overblown character of their style, the ordinary quality of the ideas expressed in their inflated phrasing. He must say to himself in advance that those who wrote them are not French, not sophisticates, not academicians nor philosophes but rather provincials, foreigners, recluses, young people, almost children, who in their romantic imaginations take the innocent frenzy of their minds to be philosophy.

8.4. Comparing Literacy Transactions

Our consideration of these two very distinct types of literacy interactions, the sacred and the useful, highlights the multiple meanings the term literacy can have when we take the social transactional stance we have proposed, and it suggests the complexity that will be involved in a full analysis of literacy in these terms. Let us consider some contrasts as they affect each of the three elements in a literacy transaction: the reader, the text, and the author.

The reader. The reader in a sacred transaction comes to the text as a member of a community or as a postulant, and interest in the text derives, in part, from its promise of community membership. The "benefits" sought by the reader include confirmation of belonging and guidance in the obligations and rights of membership in that community. Individuals may sometimes adopt certain religious or quasi-religious texts as personal guideposts for ethical or spiritual purposes without social engagement in a community. This happens, for example, when Westerners discover and study Buddhist texts. Strictly speaking, such personal "adoptions" of texts fall outside our definition of sacred literacy transactions and deserve a separate analysis.

Yet, the very fact that a text is designated sacred by a community, and thereby subject to many rereadings and to efforts to maintain its relevance even when conditions of life change dramatically, will, we think, create a pressure toward noncanonical reinterpretations. Reading of the Bible provides a prime example. Except within very tightly controlled communities, such as fundamentalist Christian churches or orthodox Jewish yeshivas, efforts of religious groups to retain loyalty to the text and to the group have spawned multiple reinterpretations. These reinterpretations often loosen certain behavioral injunctions, which come to be viewed as specific to a particular time and cultural condition rather than universal.

In another form of reinterpretation, the Bible can be treated as great literature—rich in archetypal characters, cultural myths, and memorable poetry. Opened to relatively free interpretation, interest in the Bible no longer necessarily requires religious commitment. The cultural literacy movement of today, in this view, argues for a national reestablishment of the Bible, along with certain other texts, as a kind of common cultural heritage. Those who propose "great books" forms of literacy development, are not, for the most part, suggesting that canonical interpretations be required. Rather they see these texts as a common point of reference for a society. Yet in this cultural literacy view, participation in the study of core texts would, as in the case of sacred literacy transactions, confer membership in a community.

Central to our characterization of the sacred literacy transaction is the fact that the range of interpretations of a text that can emerge in a sacred reading is constrained by community standards. No such community constraint on use or interpretation by the reader characterizes the form of literacy transaction that we have termed "the useful." Indeed, motivation for "useful" literacy is, we surmise, creation by separation from small communities of taste, residence, and production and the reader's sense that familiar ways of doing things are no longer appropriate or sufficient. On the other hand because texts for functional use tend to be written for specific conditions of use, and are discarded— or at least revised—when conditions change, there is, we imagine, little press toward the variety of interpretation that characterizes sacred texts when community constraints are at least partially lifted. In practice, then, functional literacy is likely to demand less interpretive skill and invite less interpretive elaboration than those forms of literacy transaction in which texts are considered important objects, worthy of study in their own right, rather than just vehicles for transmitting information.

The text. The preceding discussion of differences in the nature of the reading process for sacred and useful literacy already suggests some of the dimensions along which texts in these two very different kinds of transactions are likely to vary. Sacred texts need to serve communities over long periods of time. They need to be rich, complex, capable of commenting on many aspects of the human condition. They need to be "habitable," to use George Lindbeck's formulation.[23] Such texts will bear multiple readings and be capable of providing guidance for living under many specific conditions. Such texts will not be transparent, easy to understand, or direct in their form of communication. They will not simply "say what they mean." In the words of Frank Kermode, they will be "a repository of secrets."[24] In this respect, they are the opposite of useful texts. Texts useful for functional purposes ought to be straightforward and unambiguous. What makes for texts of this kind is the subject of substantial bodies of research, on "readability," on "document design," on "friendly" text structures and the like. Yet even if we don't yet know as much as we would like to about what makes texts "useful," it is impossible to imagine a set of criteria that would qualify the Bible or the Koran as elegant functional texts. That, we think, highlights an essential difference.

The author. The most striking feature of authors in useful literacy transactions is their actual or ascribed expertise in a narrow domain. Readers take up books or articles for functional purposes on the basis of a belief that the writer knows more than they do on the subject at hand. Perhaps one of the reasons that bureacratic functional texts—ranging from instruction manuals to tax forms—are so rarely successful is that there is no apparent author, no imagined or imaginable relationship between the person who knows how to do something and the person who would like to know how. This conjecture, at any rate, bears consideration and investigation.

The question of authorship in the truly sacred literacy transaction is, as the incident from the Potok story illustrates, a delicate matter, one often of concern to the community defined by its adoption of the text. The sacred text is assumed to be of divine origin. Even if the author is a known, historical individual—as in the case of the Koran, for example— he is assumed to be divinely inspired. The sacred literacy transaction, then, is not between readers who want some specific knowledge and an author able to give it to them.

8.5. *Other Forms of Literacy Transaction*

The preceding analysis establishes the kinds of questions that will need to be addressed in an eventual full characterization of the varieties of literacy. We can briefly suggest here the shape of the analysis we envisage for other forms of literacy transaction.

8.5.1. THE INFORMATIONAL

We term informational those literacy transactions in which texts are used to transmit or acquire knowledge. This form of literacy shares with functional literacy the basic relationship between author and reader. That is, the author knows something that the reader wants to find out. However, there is a fundamental difference between the useful and the informational literacy transaction: A reader of an informational text is not expected to immediately apply the information gained from that text. Informational texts—which may be on any topic from history to science to the current news and may be written in a number of different rhetorical forms—are meant to give the reader new knowledge and understanding, but not necessarily to help negotiate any specific situation. The occurrence of knowledge-conveying forms of literacy is, apparently, rather limited in society. Very probably, newspaper reading constitutes the predominant form of informational literacy for all but an elite with the taste and leisure for acquisition of "useless knowledge."

Apart from newspaper and magazine reading, the major encounters with informational text occur in schools. Indeed schools (including colleges and universities) specialize in a knowledge-conveying form of literacy that is quite distinct from literacy activities outside of school.[25] Although schools aim to convey knowledge, they have found that they cannot maintain a pure informational form of literacy. This is because they cannot count on students to *want* to gain the knowledge their texts provide. So schools use various motivators—mostly tests—that have the effect of converting informational texts into functional ones. In school, the immediate purpose of reading a textbook is almost always to pass some kind of test on its contents.

The schools' tendency to convert texts that are apparently informational (that is, they do not appear to be "about" any specific, practical situation) into texts that play a primarily functional role (preparing students to pass a specific test) highlights a major point we wish to make in this chapter—that it is not possible to understand the nature of literacy by examining texts alone. It is essential to also examine the social transactions that they mediate. This conversion of texts from their apparent intended use to another can go in the opposite direction as well. For example, people may read cookbooks (at least certain ones) for the pleasurable[26] and evocative experience they provide and to gain general information about food and eating habits, not necessarily to follow recipes immediately. Indeed, some books seem to be written with this kind of multiple social use in mind.

8.5.2. THE PERSUASIVE

Persuasive literacy occurs whenever someone uses print to try to influence the actions or opinions of others. The authors of persuasive texts may be anyone with an opinion on a topic and access to an audience. The presumed reader of a persuasive text is a person or persons whose opinions matter to the author or whom the author believes is in a position to act appropriately if persuaded. A text is persuasive in intent if the author hopes to change (or in some cases explicitly confirm) the action or opinion of the reader.

Virtually any rhetorical form can be used to create a persuasive text. Advertising copy constitutes a persuasive text according to our definition. So does a letter to the editor, testimony at a Congressional hearing, a personal letter appealing for funds or signatures, a poem if it is aimed to convince, or virtually any other piece of writing. It is the intended social exchange that qualifies a text as persuasive, rather than anything about the text itself. Of course, texts initially intended for other uses can be appropriated for persuasive exchanges, either by their original authors or by others. Once again, we encounter texts migrating from one kind of literacy situation to another, a reminder that it is not the text itself, but rather its use that is definitive for our analysis of literacy.

8.5.3. THE PLEASURE-GIVING

We come now to the category of literacy that includes, but is not limited to the reading of literature. There is much reading and writing whose only aim is to engage and give pleasure to readers. These can range from high literature, to pulp novels, from murder mysteries to poems to fairy tales. What these texts have in common is that they are read for their own sake. The intended effect on the reader is engagement and pleasure, and perhaps empathy with characters or with the author himself. The reader seeks out the writer and the text for the enjoyment of the experience. Although reading for pleasure can perform a variety of latent cultural functions,[27] there is no practical action to be taken, no specific knowledge to be gained. Unlike the author of a functional or knowledge—giving text, the author of a pleasure-giving text need have no special expertise, apart from the skill of engaging a reader. Of course, different readers will find engaging texts of very different characteristics. Texts that will engage some readers precisely because they use simple language and contain recognizable characters in recognizable situations will seem uninteresting to other readers because of their lack of complexity and nuance. There is, in other words, room within this broad category of pleasure-giving literacy for a wide range of reading habits and writing styles. There is also room for considerable change in taste over historical periods.

As for the other categories of literacy, texts can migrate out of the pleasure-giving category if they are used in social settings in which the reader's pleasure is not the primary intent of the exchange. A test, as in school literature courses, for example, can change the context for even the best of literary texts from pleasure-giving literacy to functional literacy. Too much prescribed "socialist realism" can turn books that have the form of novels or romances into persuasive texts, whose value must then be judged by the opinions they change or sustain rather than by the engagement and pleasure they provide. In the other direction, as already noted, texts with an apparent practical flavor can provide engagement-type pleasure to certain readers.

8.5.4. THE PERSONAL-FAMILIAL

We term personal-familial transactions in which the written word is used in exchanges between family members or close personal associates. The paradigmatic form of personal-familial transactions is the personal letter. Personal letters may serve functional purposes (as when families conduct business together at a distance), they may convey information, they may aim to persuade, they may have literary aspirations akin to what we have termed pleasure-giving texts. However, letters are distinguished from all of the other forms of literacy we have considered by what we take to be their primary purpose—to maintain social contact between family members and close associates who are geographically separated. The particular content of such personal-familial letters is very varied—ranging from news of self, family, and neighbors to emotional expressions as in love letters. What is constant across all of these forms is the relationship between author and reader: they already know one another and have an established relationship to one another that exists apart from the written transaction.

Letter writing is far less common in industrialized countries with high rates of advanced literacy than it once was. Family members and friends who are separated find it easier to communicate by telephone than by letter. Only when telephone communication and travel are restricted by large distances (usually different continents and very different time zones) or by conditions of isolation as when a member of the family is away in military service or in prison do letters comprise a primary means of staying in touch. In developing countries, however, ability to engage in personal-familial letter writing constitutes a major motivation for becoming literate. Patterns of migration frequently separate family members or subgroups for long periods of time. Personal economic conditions, together with limited telephone facilities and poor public transportation, make letter writing the only practical way to maintain contact. Public scribes remain a common sight in Third World cities and towns, attesting to the importance of exchanges of letters even among the illiterate. And those engaged in literacy development work find that the expectation of being able to exchange private letters with family members is the major reasons that adults give for entering literacy programs or wanting their children to learn to read. A full account of the various forms of literacy transaction must, therefore, give due consideration to personal-familial literacy transactions—while examining the hypothesis that this form of literacy may in the future (as electronic communication spreads and travel becomes easier) be dominant during only a relatively limited period of any group's history.

8.6. *An Agenda for Literacy Research*

Our framework for understanding literacy has focused on the interactive nature of the author-text-reader relationship and has encouraged us to explore the varieties of transactions that occur in different social settings. Six types of literacy transaction have been identified and a framework for comparing and contrasting those relationships has been established. Although we have a sense of some progress in our effort to understand the ways in which social settings can allow these interactions to develop, we are also aware of certain limits to our argument.

First of all, our typology of literacy transactions is not completely adequate as it stands. We have dealt only with texts that have a reader in mind, apart from the author. There is, however, another category of texts—the expressive—which are addressed to no known or expected reader other than the author. Expressive texts are those that people write to convey their intentions, emotions, needs, opinions, and so on. An expected sympathetic reader usually enhances a writer's motivation to create an expressive text. But many texts—ranging from diaries, to prison notebooks, to unmailed and some mailed letters—are written without this expectation of a necessary audience. As expressive texts gain wider audiences they are likely to function in either pleasure-giving or persuasive transactions. This happens, for example, when an individual's diary or notebooks are eventually published, or when poems written in prison pass to the outside and into either published or underground literature.

Under what conditions do people come to use writing as a form of expression, and how widespread is it in our own and other societies? Presumably, people are either initiated into the use of writing as a form of expression by participation in social communities that use it that way (the writers' workshop idea) or by extraordinary circumstances that make writing a way to maintain mental balance. The latter can happen in conditions of imprisonment or other severe social isolation. Consider, for example, the role of the diary in *The Color Purple* and of letters and notes for Natan Sharansky.[28]

Secondly, our argument about the importance of the author's intention and the social setting for the nature of a literacy transaction will need to be developed further. Within the framework of literacy transactions, we have argued that an author's intention establishes certain boundaries of expectation in the literacy act, just as in different historical environments, communities of readers place constraints on permissible interpretations for certain kinds of text. Historians have begun to try to deepen their understanding of the social and cultural meaning of texts, but this "linguistic turn" is still not fully developed.[29]

Finally, in our analysis of literacy as a transaction, we have tried to discover how larger economic and social forces, at different stages of historical development, impinge on written texts and their authors and readers, and how these in turn are influenced by the literacy transactions that follow. The relationship of literacy to these developments is complex, and it is not simply one of dependence. We have given literacy transactions a prominent role in mediating and shaping the growth of modern societies, but the constraints on that process need further exploration.

In the area of the useful, literacy transactions have helped to prepare readers to adapt to the process of rationalization that Weber identified. The decline of apprenticeship and rapid changes in technology have encouraged the interest in useful texts, just as a growth in the number of literacy transactions involving texts has encouraged a mind-set that could shape as well as adapt to those changes. It seems also to be the case, as we have argued with examples largely drawn from eighteenth-century France, that changes in family structure and family relations, tied to a variety of economic and demographic shifts, created a larger market for text-based literacy involving parental behavior and child-rearing, and that these literacy transactions, in turn, helped families adapt to patterns of child-rearing, family size and gender relationships imposed by structural changes in the economy, the population and the workplace.

The historical direction of development in literacy transactions involving the sacred is less clear. As S. N. Eisenstadt argued more than fifteen years ago, modernization theory cannot assume that rationality and secularism will dissolve traditional religious bonds.[30] The persistence or revival of premodern religious beliefs and associations in otherwise modern or modernizing societies has forced a qualification of those expectations. Historical criticism of the Bible has yielded to literary appreciation. In this perspective, the Bible appears as "a loose anthology," nine centuries of literary production including laws, history, genealogy, prophecy, and poetry. As the editors of *The Literary Guide to the Bible* put it in their preface, "the general reader can now be offered a new view of the Bible as a work of which it is entirely credible that it should have shaped the minds and lives of intelligent men and women for two millenia and more."[31] We do not know in what ways sacred text will continue to shape minds and lives, but the direction of influence is likely to be radically different in fundamental ways from that promoted by other types of literacy transactions.

8.6.1. IMPLICATIONS FOR THE CURRENT LITERACY DEBATE

This essay appears at a time of renewed public concern over literacy. Americans are convinced that current levels of literacy in this country are inadequate, and many believe that there is a higher proportion of illiterate or inadequately literate people in the society than ever before.[32] Several analysts have shown that higher expectations of literacy are responsible for our perceptions of a literacy problem. More people are expected to be able to use texts interpretively rather than in routine, catechetical ways. Such analyses help to locate the literacy problem demographically; they show that the challenge the nation has set itself is a new one in the sense that entire populations are now expected to learn what only a select few were once taught. However, such analyses implicitly assume that literacy is unidimensional, that literacy is a state of individual competence rather than a complex of actions that take place inside a web of social relationships and social assumptions.

The analysis we have begun in this article suggests that there are multiple forms of literacy which may not be unidimensionally scalable. For example, it is common to treat functional literacy—the literacy of the workplace and of everyday utility—as being intermediate on an implicit scale of *low* (routinized and catechetical) to *high* (interpretive) literacy. Yet our analysis suggests that useful literacy transactions may engage complex specific interpretive processes that would not be developed by engagement with the texts of the literary canon.

Literacy is not only an abstract "skill" that people acquire and then transfer freely from one situation to another. It is also a situated competence, shaped to particular conditions of use. If we want to know how literate we are, therefore, we must ask how much and how well people use the printed word to carry out each kind of social transaction that we consider important. Each must be considered in its own right. None can be taken to stand for the others. Instruments such as the NAEP literacy examination,[33] although they go further than most standard tests of reading and writing skill in the direction of including a variety of kinds of reading and writing tasks, are not geared to this situational analysis.

We have noted earlier that common school practice does not match well any of the types of literacy transaction we have identified here. "School literacy" has become a literacy transaction of its own, with its own kind of relationship between authors and readers and its own motivations. Most striking is the near absence of a strong author-reader relationship in most school literacy transactions. Textbook authors are anonymous, and the only person who typically reads a student's essay is a teacher who presumably knows more about the topic than the author and whose sole interest in reading is to judge and grade. Indeed, grading and the tests on which it is usually based so pervade school literacy that students almost never engage in class in the kinds of literacy transactions we have discussed here. They read textbooks not to gain information but to answer questions posed by others. They read literature not for the pleasure of reading and perhaps talking about it, but to demonstrate that they have read, either by taking tests or by writing prescribed reports.

Our analysis, then, has clear implications for educational policy. The varieties of literacy we have identified are poorly reflected in current educational practice. If our nation is to raise the literacy of its population, it should behave in ways that respect the many dimensions of literacy transactions. Schools and other educational agencies must learn to deal with each of the forms of literacy. One does not substitute for or automatically produce the other. This implies that schools will have to seek ways to create and sustain the social conditions that support each kind of literacy experience. Responding to this challenge requires not only appropriate goals and effective methods for instruction, but efforts to build a culture of reading and writing in which the multiple social purposes of literacy are recognized and valued.

NOTES

1. For readers that bring together this work, including scholarship on the medieval period, see Daniel P. Resnick, ed., *Literacy in Historical Perspective,* (Washington, 1983) and Harvey J. Graff, ed., *Literacy and Social Development in the West: A Reader* (Cambridge, 1981). A list of major books in this area, published in the past decade, would have to include, on printing and publishing, Elizabeth Eisenstein, *The Printing Press as an Agent of Change: Communications and Cultural Transformations in Early Modern Europe* (Cambridge, 1979); David Cressy, *Literacy and the Social Order: Reading and Writing in Tudor and Stuart England* (Cambridge, 1980), an important study on literacy and social classes; on changing literacy rates over time and their significance in seventeenth, eighteenth, and early nineteenth-century France, François Furet and Jacques Ozouf, *Lire et écrire: L'alphabétisation des français* (Paris, 1977) (Trans. as Reading and Writing: Literacy in France from Calvin to Jules Ferry [Cambridge, 1982]).

2. For the use of signatures as a source in seventeenth- and eighteenth-century England, see Roger S. Schofield, "The Measurement of Literacy in Pre-Industrial England," in *Literacy in Traditional Societies,* ed. Jack R. Goody

(Cambridge, 1968), 311–25; and Richard T. Vann, "Literacy in Seventeenth-Century England: Some Hearth-Tax Evidence," *Journal of Interdisciplinary History* 5 (1974): 287–93. For the historians' use of signatures in France, to gauge literacy, François Furet and Vladimir Sachs, "La croissance de l'alphabétisation en France (XVIIIe–XIXe siècles)," *Annales: Economies, sociétés, civilisations* 29 (1974): 714–37 and Furet and Ozouf, *Lire et écrire.*

3. One of the early skeptics about the value of the signature as a source for literacy was Lawrence Cremin. See his review of Kenneth Lockridge, *Literacy in Colonial New England: An Inquiry into the Social Context of Literacy in the Early Modern West* (New York, 1974), in *Review of Education* 1, no. 4 (1975): 517–21.

4. See Cressy, *Literacy and the Social Order,* 53.

5. Sylvia Scribner, "Literacy in Three Metaphors," *American Journal of Education* 95, no. 1 (1984): 6–21.

6. See Peter Burke, "Strengths and Weaknesses of the History of Mentalities," *History of European Ideas* 7, no. 5 (1986): 439–51.

7. See John Toews, "Intellectual History after the Linguistic Turn: The Autonomy of Meaning and the Irreducibility of Experience," *American Historical Review* 92, no. 4 (October, 1987): 879–907; William J. Bouwsma, "From History of Ideas to History of Meaning," *Journal of Interdisciplinary History* 12, no. 1 (1981): 279–91.

8. Nobel Prize address, "Uncommon Visage," *The New Republic,* trans. Barry Rubin, 4 and 11 Jan. 1988, 27ff.

9. Cognitive research has, by and large, been concerned with expository writing or simple narrative stories. It has not, therefore, for the most part, attended to questions of how the reader reaches out to grasp latent meaning and how the evocative powers of language work cognitively. For an excellent recent text on reading from the perspective of cognitive research, see P. Carpenter and M. Just, *The Psychology of Reading and Language Comprehension* (Boston, 1987); Walter Kintsch, "Learning From Text," *Cognition and Instruction* 3, no. 2 (1986): 87–108, distinguishes between representations of the text and representation of the situation, both constructed by the reader. For attention to readers who are required to reach into imaginary worlds to understand text, and for the uses of metaphor, see Andrew Ortony, A. W. Albrecht, S. D. Lima, P. J. Carroll, "Contextual Effects on Metaphor Comprehension in Reading," *Memory and Cognition* 12, no. 6 (1984): 558–67; W. F. Brewer, "Literary Theory, Rhetoric, and Stylistics: Implications for Psychology," in *Theoretical Issues in Reading Comprehension,* eds. R. Spiro, B. Bruce, and W. Brewer (Hillsdale, N.J., 1980).

10. Gustav Marius Bruce, *Luther as an Educator* (Minneapolis, 1928; reprint, Westport, 1979), 182. The work was translated into all the major European languages within a generation of its appearance in 1529.

11. In an earlier paper, in which we investigated the levels of cognitive demand in historically different reading situations, we placed this kind of catechetical reading at the low end of the demand spectrum. See Daniel P. Resnick and Lauren B. Resnick, "The Nature of Literacy: A Historical Exploration," *Har-*

vard Educational Review 47 (1977): 370–85. A fuller discussion of the catechetical tradition will appear in D. P. Resnick, "A Historical View of Some Literacy Environments and the Textbook," in *The Textbook in American Education*, eds. R. Selden, J. Cole, T. Sticht (Norwood, N.J., forthcoming 1989).

12. Michael Walzer, *Exodus and Revolution* (New York, 1985), 7.

13. Haim Potok, *Davita's Harp* (New York, 1985). The passage is presented in its entirety, 347–49 and reprinted by permission of Alfred A Knopf, Inc.

14. See Joseph F. Brinley, Jr., "The 1983 Consumer Research Study on Reading and Book Purchasing: A Summary," in *Books in Our Future: Perspectives and Prospects*, ed. John Y. Cole (Washington, 1987), 93–114.

15. See A. Labarre, *Le livre dans la vie amienoise du seizième siècle: L'enseignement des inventaires après décès 1503–1576* (Paris and Louvain, 1971) and the discussion in Roger Chartier, *The Cultural Uses of Print in Early Modern France*, trans. Lydia Cochrane (Princeton, 1987), 146–53.

16. For evidence that the craft mentality survived well into the nineteenth century, see William H. Sewell, Jr., *Work and Revolution in France: The Language of Labor from the Old Regime to 1848* (Cambridge, 1980), esp. 62–113. The guilds were dissolved with the other corporations in 1791, but artisans remained dominant in the production process of the small workshops and fought to reassert their common interests in the face of legal repression.

17. W. J. Rorabaugh, *The Craft Apprentice: From Franklin to the Machine Age in America* (New York and Oxford, 1986).

18. Hargrove, *The Weavers Draft Book* (Baltimore, 1972), 2, cited in Rorabaugh, *The Craft Apprentice*, 33–34.

19. Amanda Jones, *Rules and Directions for Cutting Men's Clothes* (improved ed., Middlebury, Vt., 1822), cited in Rorabaugh, *The Craft Apprentice*, 34.

20. Quoted from Rorabaugh, *The Craft Apprentice*, 35.

21. Common types of publications and individual titles are discussed in Chartier, *Cultural Uses of Print*, 170–75.

22. The discussion that follows draws on and cites material presented in Robert Darnton, *The Great Cat Massacre and Other Episodes in French Cultural History* (New York, 1984), 215–56 and "The Origins of Modern Reading," *The New Republic*, 27 February 1984, 26–33.

23. George Lindbeck, "The Search for Habitable Texts," *Daedalus* 117, no. 2 (Spring 1988): 153–56.

24. Frank Kermode, *The Genesis of Secrecy: On the Interpretation of Narrative* (Cambridge, Mass., 1979), 144.

25. This argument is developed in Lauren B. Resnick, "Learning in School and Out," *Educational Researcher* 16, no. 9 (December 1987): 13–20.

26. See sec. 8.5.3, "The Pleasure-Giving."

27. Reading romances, for example, can express, *inter alia*, a desire for combat against a socially imposed role, a need for bonding with other women, and a desire to escape through fantasy. See Janice Radway, *Reading the Romance: Women, Patriarchy, and Popular Literature* (Chapel Hill, 1984).

28. See Alice Walker, *The Color Purple* (New York, 1982); Anatoly Scharansky (Natan Sharansky), *Fear No Evil* (New York, 1988).

29. See in *Modern European Intellectual History: Reappraisals and New Perspectives,* eds. D. LaCapra and S. L. Kaplan (Ithaca, 1982), 280–310, 47–85, 86–110: Hayden White, "Method and Ideology in Intellectual History: The Case of Henry Adams"; Dominick LaCapra, "Rethinking Intellectual History and Reading Texts"; and Martin Jay, "Should Intellectual History Take a Linguistic Turn? Reflections on the Habermas-Gadamer Debate."

30. S. N. Eisenstadt, "Intellectuals and Tradition," *Daedalus* 101, no. 2 (1972): 1–19.

31. Robert Alter and Frank Kermode, eds., *The Literary Guide to the Bible* (Cambridge, Mass., 1987). These lines from the preface are also cited in Lindbeck, "The Search for Habitable Texts," 153.

32. See, for example, George A. Miller, "The Challenge of Universal Literacy," *Science,* 241 (1988), 1293–98; Resnick and Resnick, "The Nature of Literacy," 370–85.

33. For the National Assessment of Educational Progress findings on literacy, see I. Kirsch and A. Jungeblut, *Literacy: Profiles of America's Young Adults* (Princeton, 1986) and R. Venezky, C. Kaestle, and A. Sum, *The Subtle Danger: Reflections on the Literacy Abilities of America's Young Adults* (Princeton, 1987).

— 9 —

Literacy and Psychological Evaluation

John R. Hayes

As a cognitive psychologist, my perspective on the two foregoing chapters is likely quite different from that of a historian. My response to these contributions has been to relate the ideas that have been presented to psychological studies which seem to bear, at least peripherally, on the same issues. The intersection between historical and psychological views may be richer than usual because the topic is literacy, a subject psychologists have been exploring in their own way for more than 100 years.

Psychological research on literacy has focused most strongly on three areas:

1. *Basic Processes.* Basic process research has been directed to answering questions such as "How do readers perceive words?" and "How do writers revise text?"
2. *Pedagogy.* Pedagogical research has focused on evaluating methods for teaching reading such as the "whole word" and "phonics" methods and methods for teaching writing such as "sentence combining" and "peer critiquing."
3. *Assessment.* Assessment efforts have been concerned both: a. with the evaluation of capabilities of individual students so that they may be provided with the most appropriate instruction and b. with the evaluation of the effectiveness of educational delivery systems.

In addition to these areas, there has been increasing attention recently to the relation between literacy and social/cultural context. Shirley Brice Heath's work (1983) is an early and important contribution in this area.[1] An important recent synthesis is Applebee's "Contexts for Learning to Write" (1984).[2]

Although reading and writing are both obviously central to the field
of literacy, reading research has a much longer history than does writing
research. Reading research had its origins in the 1880s with Cattell's
(1885) pioneering research while writing research began in the 1970s
with Janet Emig's work.[3]

Over the years, reading researchers have explored a number of fundamental issues. For example, Conrad (1964) established that readers
represent visually presented letters as sounds.[4] In a memory experiment,
Conrad asked college students to remember lists of six written letters
which they read silently. When the letters disappeared, they were asked
to recall them in the order in which they had been presented. The errors
the students made were primarily confusions between letters which
sounded alike such as *C* and *E* rather than letters which looked alike
such as *Q* and *O*. Zhang and Simon (1985) have recently provided
evidence of auditory coding by Chinese readers of visually represented
Chinese letters and words.[5] In a follow-up of his earlier study, Conrad
(1972) found that deaf people, who do not know the speech code for
written letters, make visual rather than auditory confusions.[6] Considerable evidence has now been amassed that readers recode words as speech
just as they do letters. For example, Gough and Cosky (1977) showed
that spelling errors that preserve pronunciation, such as "werk" for
"work" were much harder for proofreaders to find than errors that did
not preserve pronunciation such as "wark."[7] It appears, then, that people with normal hearing spontaneously recode visually presented reading
material into speech code.

Another fundamental discovery concerned the relation between letter
perception and word perception. Cattell (1885) found that when words
and letters were exposed very briefly, words could be recognized with
shorter exposure times than were required to recognize any of the individual letters in the word. In a related study, Dodge (1898) found that
when words and letters were shown at a distance, words could be
recognized at greater distances than could the individual letters of which
they were composed when these were presented separately.[8] They also
showed that when exposure time was set at a duration that allowed
observers to recognize four or five unrelated letters, they could read
single words which contained more than twenty letters.

Reicher (1969) showed that it is easier for people to discriminate
letters when they are contained in words than when they are presented
in isolation.[9] For example, he showed that people can discriminate better
between *R* and *W* when they are presented in the words "ripe" and
"wipe" than when they are presented as single letters. Recent theorists
such as McClelland and Rumelhart (1981) and others interpret these

findings as indicating that reading is both "bottom up" and "top down."[10] That is, reading relies both on letter information and on knowledge of word patterns. Thus, to be fluent, readers must learn large numbers of word patterns.

Reading researchers have also been able to show that comprehension and memory for text depend critically on the readers' knowledge and beliefs. Henderson (1903) studied memory for short text passages in students from first grade through graduate school.[11] He found that the texts as remembered contained changes which made the recalled material more consistent with the experience and preconceptions of the reader than the original text had been. Bartlett (1932) asked university students to read and recall a Native American folk tale.[12] He found that the culturally different aspects of the folk tale were the parts most subject to omission or modification. Thus, in predicting how readers will respond to a text, we must understand the context of knowledge and belief that the reader brings to the text.

Results such as these, although not central to the interests of historical researchers, can be useful for some purposes. To illustrate how such result might be used, I will consider the chapter by Landes. The very interesting central argument that Landes presents in his contribution, the argument that church fathers kept the Bible from the laity because it was revolutionary, rests on the assumption that certain texts within the Bible permanently express "anti-hierarchical attitudes toward power." Landes says, for example, "The revolutionary potential of the Exodus Tale has inspired generations of political activists. . . ." and "At a basic level, which informs almost every passage of the New Testament, lies a revolutionary world view." Thus, the Landes argument requires us to believe that over widely different points in time and geography, a significant proportion of church fathers believed that these texts would inspire revolution.

Evidence from psychological research on literacy does not refute this belief but it does provide some grounds for questioning it. First, though, the idea that teaching a tale of revolution is likely to inspire revolution is not entirely consistent with common observation. We typically do not worry that students will be radicalized by reading about the French revolution, say in *A Tale of Two Cities,* and we expect that teaching about the American Revolution will promote patriotism rather than rebellion. Revolutionary tales seem more likely to inspire enthusiasm for the product rather than for the process of revolution.

The Bible is a peculiar text because, as Resnick and Resnick point out, its authors are assumed to be inspired by God. This point is relevant to Landes's assumption because Asch (1952) has shown that the interpretation of a text can depend heavily on the readers' beliefs about the author.[13] Asch conducted a series of experiments in which students were asked to interpret quotations such as the following: "I hold that a little rebellion, now and then, is a good thing, and as necessary in the political world as storms are in the physical."

Some students were told (correctly) that the author was Jefferson while others were told that the author was Lenin. Typical interpretations by students who were told that the author was Jefferson were the following:

> Jefferson did not mean both a social and political revolution. A political revolution, to him, probably meant little more than a change in the bureaucracy. However, many who have used this quotation have inserted a much different meaning.

> Jefferson wanted an America for Americans. He did not want the abuses which came from the control of the English. Therefore, he attempted to justify the American Revolution. But he did not mean that revolution itself was a good or necessary thing. It depends on the circumstances and on foreign influence.

> In order for the conditions of the people to be improved, there must be some agitation now and then so that attention will be focused on need for reforms and change.

> Jefferson probably meant rebellion as an upheaval in personal political opinions within a party, rather than a revolutionary turnover of one party by another.

> By "little rebellion" Jefferson might have meant what we would now call third parties.

Typically interpretations by students who thought that the author was Lenin are these:

> I believe that Lenin here meant rebellion in the sense of outright revolution within a country, not against aggressors.

> A statement like the one quoted would be expected to come from man like Lenin, with his revolutionary ideas.

Of the seventy-one students who were told that Jefferson was the author, only one interpreted "rebellion" as meaning "revolution." Of the fifty-six students who were told that Lenin was the author, thirty-eight or 68 percent interpreted "rebellion" as meaning "revolution." These results, if they can be generalized across time, would suggest that people would be likely to interpret the Bible as a revolutionary only if they believed God was revolutionary.

These results, together with those of Bartlett, suggest that there is some reason to doubt the assumption that the Bible was perceived by a significant number of church fathers as revolutionary.[14]

Although his argument doesn't depend on it, Landes claims, citing Diringer and Goody and Watt,[15] that it is easier to learn to read alphabetic than logographic scripts. The basis of this claim appears to be the assumption that logographic languages require the reader to learn huge numbers of word patterns whereas alphabetic languages only require the reader to learn the patterns of a relatively short list of letters. However, as we discussed earlier, fluent reading of English, and presumably of other alphabetic scripts, does require learning word patterns. It is conceivable that learning word patterns for alphabetic scripts is easier than learning word patterns for logographic scripts. If this were the case, we would expect that to learn to read, Chinese students would require more hours of instruction than American students. However, a study by Stevenson, Stigler, Lucker, Lee, Hsu, and Kitamura (1978) suggests that the rates of acquiring literacy skills in Chinese and American schools are, at least roughly, comparable.[16] The claim that the alphabet is the "democratic script," then, appears suspect.

The most important point I want to make about Landes's paper is that texts cannot be assumed to have fixed interpretations irrespective of readers' knowledge and predispositions. The text is always assimilated to the readers' world view and the process of assimilation may lead to very large differences in interpretation from one reader to the next. The idea that the Bible could have a fixed or even a single dominant "antihierarchical" interpretation through the social and cultural changes of sixteen centuries seems very questionable.

The Resnick and Resnick chapter represents a project in the early stages of development. As a result, and in contrast to Landes, Resnick and Resnick make very modest claims. Their claims are modest in two senses. First, while its general territory is literacy transactions, that is, social interactions between author and reader mediated by text, Resnick and Resnick stake out only a part of that territory. In particular, they confine their attention to the relation of author and reader *as construed by the reader.* This strikes me as an unfortunate and unnecessary restriction of the territory. In a recent doctoral dissertation on legal brief writing, Stratman (1988) notes that the success of a literacy transaction may depend critically on whether the relations of author and reader are construed in consonant ways by both author and reader.[17] In particular, Stratman describes a case in which a lawyer misunderstands the attitudes of his reader, a judge, and, as a result, writes a brief which is poorly received. Clearly, the way the author construes the relation of author and reader can have an important impact on literacy transactions.

The Resnicks are also modest in the number of categories of literacy transaction they have chosen to describe. They identify just six: the sacred, the useful, the informational, the persuasive, the pleasure-giving, and the personal/familial. I suspect that few will object seriously to the particular distinctions that the Resnicks have proposed. They seem uncontroversial. Indeed, Kern, Sticht, Welty, and Hauke (1976) have emphasized the practical importance for technical writers of distinguishing between procedural (useful) and informational texts.[18] However, it is easy to imagine many patterns of transaction between author and reader in addition to those the Resnicks discuss. All of the following appear to me to involve distinct patterns of author/reader relations: contracts, invoices, poison pen letters, ransom notes, draft notices, legal summonses, order forms, chain letters, invitations, suicide notes, school essays, petitions to government authorities, prayers, and graffiti.

Some of these, of course, can be grouped under categories the Resnicks have specified. For example, invitations and invoices might be classed with textbooks as informational texts, and prayers might be classified with ads as persuasive texts. Nevertheless, invitations and invoices involve very different social interactions between reader and author and the same is true, of course, for prayers and perfume ads. Presumably, as the Resnicks' project precedes, they will add to and refine the list of categories they have described so far.

An important omission in the Resnick paper, which I hope they will address as their project progresses, is any discussion of how their literacy transaction categories can be evaluated. There are at least three evaluating questions which could be asked about the categories: "Are they consistent?" "Are they complete?" "Are they useful?"

We have raised the question of consistency above by asking if all texts which can be classified as informational or persuasive actually mediate the same sort of social interaction. Praying and advertising seem like very different sorts of social exchanges even though they are both clearly persuasive.

We have also raised the question of completeness by suggesting a number of additional categories, e.g., chain letters, graffiti, and so on.

The question of usefulness might be addressed in several ways. One way, implied in the Resnick's discussion of sacred and useful texts, would be to determine if the frequency of production of a text category changes with interesting historical variables. For example, one might find that the frequency of publication of pattern books in various trades varies as the power of the guilds in those trades varies.

Another way to evaluate the utility of the categories would be to ask whether or not the categories have consistent and identifiable formats and whether related categories have similar formats. For example, do petitions to government authorities have a recognizable format and does that format resemble the format of prayers?

Finally, we might ask whether formats change in an interesting way with historical variables. For example, is the format of petitions to government authorities different in authoritarian forms of government than in democractic ones?

While the Resnick and Resnick project does not yet receive top marks when evaluated for consistency and completeness, I believe that as the project progresses evaluations will be much more positive. Particularly important is the utilization of the categories to pinpoint change—utilization of the consistency test, in other words, to raise issues of interest to historians and psychologists alike.

In reviewing the Landes and the Resnick and Resnick chapters, I was struck by two observations. First, there are important intersections between the historical and the psychological approaches to literacy. Psychological observations on the processes involved in reading and interpreting text can be useful to historians, and historical analysis of literacy can be useful to psychologists. For example, historians' observations, such as those of Goody (1986) on the impact of emerging literacy can help psychologists to broaden their perspective[19]—a perspective which has focused almost exclusively on literacy as seen in the twentieth-century classroom. As we saw above, psychologists' observations on the importance of word pattern knowledge in reading did not support social historians' hypotheses about the relative difficulty of learning to read alphabetic and logographic scripts.

There appear to be other conflicts between psychological and historical findings as well. For example, Goody (1977) says "Writing makes speech 'objective' by turning it into an object of visual as well as aural inspection." However, the studies of Conrad and of Zhang and Simon (1985) clearly indicate that readers translate the visual text into speech code.[20] Thus, a visual inspection may be an aural inspection.

While these findings appear contradictory, they may, in fact, not be. Even if written and spoken messages are translated into the same (or similar) internal codes in ordinary reading tasks, the differences between written and spoken forms can still have a profound impact on the efficiency with which thinking is carried out in other sorts of tasks. In

many familiar tasks, performance involves a complex interaction between internal processes and external symbols. Doing a multiplication
problem with pencil and paper is a clear example in which performance
depends on this interaction. One uses pencil and paper to help remember
partial products and to keep track of what needs to be done next. Doing
the same problem mentally (using only internal symbols) may take one
hundred times as long.

Why are external symbols so important? According to Newell and
Simon (1972), the reason is that thinking is severely constrained by the
limitations of short-term memory, which can hold only a few symbols
and those for only a few seconds.[21] However, written symbols can act as
"external memory" and effectively extend the capacity of short term
memory. Even a small increase in short term memory can lead to a
substantial increase in task preformance. Written symbols are important
because they can be used to provide external memory to facilitate a wide
variety of thinking tasks.

The psychological findings, then, indicate that the difference between
visual and aural inputs may not have important impact on the nature of
internal representations but can, even so, be very important in many
tasks for determining the efficiency of performance. These findings are
consistent with those of Goody (1977). For example, Goody is quite
explicit in asserting that the difference between literate and nonliterate
cultures is not a difference in "mind" but rather a difference in systems
of communication.[22] Clearly, he is not asserting that internal mental
processes are different for literate and nonliterate peoples. Further, those
instances in which he claims an advantage for writing over speaking are
consistent with the "external memory" interpretation. For example, he
says, "We suggested that logic . . . seemed to be a function of writing,
since it was the setting down of speech that enabled man clearly to
separate words, to manipulate their order and to develop syllogistic
forms of reasoning."[23] Again he says, "It [writing] increased the poten-
tialities of criticism because writing laid out discourse before one's eyes
in a different kind of way."[24] In this instance, at least, historical and
psychological research are mutually supportive.

My second observation is that, aside from unusual collections such as
this one, there are few stimuli to encourage psychologists and historians
to talk to each other about literacy. Generally, historians and psychologists have been working in isolation from each other. Perhaps it is time
to encourage more active interaction.

NOTES

1. S. B. Heath, *Ways with Words* (Cambridge, 1983).

2. A. Applebee, *Contexts for Learning to Write* (Norwood, N.J., 1984).

3. J. M. Catell, "Über die Zeit der Erkennung und Benennung von Schriftzeichen, Bildern, und Farben," *Philosophische Studien* 2 (1885): 635–50; J. Emig, *The Composing Processes of Twelfth Graders,* Research Report No. 13, National Council of Teachers of English, (Urbana, Ill., 1971).

4. R. Conrad, "Acoustic Confusion in Immediate Memory," *British Journal of Psychology* 55 (1964): 75–84.

5. G. Zhang and H. A. Simon, "STM Capacity for Chinese Words and Idioms: Chunking and Acoustical Loop Hypotheses," *Memory and Cognition* 13, no. 3 (1985): 193–201.

6. R. Conrad, "Speech and Reading," in *The Relationships Between Speech and Reading,* ed. J. F. Kavanagh and I. G. Mattingly (Cambridge, Mass., 1972).

7. P. B. Gough and M. J. Cosky, "One Second of Reading Again," in *Cognitive Theory,* vol. 2, ed. N. J. Castellan, D. B. Pisoni, and G. R. Potts (Hillsdale, N.J., 1977).

8. Catell, "Über die Zeit"; B. Erdmann and R. Dodge, *Psychologische Untersuchungen über das Lesen* (Halle, 1898).

9. G. M. Reicher, "Perceptual Recognition as a Function of the Meaningfulness of Stimulus Material," *Journal of Experimental Psychology* 81 (1969): 275–80.

10. J. L. McClelland and D. E. Rumelhart, "An Interactive Activation Model of Context Effects in Letter Perception," part 1, "An Account of Basic Findings," *Psychological Review* 88 (1981): 375–407.

11. E. N. Henderson, "A Study of Memory for Connected Trains of Thought," *Psychological Monographs* 5, no. 6 (1903): 1–94.

12. F. C. Bartlett, *Remembering* (Cambridge, 1932).

13. S. E. Asch, *Social Psychology* (New York, 1952).

14. Bartlett, *Remembering.*

15. D. Diringer, *The Alphabet: A Key to the History of Mankind* (New York, 1953); J. Goody and I. Watt, "The Consequences of Literacy," *Comparative Studies in Society and History* 5 (1963): 304–45.

16. H. W. Stevenson, J. W. Stigler, G. W. Lucker, S. Lee, C. C. Hsu, and S. Kitamura, "Classroom Behavior and Achievement of Japanese, Chinese, and American Children," in *Advances in Instructional Psychology,* vol. 3, ed. R. Glaser (Hillsdale, N.J., 1978).

17. J. Stratman, "The Rhetorical Dynamics of Appellate Court Persuasion" (Ph.D. diss., Carnegie Mellon University, 1988).

18. R. P. Kern, T. G. Sticht, D. Welty, and R. N. Hauke, *Guidebook for the Development of Army Training Literature* (Washington, 1976).

19. J. Goody, *The Logic of Writing and the Organization of Society* (Cambridge, 1986).

20. Jack Goody, *The Domestication of the Savage Mind* (Cambridge, 1977),

44; Zhang and Simon, "STM Capacity for Chinese Words"; Conrad, "Acoustic Confusion."

21. A. Newell and H. Simon, *Human Problem Solving* (Englewood Cliffs, N.J., 1972).

22. Goody, *Domestication*, 36.

23. Ibid., 11.

24. Ibid., 37.

PART IV

EMOTION AND
EMOTIONAL STANDARDS

— 10 —

Mother's Love: The Construction of an Emotion in Nineteenth-Century America

Jan Lewis

When the Reverend John Todd told the readers of *The Mother's Magazine* in 1839 that "God planted this *deep*, this *unquenchable* love for her offspring, in the mother's heart," he was expressing the conventional wisdom of his day. In mid-nineteenth-century America, a woman who opened any ladies' magazine or advice book would read that a mother's love was eternal, that "no circumstance, no earthly change can destroy the mother's love," that "to love children, is the dictate of [her] nature."[1] Nature and God both made women to be mothers and implanted in their hearts a love that was pure and holy. This was the premise upon which the doctrine of women's separate sphere rested. Just as the philosophy and form of democratic government proceeded from Jefferson's self-evident truths, so the nineteenth-century's description of woman's nature and role derived form seemingly incontrovertible assumptions about the nature of a mother's love.

Historians, of course, may question that which earlier generations took for granted, asking how it was that certain propositions came to be accepted as self-evident truths. We know that in 1776 belief in the equality of man was more of a novelty than Jefferson's self-confident statements would lead us to suppose. Likewise, the irrepressible nature of a mother's love was, in the 1830s, an idea whose time had only recently come. The writers who proclaimed these truths were, as much as Jefferson, the architects of an ideology. They described a world as they wanted it to be, and they could not imagine an America, as they wanted it to become, without a mother's love.

To compare the antebellum exponents of maternal love to Jefferson is, perhaps, not so strained a conceit as it might at first appear, for the idealization of mother's love was brewed in the same cauldron as Revolutionary political thought. Historians have recently recognized that the histories of politics and the family in this era are entwined. The Revolutionary brew was seasoned by a variety of ingredients—republicanism, liberalism, evangelical Protestantism, sensationalist psychology, and just as each of these strands of thought would contribute to political thought, so too would they affect the conceptualization of family roles. The late-eighteenth century's revolt against patriarchy dethroned both fathers and kings; and it said that citizens in a society, like members of a family, should be bound together by affection, rather than duty.[2]

This transformation in political and familial thought would make room for a new ideal of motherhood, one that would be flavored by all the ingredients in the Revolutionary brew. Indeed, as Ruth H. Bloch has shown, the first positive characterizations of motherhood date to this period.[3] Before the Revolution, early Americans, particularly in the Puritan colonies, were rather fearful of feminine emotion. They considered women more passionate and, hence, more dangerous than men. And even mother's love, because it was both indulgent and unqualified, was mistrusted. As Laurel Thatcher Ulrich has observed of northern New England, "Mothers represented the affectionate mode in an essentially authoritarian system of child-rearing." In a "patriarchal order. . . . mother love or any other form of human love could never be an unqualified good."[4] The Revolution undermined patriarchy, and it made of affection a political virtue, the glue of civil society. In so doing, it allowed women, who were supposedly naturally affectionate, a political role.

This new appreciation for affection was the contribution of sensationalist psychology, which had also facilitated a new interest in the education of young children. Eighteenth-century faculty psychologists argued that the characters of children could be shaped, that human nature was to some degree malleable. Sensationalist psychology, in both its Lockean and Scottish Common Sense forms, had been popularized in eighteenth-century America, softening Calvinist notions of innate depravity.[5] By the end of the eighteenth century, many Americans were accustomed to believing that children were born with a set of faculties, some of which—reason and affection, for example—were to be developed, and others of which—self-interest and the passions—needed to be controlled. To be sure, different schools placed different premiums upon certain of the faculties, with some trusting more to reason and others with more confidence in affection, just as they disagreed about how dangerous self-interest might be. By the nineteenth century, such distinctions almost disappeared, as the popular writers who adapted faculty psychology for the American audience used Lockean, Common Sense, and Calvinist assumptions almost indiscriminately.[6] Nineteenth-century didactic writers adapted eighteenth-century sensationalist psychology in another way: they said that moral education should be performed especially—indeed, almost exclusively—by mothers. Locke, the Common Sense philosophers, and Calvinist ministers had all assumed that fathers—or, at the very least, parents—played the crucial role in the education of the young. Why, in the nineteenth century, was this responsibility shifted to women? Much of the answer lies in the growing belief that the work of moral education had to begin even earlier, for the child's character was formed in the early years, while it was still in the mother's care.

Moreover, once evangelical Protestant denominations were prepared to accept the validity of childhood conversion, as they increasingly were by the mid-nineteenth century,[7] mothers acquired an important new role. Evangelical views about youthful conversion built upon secular ones about the malleability of character, giving mothers a new responsibility. The work of redemption had to begin early, when a child was still in its mother's care, and, to the extent that evangelicals believed that the world had to be reclaimed individual-by-individual, the home became the main arena for conversions. As the Reverend John Abbott put it, *"Mothers have as powerful an influence over the welfare of future generations, as all other earthly causes combined."*[8] The redemption of the world depended upon "the power of divine truth . . . Christianity, as taught from a mother's lips. In a vast majority of cases the first six or seven years decide the character of the man . . . the mothers of our race must be the chief instruments of its redemption." Mothers, thus, had it in their power to achieve not only the salvation of their children, but also that of the entire world. Mothers occupied the key "place in the grand scheme which shall renovate the world." Mrs. Elizabeth Hall expressed the millenial hopes of evangelical maternal advisers when she told American mothers "the destiny of a redeemed world is put into your hands; and it is for you to say, whether your children shall be . . . prepared for a glorious immortality."[9]

Women were called by God to be mothers; their work was nothing less than His own. But it was a work that was to be performed first and foremost in the United States, giving the mothers' mission both a sacred and a secular cast. One author who advocated the conversion of the young insisted that, "The designs which God seems to have respecting this Republic, are to be accomplished by the moral renovation of the young."[10] Religious writers believed that American society in the early-nineteenth century was approaching a crisis; they looked to mothers for the solution. "By what means," asked *The Mother's Magazine* in 1833, "can the population of this great country, increasing as it is, with fearful rapidity, be so enlightened and reformed, that our boasted liberty shall not disintegrate into gross licentiousness?" Sarah Josepha Hale provided the answer: "If the future citizens of our republic are to be worthy of their rich inheritance, they must be made so principally through the virtue and intelligence of their mothers."[11] Secular and sacred advocates of the importance of maternal influence shared certain assumptions about the crisis "in a country where the people govern." Many would have agreed that, "*Self-government* both for adults and children seems almost the only available resource left us in the present state of society in this country."[12] Self-government, of course, was a term with a resonance in both religious and political discourse; in a democratic society, which had rejected authoritarian forms of control, it became all the more necessary for individuals to learn to govern themselves, to control their sinful and anti-social impulses both.

Indeed, in the minds of the authors of maternal advice literature, sin and selfishness were usually considered one and the same. Although we may distinguish between the sacred and secular elements of the motherhood paradigm, they were often fused in the popular mind. The didactic writers who idealized motherhood envisioned an American empire that was also the Kingdom of God on earth,[13] precisely because their ideal for society drew jointly from evangelical Protestantism, late-Enlightenment political thought (both republican and liberal), and sensationalist psychology. These separate strands became part of the fabric of American culture; all were woven, for example, into an essay published in *The Mother's Magazine* in 1833: "It is the province of the mother, to cultivate the affections, to form and guard the moral habits of the child, for the first ten years of its life, and to all intents and purposes the character of the *man* or *woman* is substantially laid as early as that period of life." So argued the author of "Family Government Essential to National Prosperity." "While, therefore, the father is engaged in the bustling affairs of active life, the mother, with almost irresistible sway, is forming the characters of the future defenders of our faith, the administrators of our laws, and the guardians of our civil liberties and lives."[14] Here we see all the elements of the new paradigm: A liberal appreciation of civil liberties is grafted onto the older, republican insistence upon the importance of the character of the citizenry and a Scottish Common Sense philosophers' concern for the cultivation of the affections. And we see, also, the separation of the private sphere of the home from the "bustling"—and presumably corrupt—"affairs of the active life" in the public arena. As many historians have noted, the responsibility for training children fell to mothers almost by default, as more fathers began to work outside the home.[15] By the time this structural change had taken place, however, women were already assumed to be peculiarly suited to the task at hand.

The intellectual basis for the separation of woman's private sphere of the home from the public sphere of the world had been laid well before the United States turned into the industrial and urban nation early-nineteenth-century critics feared it would become. Women, and consequently mothers, were assumed to be more moral than men because they were isolated from the world. As Nancy F. Cott has noted, Christian doctrine had always contrasted the virtues of heaven with the vices of the world; in the early-nineteenth century, as women and men increasingly were segregated into separate spheres, and—as the masculine, public sphere of the world became ever more suspect—women and their arena profited from the comparison, and the home took on the attributes Christians had once reserved for heaven.[16] The authors of maternal advice literature accepted this assumption when they likened home to Paradise and mothers' work to that of Christ. "Our first mother found a paradise," Catharine Sedgwick wrote, and "her daughters have each the more enviable privilege and distinction of creating one at pleasure."[17] The home was designed to redeem the world.

Although a mother's work was performed at home, in private, it had enormous public importance; it was, fundamentally, of a political and religious nature, for it aimed at preparing children for entry into a particular society.[18] And it was this logic—the needs of nineteenth-century American society, as informed by both political and religious thought—that would dictate the characteristics of the children who should be created and the qualities of the mothers who would create them.

So if the work of salvation were to be performed in woman's sphere, it necessarily meant that women were especially suited to the task. Much as the nineteenth century fragmented the world into a private, heavenly sphere and an amoral public domain, so it would divide the set of faculties that once had been thought to belong to men and women both. In the process, the rational faculties were assigned to men, and the emotional ones—which the rise of sentimentalism had endowed with a higher value—to women. This new formulation is evident in the new view of marriage that had become popular by the beginning of the nineteenth century. In this paradigm, man's reason was thought necessary to check woman's emotion, while feminine affection was required to socialize masculine rationality.[19] Thus, under the influence of faculty

psychology, feminine qualities were deemed necessary to the social order, for it was women who fit men for society. In the early decades of
the nineteenth century, this paradigm of republican marriage—like republican political thought itself—would collapse, but one of its fundamental assumptions—that feminine qualities served a social function—
would endure, as the focus of feminine socializing was shifted from adult
men to children.

By 1830, the feminine social role had been redefined: women were to
prepare their children, and especially their sons, for membership in
society. If this society, with its separate private and public spheres was
recognizably that of the nineteenth century, it still retained eighteenth-
century moral philosophy's belief that social order could be maintained
only by the affection that men bore for one another, the sympathies that
they shared. "What," asked the *American Ladies' Magazine,* "are the
good works of women which she was created to perform? She was born
to perpetuate the reign of all good and gentle affections in the world,
and to diffuse through all society a spirit of love, of forebearance, of
happiness." Evangelicals agreed that "it is the province of the mother, to
cultivate the affections,"[20] and, like more secular writers, they believed
that such qualities were necessary to society.

Like their colonial ancestors, nineteenth-century American family advisers still thought of the family as a little commonwealth; as one magazine writer put it in 1830, "A family is society in miniature; home is its
location." But now, "woman is its presiding spirit."[21] Put another way,
the family represented society as these writers wanted it to be. In the
"world . . . we behold every principle of justice and honor, and even the
dictates of common honesty disregarded, and the delicacy of our moral
sense is wounded; we see the general good, sacrificed to the advancement
of personal interest." Only in the family could we "expect pure, disinterested attachment." Only "there sympathy, honor, virtue, are assembled;
. . . there disinterested love, is ready to sacrifice everything at the altar of
affection."[22] It was this love, expressed in its perfect form by mothers,
that was to remake and redeem the world. "Can a more charming
picture be drawn," asked *The Mother's Magazine* rhetorically, "than a
family cemented together and governed by the control[l]ing influence of
love? Love—flowing from the hidden spring in a mother's heart . . .
flowing deeper and wider as it goes, till neighborhood, friends, and
country are refreshed by its living waters!"[23] Mother's love was the very
basis of the social order, its blood and sinew both.

At a sociological level, the doctrine of maternal influence said that the
feminine principle of love was necessary in order to temper the selfishness evident in an increasingly individualistic age. At a psychological

level, it insisted that men, to some extent, ought to be feminized; it was the responsibility of mothers to implant in their sons, in particular, an affectionate heart. To be sure, many maternal advisers, such as Catharine Beecher,[24] believed women responsible for the intellectual education of their children, but more often it was emphasized that "the mother holds, as it were, the hearts of her children in her hand," and it was the heart that she was intended to train. She was supposed to teach her children how to love; that is, to teach them what she knew best. She was to make her children like herself. As one adviser explained it, "The control of youthful appetite and passion, is . . . best committed to those whose nature and situation best prepare them to enforce by example what they teach by precept . . . . The plastic hand of maternal affection moulds the susceptible being after the likeness of its own loveliness."[25] Properly trained, a mother's sons would meet adulthood with a woman's heart. Thus it was, explained one writer, that "the talents of the female are the transmitted inheritance of her sons."[26]

And by what process were children to be made like their mother? It was generally believed that "children learn more by example than by precept." Thus a mother was to be what she wanted her children to become. A mother was supposed "not . . . to teach virtue but to inspire it." This she would accomplish simply by being herself, experiencing her natural and irrepressible love for her children. The secret of "The Mother's Power" was "the principle of attachment [that] is as much a part of a mother's nature, as the heart and blood parts of the human frame."[27] A mother's love would inspire her children's love in return. The mother "teaches our hearts the first lesson of love . . . around [her] our affections twine as closely and surely, as the young vine clasps itself about the branch that supports it: our love for [her] becomes so thoroughly a part and portion of ourselves, that it bids defiance to time and decay." The children of such a mother would come to "revere her as the earthly type of perfect love. . . . they cannot but desire to conform themselves to such models."[28] From their mothers' example, children would learn how to love. They would carry this affection with them always, not merely as the memory of maternal tenderness, but as the standard for human behavior in an unredeemed world.

The conventions of mother's love held that it was eternal; it was "untiring," "imperishable," "unquenchable," and "irrepressible."[29] Such judgments carried a double meaning: the mother's love was eternal not only because it outlived the mother herself as it was preserved in her children's memories. It was eternal in another sense, as well, for it was reincarnated in her children, who carried it with them always, as a talisman and an almost corporeal part of themselves. *The Mother's*

Magazine advised that "the mother must dwell in the heart of the child, and be, as it were, the soul of its every action—enter into all its joys— feel its every sorrow." This characterization of maternal love reflected Christian doctrines of eternal life. But if standard evangelical exhortations advised sinners to accept Christ into their hearts so that they might be born again, the paradigm of mother's love conveyed the message from Christ's point of view: you will live again. And so mothers were told that their children "will go forth with the impress of a mother's hand, deep, imperishable. Yes! you will live in your children."[30]

Different writers expressed the same idea in different ways, but always the message was the same: the child was the mother reborn. Mary Virginia Terhune instructed mothers to "ask your heart . . . if there is not a strange ful[l]ness of joy in watching the reproduction of your traits, physical, mental and moral in your child?"[31] Another writer regarded the influence of the mother on her child the same way: "Her expressions, her feelings, her passions become almost imperceptibly a part of his nature."[32] By this process of moral and emotional replication, the identities of mother and child were merged. If the mother's love was irresistible, it mean that the mother had "in her own hands" the *"perfect formation* of [her children's] *entire character."* She could not resist making "impressions" that would "stamp" her children "not only *indelibly,* but *eternally."* The mother's child became, as Lydia Sigourney put it, her "twin-soul." Although most advisers alerted mothers to the "great diversity in the natural dispositions of children," they never seriously considered that the child should become anything other than the mother writ large, in Dr. Joseph Hanaford's phrase, "a mental and moral daguerrotype of herself."[33] From the mother's perspective, then, the child was self, rather than other. That is why Lydia Sigourney, in another remarkable turn of phrase, could instruct her mother to regard her baby as "a fragment of yourself."[34]

We have come, then, to the kernel of the emotionology of motherhood.[35] A mother focused her love upon a susceptible infant mind. "Working like nature . . . she . . . sends forth from [her] heart, in pure and temperate flow, the life-giving current. . . . her warm affections and irrepressible sympathies." The influence of eighteenth-century faculty psychology is clear; and, according to its doctrines, the infant would necessarily bear the imprint of his mother's love. He would mimic her affection, learning to love just as he was loved. Yet the object of this love was the mother herself; the very process of loving would obliterate the distinctions between—the separateness of—mother and child. The popular writer Fanny Fern understood the dynamic perfectly when she described the essence of motherhood: "Another outlet for thy womanly

heart; a mirror, in which thy smiles and tears shall be reflected back; a
fair page on which thou, God-commissioned, mayst write what thou
wilt; a heart that will throb back to thine, love for love."[36] Like Narcis-
sus, looking into the mirror, the loving mother adored her own reflection.

Here, in the doctrine of motherhood, we can see the creation of a
powerful mythology. It offers the mother a sort of omnipotence. It
denies, or offers the means for denying, the strangeness and separateness
of her children, by making them part of the mother herself. In defining
children as beings who are designed to embody and return their mother's
love, it authorizes a profound form of self love. And in suggesting that
the mother's love will be replicated in the child, and the child's child, for
generations to come, it promises immortality. No wonder that "maternity," could become, for women, "part of our religion."[37]

Yet if the nineteenth-century doctrine of motherhood was, in part, a
religion that established rather grandiose notions about the power of a
mother's love, it must be remembered that this effect was incidental. The
doctrine was not designed to increase feminine power or even a sense of
power, for it grew out of an ideology whose very objective was to
vanquish power with love, to replace selfishness with affection and
virtue. Thus, the doctrine of maternal influence was bound to take away
with the same hand that which it gave. Mothers could be powerful only
if they renounced power, loved only if they renounced self, immortal
only if they were willing to die.

Consider Catharine Sedgwick's description of an ideal mother, her
friend Anne, "one of those strong characters that must do for itself the
hardest work." And how did she train her children? "By the atmosphere
of affection and kindness with which she surrounded herself [rather]
than by any direct bearing of authority upon them." The mother had to
be what she wanted her children to become. Then, in the confines of the
family circle, the "exercise of absolute power" might be "softened by
perfect love."[38] Somewhat like Christ, a mother was to be active only in
"the exercise of those virtues denominated *passive*." Indeed, mothers
were barely to "exercise" at all. When observing her growing children,
would not a mother naturally "say, with a smile, a sigh—perchance a
tear—'I felt, or thought, or longed the same at her years.'"[39] A mother
could not act; she might feel, or think, or long; she should "surround
herself" with an "atmosphere"; she could smile, sigh, and shed a tear.

The mother was, as the maternal advisors liked to say, "the first book
read, and the last one laid aside, in every child's library. Every look,
word, tone, gesture . . . makes an impression."[40] Because everything
about her could leave an indelible mark, she had to make certain that

everything about her was designed to create the right impressions. It was not only what she did, but how she looked, sounded, and seemed that was important. Although advisors might tell them how to feed, clothe, and instruct their offspring, much of their attention was devoted to less active endeavors. An article on "How to Speak to Children" described not the words and ideas to be conveyed, but how to achieve the right tone of voice.[41] In this sense, the real work of childrearing was to be focused upon the woman herself, as she tried to make herself a fit model for imitation.

Even her appearance had to be altered to make her a good mother. T. H. Gallaudet reminded the mother of "the influence of her *countenance, voice, and general air and manners.*" Adapting eighteenth-century psychological assumptions for his own age, addressing the nineteenth century's anxieties about the discrepancies between appearance and reality, he argued that the face was the *"index and agent of the soul."* Character and countenance mirrored one another. Like a phrenologist, Gallaudet believed that the exterior of the person reflected her moral qualities. And like a Common Sense philosopher, he believed that the moral qualities of the parent might by "the sympathy of sentiment" be communicated to her offspring. Therefore, it was imperative that the mother learn "to improve in all the heaven like expressions of countenance," making herself look like Christ.[42]

If children were such impressionable creatures that they could absorb their mother's character from the expression upon her face, then she would have to be enormously careful not to disclose, even inadvertently, any thought or feeling she did not want her child to acquire. Mothers were warned not "to permit the anxieties of your mind to mantle your countenance with forbidding gravity or gloom." And because the countenance and the voice were reflections of the mother's character, it was likewise necessary for her to control her thoughts and feelings, lest they betray her and ruin her child. The mother "must always be dignified, calm, consistent with herself. . . . She must never be observed to betray a weakness, changeableness or vascillation *[sic]* of character. . . . the mother must be at all times, agreeable, entertaining and tender."[43] Mothers were urged to suppress all negative emotions and to cultivate a placid cheerfulness. Again and again mothers were told which feelings might be enjoyed and which were to be denied. Lydia Sigourney advised that "every irritable feeling should . . . be restrained." She asked her readers to forgive her "for repeatedly pressing on mothers, to wear the lineaments of cheerfulness." Similarly, Alphonse Perren told mothers that "an even temper is indispensable to the cheerfulness of home," while *The Mother's Magazine* insisted that "a good disposition," one that was kind, considerate, and unselfish, was "the most important requisite in domestic life."[44] All these advisors assumed that women could manipulate and control their emotions, that a mother was able "to cultivate all good dispositions and noble aspirations—to overcome and subdue all evil propensities."[45] Emotion could be overcome by will.

Although women were believed to be, in a general sense, more emotional than men, "possessing superior strength of heart,"[46] that did not mean they were to express whatever they felt. Feminine emotionality was fundamentally passive; women might register feeling, deeply and indiscriminately, but they were not to transmit everything they might feel. The nineteenth century expected women, no less than men, to exercise self-control. Indeed, for mothers to be able to teach their sons essential lessons in self-control, they must be able to control themselves. Hence, advisers told women to "bear in mind, that, in governing, we should begin with ourselves." A woman endowed with "warm feelings" and "quick apprehension" would have to exercise "self-control" so that she might display only a "calm good sense."[47] Emotion was not in itself an unqualified good. Rather, mothers were enjoined to govern and, indeed, to manipulate their feelings for the benefit of their children. Thus, in a chapter entitled "The Mother's Difficulties," John Abbott insisted, "We must bring our own feelings and our own actions under a rigid system of discipline, or it will be in vain for us to hope to curb the passions and restrain the conduct of those who are looking to us for instruction and example."[48] Put another way, the natural and spontaneous outpourings of a mother's heart might interfere with the mother's true mission. Her most strenuous efforts would have to be directed at herself.

Is there a contradiction here? After all, the maternal advisers certainly believed that the mother's love was natural and irrepressible, and they agreed that one of the attributes that qualified women for motherhood was their ability to sympathize with their children, to feel what they felt. Were women born to be mothers, or was it an office that was to be achieved? Were women suited as they were, or did they have to be changed? The maternal advisers did not confront this question directly, but taken as a body, their writings offer this answer. Individual women were to strive to realize their feminine potential, by deliberately cultivating that within themselves which was supposed to be the most naturally and essentially feminine. The advisors thus betrayed their suspicion of female emotionality in the full range of its possible manifestations; they idealized feeling only to the extent that it was an expression of the generalized, socializing affections or sympathies that Common Sense philosophers had glorified. More particular, individualized emotion was

quite another matter. It was the feelings that a woman had in common
with other women that were prized, not intense or idiosyncratic emotions.

Emotion was construed instrumentally; it had certain purposes and
was to be shaped to serve those ends. Only in this context does the
advice given by *The Mother's Magazine* in 1833 make sense. P told
mothers to *"feel* for your child . . . for whatever your feelings are, he
will know them; you cannot elude his eagle eye." So mothers must feel
the right feelings, but they "must beware of disclosing [their] feelings, or
at least, let there not be an apparent *attempt* to exhibit them, either to
himself or to others. This would be most ruinous. Rather let him feel
that there exists in your bosom a well spring of feeling and anxiety,
which others know nothing of, and which even he cannot fathom." P
told mothers that they must craft a maternal persona, a woman who
was quintessentially feeling and self-effacing. She must eradicate almost
entirely all evidence of will and intention, perhaps modeling herself after
P's own mother, who prayed early in the morning, before her family
awoke, almost—but not quite—eluding the watchful eye of her child.
She must create the illusion that she had subdued all feeling, any interest
in self, and all desire to exercise power. She might reveal only the
scintilla of the crafted self that escaped her extraordinary efforts as self-
suppression.

The mother was an actor on the stage of eternal life and death. She
must see herself as her children would see her; she must observe herself
playing her assigned role. "Mother, watch yourself," wrote P. "Your
child watches you; his eye watches every motion; his ear is bent to catch
every sound from your lips." Again P warned, "Mother, watch yourself;
how can you expect your Saviour's blessing if you slight his most solemn
and repeated injunction to watchfulness?" And a third time, most emphatically, "Mother! watch yourself! Should the inquiry be made about
your children—Who slew all these? How could you bear to have all eyes
turned on you, as their murderer?"[49]

The mother had it in her power to secure for her child eternal life, or
to consign him to perdition. Because the stakes were so high, it was "a
mother's imperious duty to make any and every sacrifice, to rescue her
child." Maternal advisers insisted unequivocally that "a mother's duties
ought to take precedence before everything else." Quite simply, a mother
had "no right to seek her own pleasure more than that of her children,
or her own improvement more than theirs."[50] Americans could exhort
mothers to self-sacrifice because they considered unselfishness a cardinal
virtue; indeed, it was just what mothers were supposed, by precept and
example, to teach.[51] Moreover, self-sacrifice was thought to bring its

own sort of pleasure. So reasoned Lydia Sigourney, who observed that "the disinterested, have the best materials for being happy. . . . May it not therefore be assumed," she asked, "that the subjugation of self, is happiness?"[52] The mother's mission was to live for her child; this would bring her happiness here, and her child happiness hereafter.

Curiously, the maternal advisers never predicted whether the mother herself might look forward to salvation; their interest was only in the future of the child. Indeed, mothers were reborn not in heaven, but in their children; they sacrificed themselves in a most profound sense. Here is the way Lydia Sigourney explained the "Privileges of the Mother": "No longer will you now live for self,—no longer be noteless and unrecorded, passing away without name or memorial among the people. It can no more be reproachfully said of you, that 'You lend all your graces to the grave, and keep no copy.' "[53] Life everlasting came to a woman only through her child. The subtext of the maternal advice literature was that women, like Christ, were the instruments of someone else's salvation.

And like Christ, they would have to die that their children might live. The maternal advice literature makes this point effectively, if indirectly. We may consider the exhortations to self-sacrifice and the suppression of feeling as a generalized expression of the belief that mothers must pay dearly for the happiness of their children. But it is in fiction, especially in short, instructive tales, that this message comes through most clearly.

Again and again, maternal advisers imagined the moment when mother and child separated. This was the test of maternal influence: had the child learned from his mother's example? John Abbott summarized the basic assumption: "When a son leaves home, and enters upon the busy world, many are the temptations which come crowding upon him. If he leaves not his mother with established principles of religion and self-control, he will most assuredly fall before these temptations."[54] If all went as it was supposed to, the child would have internalized his mother's values, her voice, her countenance, and her prayers; they would serve as his conscience. Many men who wrote for women's magazines testified to the efficacy of maternal influence. S, for example, described his falling away from God after he left his mother's home and his later conversion, which he credited to his mother: "If my heart has ever been renewed—if my sins have been forgiven, I feel I owe it, through the mercy of God, to a *pious mother's prayers*. . . . The memory of those prayers, wherever I am, still, like a guardian angel, hovers over my heart to restrain me from evil, and cheer me onward in the way of live."[55] Just as the maternal advice literature postulated, S carried his mother with him, in his heart; Christ's surrogate, she effected his salvation.

That is the way the paradigm worked, from the perspective of the child. Many confessions—or pseudo-confessions, for it is impossible to assess the veracity of these tales—told the same story.[56] Only occasionally were such tales recounted from the mother's point of view. If children, when grown, might expect to enjoy the fruits of their mothers' labors, the mothers themselves would have to trust to faith. The *American Ladies' Magazine* put it this way, beginning with the standard sentiment: "The Maternal influence in molding these wonderful minds, is a triumph of which our sex may well be proud. . . . there is a connexion between duties performed and blessings secured, which is always certain." Then follows the caution. "The faithful mother may not see this fulfillment during her life; but she can and will feel its benignant and cheering hope."[57] Mothers, then, should not expect fulfillment on this side of the grave. Implicit is the assumption that mothers will not see their labors rewarded; for that they will have to trust to God.

It is necessary to read these stories from the mother's perspective to understand fully the nature of the mother's mission and the purpose of maternal love as they were defined by nineteenth-century maternal advisers. One tale may serve to represent them all. Fanny Fern's "A Mother's Influence" focuses upon the moment when a young man takes his leave from the parental home. Young Will Low has decided to go to sea. His father, an old-fashioned patriarch, has made his life unbearable. The son, however, will miss his mother, who is, as he tells a friend, "the only humanized portion of my heart—the only soft spot in it. She came to my bed-side last night, after she thought I was asleep, gently kissed my forehead, and then knelt by my bedside. . . . I shall never be an infidel while I can remember my mother." Mrs. Low has mastered the conventions; she reveals her emotion only when she thinks she is unobserved. She tries to suppress her feelings, but the next morning her "hand trembled as she passed her boy's cup" at his last meal at home. "She did not trust herself to speak—her heart was too full." Will, of course, observes the signs of his mother's emotion, her "swollen eyelids" and "his favorite little tea-cakes that she had busied herself in preparing for him." All that she could utter was the simple prayer, " 'God keep my boy!' " This was the ritual mother's prayer, an incantation to protect her son and secure his salvation.

And so Will Low went to sea, enacting a scenario that seems to have been the realization of a mother's greatest fears. In tale after tale, separated sons went to the city, or, more often, to sea—the masculine communities that appear as the antitheses of the female-dominated home. And, as in all of these tales, the son gave in to temptation. Of course he felt guilt, but "when the angel whisper, 'God keep my boy,' palsied his

daring hand," he would drink another cup "to drown again more reck-
lessly 'that still small torturing voice.' " He was too ashamed even to
write home. Finally satiated, Will returned home, on what proved to be
the day of his mother's funeral. A neighbor explained that after Will left
home " 'she began to droop like a willow in a storm, and lose all heart,
like. Doctor's stuff didn't do any good, as long as she had no news of
the boy.' " Will's sins, then, have killed his mother.

Will's "conscience," however, "did its office. Long years of mad folly
passed in swift review before him; and over that insensible form a vow
was made, and registered in Heaven." Mrs. Low's death worked her
son's conversion, and he, in turn, persuaded his father also to repent.
The story ends with the two men entering church, as the older Low
comments, " 'Your mother should have lived to see this day, Will.' "[58]
But of course, she could not have. So directly is Will Low's conversion
linked to the death of his mother that we cannot miss seeing the causal
connection. Finally and firmly transplanted into her son's heart, Mrs.
Low has served her life's function: she now *may* die. And in order to
secure her husband's and especially her son's rebirth, she now *must* die.
The narrative and the logic both are established by the life of Christ.
Mrs. Low's death, like that of Christ, was necessary for her son and her
husband to be reborn. She made the greatest sacrifice that a mother—
and a Christian—could make; she gave her life for her child. Ultimately,
a mother's influence depended upon her willingness to give herself fully
and to deny herself finally. And it was only after she had gone to this
extreme that she realized her destiny. A correspondent to *The Mother's
Magazine* explained the effect of a mother's death this way: "Blessed are
they, in the earth, who possess the inestimable dowry of a pious mother's
grave!—I had almost said, the example and counsel of a living mother
could hardly equal in power, upon the filial heart, the silent but thrilling
preaching of a departed one."[59] There was no "almost" about it. The
mother atoned for her child's sins; she forgave him still; she died that he
might achieve eternal life. The mother was Christ.

The paradigm of mother's love must be read as an elaborate parable that
patterns the mother's nature and destiny after that of Christ. Not only
the moral tales invented by Fanny Fern and the others, but the entire
corpus of maternal advice literature in early to mid-nineteenth-century
America was directed to achieving the conversion of the nation's children. Sometimes the message was secularized, and mothers were enjoined to prepare their children for entry into a democratic society. But
even in those cases, the design bore an evangelical imprint: citizens of
the republic were supposed to manifest the recognizably Christian traits

of self-sacrifice, sinlessness, and benevolence toward their fellow man. So it is not surprising that, if mothers were designated the instruments of conversion, a mother's life story, as it was imagined by the maternal advisers, would read like a parable. Endowed with "a love, next in patience to that of a Redeemer,"[60] her career would be like that of the great Converter; to redeem, she must die. The logic of the paradigm of maternal influence could have it no other way, so closely was it patterned after the narrative of Christ's life.

We see, then, theology and democracy, engaged in a dialectic that would determine the shape of nineteenth-century American culture. The paradigmatic mother was this dialectic's creature, designed to serve its ends. Historians have usually linked the nineteenth-century's idealization of motherhood to the early stages of industrialization and the removal of men's work from the home.[61] Yet if structural changes alone could explain the exaltation of self-sacrificing motherhood, that ideal surely would have been modified as the society and economy continued to change; in our current, postindustrial age, it might seem an anachronism. But because the ideal is part of our national civil religion, reflecting an American fusion of democratic and Christian thought, it persists. Even though most Americans no longer expect mothers to act as agents of conversion, they still think that maternal love can redeem.

Indeed, since the early nineteenth century, Americans have increasingly looked to love for salvation; they have attached to love a transcendent importance.[62] Yet love is an emotion, a feeling that can be experienced and expressed in a variety of ways. In commenting upon an earlier version of this article, John Demos suggested that those of us who study the history of emotions should consider making a commitment to a theoretical position regarding the study of emotion. He noted that he has found Silvan Tompkins' account of affective experience particularly useful. Tompkins has "identified eight 'primary affects,' " which are "inborn and intrinsic to the species": "(1) Interest/Excitement; (2) Distress/Anguish; (3) Fear/Terror; (4) Anger/Rage; (5) Disgust/Contempt; (6) Shame/Humiliation; (7) Surprise/Startle; (8) Enjoyment/Joy." Readers of *Entertaining Satan: Witchcraft and the Culture of Early New England* have an example of how effectively a historian may use Tompkins' work to illuminate a chapter in history.[63] But as Robert Levy noted in discussion, "love" nowhere appears on Tompkins' list; it would not seem to be a "primary affect."

Instead, "love" is a social construction, a term that, in different times and places, takes on different meanings. Historians, then, have a role in analyzing the changing cultural meanings of love, of helping us to understand—to use Raymond Carver's words—"What We Talk About When

We Talk About Love."[64] When Freud said that "a mother is only brought unlimited satisfaction by her relation to her son; this is altogether the most perfect, the most free from ambivalence of all human relationships,"[65] he was talking about love in a way not very different form the antebellum maternal advisors who also believed that a mother's love was pure, unconflicted, and fundamentally self-denying. Yet we must wonder about the effect of this advice literature upon the women who read it and, perhaps, took it to heart; family historians have barely begun to study the experience of mothers in the nineteenth century.[66] As in the paradigm, living, fully dimensional mothers slip from our view. Still, we may speculate whether certain pathologies that psychologists and psychoanalysts have attributed to women—their masochism, their narcissism, their calculated presentation of self—may be the unintended result of the peculiar definition Americans have attached to the term *mother's love.*

In Robert Stone's novel *Children of Light,* the protagonist responds to his lover's plea for help: " 'I would die for you,' he said. It was true, he thought, but not really helpful."[67] Nor, surely, is it very helpful for mothers to liken themselves to Christ or to see in their willingness to die for their children an appropriate test of their love.

NOTES

The author wishes to thank the National Endowment for the Humanities for a Fellowship for Independent Study and Research, the Newberry Library for a Short-Term Research Fellowship, and the Philadelphia Center for Early American Studies for a Senior Fellowship; and Barry Bienstock, John Demos, Peter Stearns, and the participants in the First Biennial Conference on Social History for their valuable suggestions.

1. Rev. John Todd, "Address to Mothers," *The Mother's Magazine* (Nov. 1839): 249 (hereafter referred to as *MM*); E. L., "The Mother's Affections," *American Ladies' Magazine* (July 1833): 320 (hereafter referred to as *ALM*); Lydia H. Sigourney, *Letters to Mothers* (Hartford, 1838), 47.

2. See Jay Fliegelman, *Prodigals and Pilgrims: The American Revolution Against Patriarchal Authority, 1750–1850* (New York, 1982); Melvin Yazawa, *From Colonies to Commonwealth: Familial Ideology and the Beginning of the American Republic* (Baltimore, 1985); Ruth H. Bloch, "The Gendered Meanings of Virtue in Revolutionary America," *Signs* 13 (1987): 37–58; Jan Lewis, "The Republican Wife: Virtue and Seduction in the Early Republic," *William and Mary Quarterly* 44, 3d ser. (1987): 689–721 (hereafter referred to as *WMQ*).

3. Ruth H. Bloch, "American Feminine Ideals in Transition: The Rise of the Moral Mother, 1785–1815," *Feminist Studies* 4 (1978): 101–26.

4. Laurel Thatcher Ulrich, *Good Wives: Image and Reality in the Lives of Women in Northern New England, 1650–1750* (New York, 1982), 154. See also Nancy F. Cott, "Passionlessness: An Interpretation of Victorian Sexual Ideology, 1790–1850," *Signs* 4 (1978): 219–36.

5. Useful discussions are provided by Fliegelman, *Prodigals*, esp. 9–29; Daniel W. Howe, "The Political Psychology of *The Federalist*," *WMQ* 44, 3d ser. (1987): 485–509; Garry Wills, *Inventing America: Jeffersons' Declaration of Independence* (Garden City, N.Y., 1978), esp. part 4. Consider also Perry Miller, "The Rhetoric of Sensation," in his *Errand into the Wilderness* (New York 1956), 166–83.

6. See, for example, Rev. John S. C. Abbott, *The Mother at Home; or, The Principles of Maternal Duty* (Boston, 1834), 66; "Hints for Maternal Education," *MM* (Aug. 1834): 113, 114; S.F.W. "Woman's Sphere," *ALM* (May 1835): 264; Sarah W. Gordon, "It Should Be Love," *The Mother's Assistant and Young Lady's Friend* (March 1849): 53 (hereafter referred to as *TMA*); Rev. V. Clark, "The Ruined Son," *TMA* (Oct. 1845): 74; "The Beginning," *ALM* (Jan. 1829): 4; "On Early Domestic Education, *Mother's Monthly Journal* (1837): 6 (hereafter referred to as *MMJ*); Mrs. *(sic)* C. Sedgwick, "A Plea for Children," *ALM* (Feb. 1835): 95; Virginia Cary, *Christian Parent's Assistant; or Tales for the Moral and Religious Instruction of Youth* (Richmond, 1829), x; G. W. H., "The Disadvantages of Childhood," *MM* (1867): 7; "What Virtue Is," *MM* (Aug. 1834): 115; D. M. L., "Early Habits of Industry," *MM* (Feb. 1834): 17; "Let Reason Dictate," *MMJ* (Nov. 1837): 170–71.

7. See "The Conversion of Children," *MM* (Nov. 1835): 161–64, (Dec. 1835): 179–81; "Remarks on the Conversion of Children," *MM* (Feb. 1836): 24–25; C. A. Goodrich, "Hints on the Conversion of Children," *MM* (May 1838): 97; *Religious Remembrancer*, 20 July 1816, 187.

8. Abbott, *Mother*, 159.

9. "Be Wise to Do, as Well as Learn," *MMJ* (April 1837): 56; "A Mother's Influence," *TMA* (Feb. 1849): 25. See also "Third Annual Report of the Louisville Baptist Maternal Association," *MMJ* (Feb. 1846): 50.

10. "The Conversion of Children," *MM* (Dec. 1835): 179–81.

11. "Family Government Essential to National Prosperity," *MM* (Mar. 1833): 35; "The Beginning," *ALM* (Jan. 1829): 3.

12. "Letter from D. B. L. Wade to Sister Allen," *MMJ* (Jan. 1846): 13–15.

13. H. Richard Niebuhr, *The Kingdom of God in America* (New York, 1937).

14. "Family Government," 36.

15. For evidence that would support this analysis, see S. F. W., "Woman's Sphere," 266.

16. See Nancy F. Cott, *The Bonds of Womanhood: "Woman's Sphere" in New England, 1780–1865* (New Haven, 1977).

17. Sedgwick, "A Plea for Children," 94. See similarly, S. F. W., "Woman's Sphere," 262.

18. See Mary P. Ryan, *Cradle of the Middle Class: The Family in Oneida County, New York, 1790–1865,* (New York, 1981), 15, for her analysis of the family's function as that of "social reproduction . . . whereby people, rather than goods, are created."

19. See Lewis, "Republican Wife."

20. Sedgwick, "A Plea for Children," 93; "Family Government," 36. See similarly, "The Beginning," 4.

21. "Woman," *ALM* (Oct. 1830): 441. See John Putnam Demos, *A Little Commonwealth: Family Life in Plymouth Colony* (New York, 1970).

22. L. E., "Home," *ALM* (May 1830): 218, 217, 218.

23. "The Happy Family," *MM* (May 1839): 111.

24. See Kathryn Kish Sklar, *Catharine Beecher: A Study in American Domesticity* (New Haven, 1973).

25. S. F. W. "Woman's Sphere," 264; "The Peculiar Faculties Afforded Mothers for Training Up their Children for Good," *MM* (May 1837): 104.

26. "The Mother of Washington," *ALM* (Nov. 1831): 385.

27. "The Connection Between Piety and Usefulness in Mothers," *MMJ* (Jan. 1837): 12; "Maternal Influence," *MM* (April 1841): 84; "The Mother's Power, *MM* 35 (1867): 221. Such language became conventional. See also Sigourney, *Letters,* 16.

28. John A. Bolles, "The Influence of Women on Society," *ALM* (June 1831): 256; Maria J. McIntosh, *Woman in America: Her Work and Her Reward* (New York, 1850), 77.

29. Rev. E. H. Chapin, "A Mother's Love," *TMA* (July 1845): 9; Frederick, "Maternal Affection," *The Casket* (April 1827): 134. Also, see note 1 above.

30. "Extracts from Reports of Maternal Associations," *MM* (Feb. 1841): 46; "Be Wise to Do," 56. See similarly Sedgwick, "Plea for Children," 97.

31. Marian Harland [Mary Virginia Hawes Terhune], "A Christmas Talk With Mothers," in *The Christmas Holly* (New York, 1866), 53.

32. "Extract," *MM* (Jan. 1830): 24; "Training," *MMJ* (Jan. 1846): 2; "Prospectus," *MM* (Jan. 1833): 3.

33. Sigourney, *Letters,* 25; Abbott, *Mother,* 40; "Friendly Suggestions to Mothers," *TMJ* 20 (1855): 189. See also T. S. Arthur, *Anna Lee; or, The Maiden, The Wife, and the Mother* (repr. London, n.d.), 186.

34. Sigourney, *Letters,* 31.

35. This very useful neologism has been coined by Peter N. Stearns and Carol Z. Stearns to denote "the collective emotional standards of a society." See "Emotionology: Clarifying the History of Emotions and Emotional Standards," *American Historical Review* 90 (1985): 813–36; quotation on 813.

36. McIntosh, *Woman in America,* 25; Fanny Fern [Sarah P. Parton], *Ruth Hall and Other Writings,* ed. Joyce W. Warren (New Brunswick, 1986), 24.

37. "Maternity," *The Casket* (Oct. 1828): 472.

38. "Look Before You Leap," *Columbian Lady's and Gentleman's Magazine* (Jan. 1846): 13; "Thoughts on the Education of Girls," *MMJ* (July 1837): 106.

39. "Woman," 445; Harland, "Christmas Talk," 53.

40. *MMJ* (April 1846): 119. See similarly P., "Parental Consistency," *MM* (Feb. 1833): 22.

41. "How to Speak to Children," *TMA* (Jan. 1850): 12.

42. "The Mother's Face," *MM* (Jan. 1838): 16; ibid. (April 1838): 74; ibid. (Jan. 1838): 17; ibid. (April 1838): 74; ibid. (Feb. 1838): 30: the ideal mother exhibited a "Christ like loveliness." See similarly "The Mother," *MM* (1867): 57: "Heaven has imprinted on the mother's face something which claims kindred with the skies." For the nineteenth century's concern for sincerity, see especially Karen Halttunen, *Confidence Men and Painted Women: A Study of Middle-Class Culture in America, 1830–1870* (New Haven, 1982); Fliegelman, *Prodigals*, 240–42; Lewis Kern, *An Ordered Love: Sex Roles and Sexuality in Victorian Utopias—The Shakers, the Mormons, and the Oneida Community* (Chapel Hill, 1981), 35–40.

43. "How Shall a Mother Secure the Confidence of Her Children," *MM* (June 1830): 105; "For Who Hath Despised the Day of Small Things," *MMJ* (July 1837): 101.

44. Sigourney, *Letters*, 28, 63; "Home and Its Influences, *MM* (March 1853): 80; L. L. H., "The Most Important Requisite in Domestic Life," *MM* (March 1854): 88. See similarly Rev. Ralph W. Allen, "Family Government," *TMA* (Dec. 1849): 126.

45. "Mental and Moral Qualities Transmissible from Parents to Children," *MM* (Feb. 1841): 41.

46. "Maternal Traits of Feeling," *ALM* (Aug. 1830): 373–74. See Peter N. Stearns and Carol Z. Stearns, *Anger: The Struggle for Emotional Control in America's History* (Chicago, 1986), 49.

47. "Report of the Philadelphia Union Maternal Association," *MMJ* (June 1837): 93; "The Satin Pelisse," *ALM* (Dec. 1830): 540.

48. Abbott, *Mother*, 66.

49. P., "Parental Consistency," 23–24.

50. A Mother, "Thoughts on Mothers' Responsibility," *MMJ* (March 1837): 41; Arthur, *Anna Lee*, 221; Sedgwick "Plea for Children," 96–97.

51. See, for example, "Extract from a Letter," *MM* (April 1835): 63.

52. Sigourney, *Letters*, 193; see also 56.

53. Sigourney, *Letters*, 9.

54. Abbott, *Mother*, 15.

55. "The Mother in Her Closet," *MM* (Oct. 1840): 226.

56. The following discussion is based upon: C. D., "Maternal Influence," *MM* (July 1840): 160–64; "I Had a Mother," *MM* (July 1838); 157–58 P. R. W., "Maternal Influence," *MM* (Nov. 1840): 254–55; Rev. William H. Thayer, "The Mother's Grave," *TMA* (March 1849): 83–84; "My Mother's Grave," *The Casket* (May 1829): 84; "My Mother's Death," *MM* (March 1833): 94–95; S. M. D., "The Deathless Influence of a Mother's Love," *MM* (1867): 75–77.

57. "Woman's Way to Eminence," *ALM* (Sept. 1834): 388.

58. Fanny Fern [Sarah P. Parton], "A Mother's Influence," in *Fern Leaves From Fanny's Port-Folio*, 2d ser. (Auburn and Buffalo, 1854), 252–56.

59. H. M. S., "A Mother's Grave," *MM* (June 1837): 138.

60. Sigourney, *Letters*, 55.

61. See, for example, Cott, *Bonds;* Ryan, *Cradle;* Ann Douglas, *The Feminization of American Culture* (New York, 1977); Bloch, "Moral Mother."

62. See, for example, Jan Lewis, *The Pursuit of Happiness: Family and Values in Jefferson's Virginia* (New York, 1983). Consider also this observation by Robert N. Bellah, Richard Madsen, William M. Sullivan, Ann Swidler, and Steven M. Tipton, in *Habits of the Heart: Individualism and Commitment in American Life* (Berkeley, 1985), 291: "Many Americans are concerned to find meaning in life not primarily through self-cultivation but through intense relations with others."

63. John Putnam Demos, *Entertaining Satan: Witchcraft and the Culture of Early New England* (New York, 1982), 184, 461; for Demos's use of Tompkins, see 184–94.

64. This is the title of Carver's collection of short stories, *What We Talk About When We Talk About Love,* which includes the story of the same title. (New York, 1981).

65. Sigmund Freud, *New Introductory Lectures on Psychoanalysis,* ed. and trans. James Strachey (New York, 1965), 118.

66. See for example Nancy Schrom Dye and Daniel Blake Smith, "Mother Love and Infant Death, 1750–1920," *Journal of American History* 73 (1986): 329–53; Ulrich, *Good Wives;* Lewis, *Pursuit of Happiness,* chaps. 3 and 5; Sylvia D. Hoffert, " 'A Very Peculiar Sorrow': Attitudes Toward Infant Death in the Urban Northeast, 1800–1860," *American Quarterly* 39 (1987): 601–16.

67. Robert Stone, *Children of Light* (New York, 1986), 231–32.

— 11 —

Suppressing Unpleasant Emotions: The Development of a Twentieth-Century American Style

Peter N. Stearns

What do Americans in the late twentieth century do about emotions regarded as personally or socially damaging? How is emotional suppression* handled in an age that often seems to regard suppression as a shadowy vestige of an unenlightened past? This essay sketches some ingredients of the contemporary suppressive apparatus by looking at the evolution of the management of two unpleasant emotions—unpleasant at least by twentieth-century criteria: jealousy and anger. It argues that an examination of these two emotions in dynamic terms—in terms that is of a movement from one style of control to another—reveals the emergence of a new approach to disapproved emotions, a third style different both from the traditional approach visible among many Americans in the colonial era and the Victorian approach that swelled in the nineteenth century. The contemporary suppressive style rests on a number of novel factors in the emotional context of American life, and produces an interesting balance of strengths and weaknesses, all of which can be explored in part by dealing with suppression in terms of historical change. This same historical exploration helps explain why so

---

*I will be using the term *emotional suppression* in this chapter, in order to focus on socially determined goals and strategies to limit undesirable emotions, and partially self-conscious personal efforts in the same direction, as opposed to the more strictly individual, and largely unconscious, phenomenon of repression. One element of the argument is the fact that the twentieth-century controls do involve some awareness of the emotions to be squelched, even though the process of suppression becomes partly instinctive.

much contemporary suppression became implicit and unacknowledged, clothed in vocabulary of in-touch openness.

Contemporary emotional control in the United States has not been easy to characterize, particularly because its architects have largely eschewed explicit advocacy of suppression, bedecking their strategies with a vocabulary of permissiveness and attacks on Victorian shibboleths from the past. As a result many commentators worry not about suppression but about lack of restraint; their specific comments may be on target in noting areas where suppression is inadequate or unsuccessful, but their approach may wrongly conduce to a belief that suppressive norms do not exist.[1] Evaluation of suppression is also hampered by the microscopic experimental approach dominant in many branches of emotions research, which is very successful at identifying certain kinds of replicable emotional responses but less adequate in capturing larger suppressive styles that operate in social contexts. In this sense a historical overview not only usefully focuses on contemporary suppression as a process to be described and explained in terms of change, but also emphasizes the need to develop a balance between experimental and more macroscopic, observational analyses as the basis for understanding how emotions actually work.[2]

Happily, important findings from social psychology and the burgeoning field of the sociology of emotion already provide some important signposts. Comparative data have shown that contemporary Americans rank high, compared to Greeks, Chinese, West Indians, and several other cultures, in labelling certain emotions as undesirable.[3] They are also unusually prone to equate the undesirable with the unpleasant, unlike certain cultures, such as the Chinese, who show an interesting propensity to find utility in some emotions recognized as personally uncomfortable. Furthermore, revealingly, Americans are particularly likely to seek to disguise those emotions they regard as simultaneously undesirable and unpleasant, ranking at or close to the top in desiring concealment for reproved feelings. These characteristics are not timeless, but rather result from changes in the American emotional context over the past sixty years. The historian can pinpoint how the combination of pronounced revulsion and desire to shun the unpleasant came into being as part of a new suppressive pattern, and why the interest in concealment was a logical part of the process. The historian can also put the exciting findings of sociologists about the role of work norms in contemporary emotional suppression into a clearer time frame, deepening our grasp of how current emotional suppression functions and what caused it to come into being.[4] The historian, in other words, far from working in a vacuum in sketching the development of contemporary suppressive styles, can build instead on available data from other disciplines in an analytical agenda that increasingly crosses conventional lines.

A historical approach must also take into account a more general sense, again issuing from several disciplinary perspectives, that contemporary emotional styles differ importantly from their counterparts during previous periods of the American past. Indeed, examination of the origins of the twentieth-century suppression largely confirms the judgment that contemporary Americans are engaged in some fundamental emotional reevaluations. Here, however, a focused historical inquiry also imposes caution. Some prevailing models of historical change are wrong, either because they misconstrue past standards or misinterpret the present or both. Others, not wrong, are excessively vague, offering grand views that have not been pinned down through attention to particular emotions.

Most obviously, an attractively systematic modernization approach, developed in this area primarily by sociologists, misleads more than it informs.[5] Modernization in this context has been used to argue for an increasingly liberated and individualistic emotional style, in contrast to a rather undifferentiated concern for suppression that presumably prevailed through the nineteenth century. The argument, certainly echoed in many facile popular assumptions (some moralistically critical, others blissfully enthusiastic about contemporary trends), points to a set of traditions which used guilt, shame, or some other set of mechanisms to curb people's natural sexual and emotional proclivities. The twentieth century, with its emphasis on individual personal expressiveness and freedom from constraint, gradually ate into these suppressions, yielding a spontaneity, an emotional openness, that has become fundamental in American personal life. This formulation is simply wrong. It fails to take into account the differentiation among emotions, from approved to disapproved, that has also characterized the twentieth century, often amid a rhetoric of emotional laissez-faire pitted against Victorian or Puritan hobgoblins. It mistakenly equates trends in emotions with trends in sexuality, while exaggerating liberation even in this latter area. It ignores necessary distinctions in the pre-twentieth-century past, that must be made even when one's primary interest lies in contemporary issues. The modernization model does accurately pick up on some real shifts in the uses of guilt, but aside from this contribution it should, in the emotions area at least, be laid to rest.

Other implicitly historical models have greater potential. The idea of some basic alterations in modal personality styles, recurrently trumpeted in research since the 1950s, relates closely to the present subject of emotional repression. David Riesman's distinction between inner- and other-directed personalities, though mainly descriptive, bore strongly on emotional styles.[6] Americans concerned with peer relations and standards might become newly uncomfortable with certain emotions that impeded easy social interchange. In contrast the more individualistic personalities previously dominant could utilize intense emotion more readily and might be driven, as well, by guilt-induced suppressions. Christopher Lasch, dealing with a similar differentiation between nineteenth-century character and the personality types that began to develop from the 1920s onward, confronts emotion even more directly.[7] Lasch's twentieth century is marked by a decline in parental guidance and the working-through of inherent emotional tensions, leaving children groping for direction from peers and media, alternating between conformity and outbursts of ungoverned rage. The more consistent styles of the nineteenth century, involving strong but regulated emotion, increasingly yield to the odd and troubling blend of vapidness and fits. Lasch's examination of the emotional styles of the American majority is somewhat indirect, as he focuses on the exemplary power of a shift from neurotic to narcissistic personality disorders (a shift which has been contested on empirical grounds).[8] Furthermore, the bleak and condemning tone of his characterization, while exhilarating reading for moral masochists, distracts from a consideration of the causes of change (a point on which Riesman is also vague) and from the probability that a twentieth-century style of emotional management, though novel, must in some ways be serviceable.

The following essay attempts a limited but more explanatory inquiry into emotional ingredients of what may indeed be a new twentieth-century modal personality in the United States. It tries to cut beneath more sweeping statements about narcissistic personalities and peer groups toward greater empirical detail. It focuses not just on before-and-after contrast, but on the process by which contemporary suppression replaced earlier systems; it thus deals seriously with the twentieth-century emotional index as a historical artifact, with appropriately distinctive labels that allow contrast not simply with the Victorian era but with earlier periods as well, and it attends to issues of causation.

There are, of course, huge gaps in this sketch, and not only because of its brevity. The results of the new suppressive style can only be suggested, though some of them parallel the formulas available in Riesman and Lasch. The sketch involves some essential simplifications, most notably in avoiding for the moment extensive comment on the subcultures of region, class, religious affiliation, or race and ethnicity. The focus is on middle-class standards, with some attention to their avowed application to other groups. For it was the middle class that took the lead in redefining certain emotions as "bad" and in divising new strategies to limit their incidence and impact, with implications not only for other segments of society but for a reconsideration of standards once-basic to the middle class itself. Finally the attention in what follows rests on standards and their expression in prescriptions and institutions, more than on measurable changes in actual emotional experience;[9] though here, as part of the final assessment of results, some bridges will be essayed toward real as well as perceived emotional life. The overall result is, I hope, a solid sense of the evolution of key standards in middle-class emotional life, plus a research agenda for the wider issues of direct experiential change and of emotional diversity in the key subgroups that make up American society.

Forty years ago Ruth Benedict sketched the following shift in American modes of suppression:

> The early Puritans who settled in the United States tried to base their entire morality on guilt, and all psychiatrists know what trouble contemporary Americans have with their consciences. But shame is an increasingly heavy burden ... and guilt is less extremely felt than in earlier generations. In the United States this is interpreted as a relaxation of morals, because we do not expect shame to do the heavy work of morality. We do not harness the acute personal chagrin which accompanies shame to our fundamental system of morality.[10]

Benedict's judgment usefully focuses on the idea of a recent shift in suppressive stance, but also on its link to a longer-standing historical background. It errs at least by historical standards in defining shame as a twentieth-century mode, and may err as well in suggesting a diminution of moral chagrin in contrast to a guilt-based reaction. These are questions best explored, however, by taking Benedict's cue that a guilt regime has given way to something else in the twentieth century, but extending it through a historical framework more complex than this particular version of the traditional-modern contrast. For the emphasis on guilt was itself a historical product, not an inheritance of the ages, and its application to reproved emotions was not as rigid as some of our images of Victorianism might suggest. Getting the background right, in sum, is a first step toward building on Benedict's insight concerning the contemporary shift and our undeniable tendency to equate change with laxness.

Despite its religious thunder, Puritan society based emotional standards less on fear of damnation than on community control through shame.[11] In this, despite somewhat greater tendencies toward introspection,[12] it resembled most of Western society in the seventeenth and eighteenth centuries. Religious injunctions created discomfort with certain emotions such as anger, but on the whole attention to emotional discipline was relatively imprecise because of the manageability of behaviors, however emotion-driven, through community sanctions and attendant shame. Individuals were not encouraged, for example, to identify anger as a personal trait—indeed, recognition for Puritans might produce anxieties about a lack of humility. But anger could be expressed as part of appropriate social hierarchy, as against servants; or as a vessel of divine wrath, as against unbelievers; or indeed against neighbors so long as certain constraints were observed.[13] Children were thus taught how dangerous it was to become angry against certain individuals, such as parents—but not that anger was an emotion to be carefully monitored in and of itself. Villages tried to restrain violence against neighbors— with incomplete success, given relatively high murder rates; but they did not seek more direct controls over its possible emotional base. Hence angry insults were seen as a normal part of community life. Other approved outlets for emotions such as anger existed; practices such as charivaris, directed against disapproved behavior, as well as more informal insults and hazings could express anger in sanctioned ways, while vengance might not only be accepted but even expected as a result of jealousy. Even normally-protected targets were exposed to some hostile emotions when community roles were symbolically altered through changes of costume, as part of the topsy-turvy aspect of festivals.[14] The overall point is obvious: specific emotions were not seen as bad, though they might be recognized as ambivalent. To the extent that they had bad consequences, behavioral controls were imposed. Children were taught to be attuned to community norms and were widely exposed to the punitive power of shame. They were not taught an elaborate agenda of personal emotional suppression. They were not taught guilt. They might readily, as a result, find outlets for emotional tensions produced by their upbringing or by community constraints, by selecting suitable targets, including even once-protected individuals such as older parents when these had lost their power. Emotions such as anger and jealousy might even prove useful in spurring community action against unlicensed behavior.

This traditional emotional regime began clearly to change in the eighteenth century, in two related directions. In the first place, more specific labels were applied to individual emotions and a new list of suitable and unsuitable sentiments began to take shape. Heightened approval of familial love—both warm emotional ties between parents and children and romantic love as the basis of marriage formation—had as its counterpart a growing hostility to anger. Loving families maintained a degree of equality, at least in principle, with which power-enforcing anger was incompatible.[15] Hence family manuals began to caution against this emotion, and diarists applied new zeal to its supervision. Jealousy also came under new scrutiny, though somewhat more obscurely. In the American north, a growing sense that defense of honor constituted uncivilized lack of restraint undermined one traditional use of jealousy. At the same time the new emphasis on love produced increasing belief that romantic unions should be free and untrammeled, not marred by the possessiveness—and frequent anger—that jealousy involved. This new disapproval of jealousy was in no sense inevitable, but it did surface with growing frequency as against older sentiments, dating back to the days of courtly love, that jealousy was indeed an inseparable part of romance, a cherished whetter of appetite.[16]

Along with a new list of good and bad emotions came a growing tendency to rely on guilt rather than shame for enforcement of standards.[17] Growing movement of people, including outright urbanization, made the implementation of community norms more problematic by the early nineteenth century—quite clearly and menacingly in the case of sexual behavior. Emphasis on the distinctness of the family unit, and on growing individual privacy within the family, simultaneously pushed for the creation of internalized standards that would not depend on outsiders' judgment or enforcement. This in turn meant that emotions themselves, and not simply behaviors, were manipulated as part of a control apparatus. Hence the undeniable Victorian distrust of unbridled emotion and reliance on rational restraint, which could lead to assumptions about mastery over impulse that contemporary Americans readily find either brutal or naive. Thus an angry young child, clearly prone to ungoverned temper, is sent to his room for several days to meditate on his wicked ways, deprived of his family's love and society and made to feel the kind of guilt that would recur should any outbursts crop up again, a point driven home by the insistence on an elaborate apology when the incident ended—this from one of the most popular early nineteenth-century American family manuals, by Catharine Sedgwick.[18] Thus a more precise vocabulary was introduced to designate, and chastise, bad emotions and lack of restraint—such as the word tantrum, coined in the later eighteenth century.

The twin transformations that took full shape about two centuries ago in mainstream Western emotional standards, involving the new emotional rating system and new use of guilt, were profoundly important. Partly because they were so novel, however, their significance should neither be exaggerated nor simplified, even for a group such as the Protestant middle class in the United States that took a lead in proclaiming the new emotionology. The kind of thorough emotional suppression undertaken for example by groups such as the Utku, whereby an emotion like anger may not even be acknowledged after infancy, was not widely attempted in Western society.[19] There was, to be sure, a brief period around the middle of the nineteenth century in which, if one were to judge strictly by the prescriptive literature, a perfect emotional placidity seemed to be sought. Children were held up as innocents, corruptible only by adults who could not restrain their bad passions. While this sentimentalized version of family emotions had no small power, there is scant indication that idealized formulas were accepted, whatever their intent, as terribly precise guides to actual emotional management.

For the actual Victorian approach toward emotion was unquestionably subtle, and even the use of guilt as a new suppressive tool had its complexities. These points must be recognized despite the pleasure contemporaries may still take in potshots at Victorian stiffness and insensitivity as contrasts to our presumably more enlightened outlook. Of course Victorians distrusted too much indulgence in impulse, urging curbs on anger or cowardly fear. But they also encouraged some new intensities, as in expressions of grief, and even in dealing with the newly precise list of suspect emotions their approach was hardly rigid.

Several general factors qualify any impression of tight suppressiveness through guilt. There was in the first place the heightened distinction between genders in emotional standards. In important respects, ironically given the labels of volatility often applied to them, women were held to stricter emotional standards than men, assumed thus to be angerless even more than sexually passionless. Men's impulses, though they might be subject to strong controls, were seen to be more complex. Women, in other words, came closer than men to a really suppressive regime, forced in some cases to express emotions such as anger indirectly through tears or illness.

Emotional suppression in the nineteenth century was also colored by the familiar division between public and private spheres. The family was a place for a number of deep feelings, but also the context where certain other emotions, such as anger, were supposed to be held in particular check. A good Victorian, particularly but not exclusively a good Victorian male, had thus to learn a rather subtle sense of emotional appropriateness quite different from across-the-board control. A great deal of attention to the targetting of emotion resulted. Even adult women, though presumably guardians of domestic emotional felicity, might find some outlets in public causes.

Victorian emotional suppression, furthermore, was also seen as a lifelong agenda of character-building. While launched in childhood, it was tempered by assumptions of childish innocence and a strong sense that self-control of specific impulses might come more readily in youth. Victorian parents, in other words, sought to establish a certain framework for self-control in childhood, but did not work as consistently toward repression of specific emotions as might be imagined. This point needs to be established carefully, particularly since we do not know as much about actual middle-class childrearing practices in the nineteenth century as might be desired. Girls were held to stricter standards than boys; the gender gap in childhood standards surpassed that in later life. Victorian parents certainly attended to repeated outbursts of unacceptable emotion, as in the Sedgwick example cited earlier. Really unmanageable temper would be attacked. But thorough-going suppression was not the normal alternative, even for girls. Many parents were doubtless still more concerned about moderating behavior than examining its emotional undercurrents. Hence there was much more discussion of excessive fighting or disobedience to parents than of emotional excess in itself, in the middle decades of the nineteenth century. These emphases might produce emotional suppression as side effects, and would certainly discourage huge displays of anger, but they did not produce the precise targeting of particular emotions characteristic of the treatment of children in more fully suppressive societies—or of American society a century later. Again, it was assumed that some of the chores of emotional self-governance would be picked up in youth, when character-building could become more specific. Even sexual control in fact involved more explicit attention to youth than to earlier childhood, again in some contrast to the patterns of the twentieth century.

Finally, thorough suppression of reproved emotions was qualified by the regime of guilt itself. Guilt could, after all, enhance some of the emotions that underlay behaviors against which guilt was applied. A child taught to be guilty over angry disobedience of a parent, through isolation or other marked chastisement, might indeed learn that the parent must be handled with care—often indeed with unexamined respect and love[20]—but he or she might not learn that anger was bad. The discomfort caused by guilt might indeed increase anger. This could, to be sure, turn inward, producing some of the oblique emotional expressions often attributed to some Victorian women; but it could seek more direct outlet. In their greater concern for appropriateness of target than for emotion per se Victorians continued some of the preference for behavioral over emotional control characteristic of earlier centuries, even though they relied more on guilt than on shame as goad.

The Victorian approach to emotional control, then, involved more than a simple list of bad emotions to be bathed in childhood guilts. Self-control was stressed and emotional excess punished, but restraint was qualified by distinctions of gender and locale; by a certain lack of specificity during childhood; and by a willingness to countenance some of the strong feelings which a guilt regime might generate. These complexities can be traced in a brief review of the ways two of the emotions officially on a reproved list were actually handled, in childhood and beyond.

The keynote of the recommended approach toward anger, at least for boys, by the later nineteenth century involved an emphasis on channeling, rather than suppressive uprooting.[21] Not only emotionological standards, but actual parental strategies, tried to install simultaneously a disapproval of anger and a positive embrace of its utilization in socially or personally fruitful directions. In this unusual combination was expressed the distinction between family, in which ire was officially forbidden, and the wider world where it might be essential; in this combination as well the stress produced by familial guilts might find approved release in controlled anger outside the home. In socializing boys, parents were urged to clamp down firmly on anger in the bosom of the family, but to avoid extirpating the emotion itself, which could serve as a goad for appropriate competitive behavior or quest for social justice in later life.[22] Specific strategies, such as urging angry attacks on bullies or practicing sports such as boxing which would vent but not eliminate anger, were suggested to implement the complex combination. And a series of comparative studies, during the first half of the twentieth century, demonstrated that American parents did indeed attempt an unusual mixture of severe disapproval of anger at home—particularly if directed against themselves—but considerable latitude in relations with peers.[23]

Whether the channeling approach applied to actual patterns of anger in adulthood is more difficult to determine. Certainly both men and women were urged, in family manuals, to avoid serious domestic anger. A certain amount of anger in public, however, either as the basis for reformist zeal or to enforce rights at work—including, in the judgment of middle-class managers, the right to respond aggressively to working-class challenge—was tolerated in most discussions of character standards and visible in actual public and labor life. Even women, as adults, might modify earlier upbringing to combine obeisance to the emotionology of domestic tranquility with considerable anger in public causes—an indication that thorough suppression of anger had not been attempted even where emotionological ideals seemed most extreme. Anger remained an emotion to use in controlled ways, so that careful lessons in appropriate targeting, more than across-the-board suppression, characterized the dominant approach.

The Victorian management of jealousy paralleled that of anger is some respects—not surprisingly, given the role anger played in jealousy as a composite emotion—but there were also some distinctive facets. Advice-givers whose popularity suggests some serious role in reflecting emotional standards saw some positive uses for a jealousy that was kept from excess. Some noted jealousy's relationship, emotionally and etymologically, to zeal. A bit of jealousy could spur achievement, as in school. It might also enhance romance. "A proper amount of this passion is most desirable . . . in romantic love."[24] Marriage consultants both in the nineteenth century and in the early twentieth—at which latter point some experts claimed a veritable science of courtship and marriage—talked about the role of jealousy in turning friendly interest into deeper passion and commitment.[25] In these senses the governance of jealousy, not its extirpation, should be the goal of any sensible emotional regime, in a pattern of channeling not dissimilar from that of anger.

The dominant emotionology, however, remained committed to the notion that jealousy was bad, a contradiction of the voluntary, spontaneous quality of real love and the independence that participants in shared love should be able to maintain. Love, the readers of *What Women Should Know* were told in 1873, was a "strong, unselfish affection blended with desire,"[26] which in its ennobling qualities contrasted starkly with the baser passion of jealousy. Jealousy certainly had no positive role in family life, and there were many statements in Victorian prescriptive literature, and in fiction, about the importance of overcoming jealousy when a beloved sister or brother developed a romantic interest in someone else or even when two siblings rivaled for the affection of the same suitor.[27] Many young women prided themselves on a lack of jealousy when fiances relieved their baser needs with paid prostitutes. Less overall emphasis was placed on jealousy's usefulness than prevailed in the case of channeled anger, which explains why there were fewer concrete suggestions about how to preserve the emotion while keeping it under proper safeguards.

Given this reproval, what is surprising, in Victorian emotionology, is how little attention was directed to the suppression of jealousy itself. Most notably, the abundant and widely-sold prescriptive literature of the Victorian decades included almost literally no warnings about jealous rivalries among children, and therefore no advice on how to launch a campaign that would bring jealousy under proper control.[28] Various authorities discussed children's disputes and certainly offered some ideas on how to minimize them, but they rarely treated the issue as a systematic problem and almost never discussed any emotional base. Episodes that by our standards should have provoked some comment on sibling rivalry were dismissed as atypical: a sister strikes her younger brother but is immediately sorry, for "she had no animosity against her little playmate; on the contrary, she loved him dearly."[29] As late as 1904 a clear case of sibling jealousy was virtually brushed aside, when Mrs. Theodore Birney described a child biting her baby sister. The advice to parents was to strike the girl "lovingly" in the same place to show her it hurt; there was really no emotional problem for the two girls really loved each other.[30] The management of jealousy was simply not seen as an issue for parents of young children. The absence of contrary indications from parents themselves suggests that the silence of advice literature mirrored some actual socialization goals. As one revealing result, adolescents and young adults in the nineteenth century—though particularly women—talked readily of the jealousy they felt in family settings (not so clearly in romantic situations) in ways twentieth-century adolescents would routinely dismiss as childish. Thus, from a twenty-year-old to her mother in 1887: "I suppose Papa told you of how jealous I was when I heard you are going to allow Emily to go to the Phi Psi musical for it did not seem at all like you to let a *child* like her go to any such things." In contrast, Arnold Gesell's consistent report that, by age eleven, most American children had learned to dominate jealousy of younger siblings as a childish passion that was now beneath them, showed how even prepubescent standards had shifted less than a century later.[31]

The Victorian neglect of specific strategies to manage jealousy, at least in what we would regard as its early manifestations, resulted from a number of factors. There may well have been, in large families, less rivalry among young children to start with. Some control of jealousy doubtless came under the more general heading of insisting on obedience and on avoidance of anger, though here it remained interesting that more specific labelling was not applied. A common conviction that jealousy was a characteristic female emotion, and therefore perhaps trivial, or inevitable, or useful to girlish romance may have played a role in the widespread silence. More generally, a considerable belief that jealousy did indeed have some uses, though not well articulated in a prescriptive literature bent on high-minded definitions of love and on covering family life with a sentimental veneer, may have reduced interest in strategies for control. Finally, it was unquestionably assumed that the proper governance of jealousy was an issue for youth, not younger children, to confront. Jealousy among older siblings, jealousy linked to romance—these were emotional concerns to be handled as part of on-going character development, not as occasions for some suppressive crisis management. Without generating such a clear model as the chan-neling approach, jealousy resembled anger in commanding a certain degree of flexibility in the Victorian emotional lexicon. Disapproved, sometimes in ringing tones, both emotions evoked in fact considerable ambivalence and some surprisingly lenient, or at least imprecise, control strategies.

In dealing both with jealousy and with anger, Victorians were not convinced that disapproval must lead to a fixation on suppression. They were in this, as in other areas, comfortable with a certain amount of useful hypocrisy, in which condemnation was less than absolute;[32] this followed from the emotional distinctions encouraged by private-public and gender divisions. They were also persuaded that unpleasant emo-tions could be useful in certain contexts; only in family life, and particu-larly for women, did they tend to insist that the discomfort of obtrusive emotions should be avoided. Finally, they were not convinced that chil-dren must be converted quickly into paragons of emotional maturity. Their belief in obedience and behavioral control, though resting on different bases from those current in previous centuries, obviated the need to set detailed standards for children, who were in any event, at whatever cost to the actual utility of prescriptive advice to parents, bathed in a sentimental glow of innocence. It was not assumed to be an arduous task to teach children the appropriate strategy for difficult emotions, particularly since targeting, not complete suppression, was the aim. Continued efforts at emotional control would form an ongoing part of good character, based on an ability to respond to rational emotional rules.

An essentially "Victorian" approach toward managing emotions lasted in some respects well into the twentieth century, particularly of course in middle-class and Protestant families. It was in 1950 that Lloyd War-ner correctly noted that lessons about anger, like those concerning sex, formed a strangely problematic agenda for boys in middle-class families, because of the inherited combination of encouragement and restraint.[33] Yet, despite persistence both in standard-setting and apparent socializa-tion strategies, the dominant reactions toward anger and jealousy began to shift much earlier in the twentieth century. A new level of disapproval developed, with suppressive intensity to match, though the full fruits of change became clear only after mid-century. The shift, though at first focused somewhat differently for anger than for jealousy, responded to the same basic causes and led ultimately to the same formula for suppression, a formula distinctive both from Victorian guilt-based and more traditional shame-based regimes.

Innovations in the American management of anger, taking shape from the 1920s onward, are increasingly familiar.[34] Their convergence with the less familiar innovations concerning jealousy is the special point to note here.

Beginning in the 1920s, American industrial psychologists and other personnel authorities launched a new effort to limit anger expressed in the workplace and to develop appropriate mechanisms to accomplish this end. Essentially they cast aside the older willingness to distinguish between home and public emotional contexts, arguing that anger had no legitimate role anywhere. Most workplace anger was thus held to be irrelevant to any real issue, the fruit of poor character or of frustrations imported from the worker's personal life. Certainly in sales or management operations, or for service-sector work such as secretarial jobs, anger was not only unjustified but positively detrimental to appropriate functioning. Secretarial training, which had once stressed the importance of trustworthiness and other less specifically emotional qualities, in the 1920s shifted toward insistence on firm emotional control. Foremen were taught that anger control was a key part of their job, and by the 1940s an array of retraining programs attempted to inculcate the lesson that smooth human relations constituted an end in itself.

To achieve the new goals of anger control, a series of strategies were devised. Collectively these highlighted, first, a growing effort to avoid situations that might provoke emotional response—hence the new-model foreman, who listened instead of shouting. Second, they involved a ventilationist tactic when, despite best efforts, anger boiled up: Have an aggrieved worker repeat his angry complaint several times, so that the emotion would wear off and be replaced, hopefully, by an embarrassed willingness to drop the whole affair. Certainly wrath could be talked away, even if occasionally a valid issue remained.

The interest in anger-free work suggested a third implementation technique, which entered mainstream family emotionology by the 1940s: stress, in first socializing children, a ventilationist parental response that would prevent anger from becoming a durable personality feature. Parents were urged of course to avoid anger-provoking situations, but they were implored even more strongly to guard against the festering qualities of childish wrath. Let children talk it out, label it, but in the process defuse the whole emotion. Gone was the idea that anger could be disciplined but channeled; references to the utility of anger-charged emotion disappeared in the prescriptive literature, and key channeling symbols such as boxing-gloves similarly faded from the domestic arsenal of middle-class boys. Anger was unequivocally bad, though not entirely avoidable in children. The good parent would aid a child in maturing without seeing anger as anything but an unpleasant experience, to be voided without behavioral result.

Even as the new campaign against anger entered the homes of up-to-date parents, virtually unprecedented concern about jealousy among young siblings reached a fever pitch.[35] Thus the transformation of the word tantrum to designate specifically a childish outburst culminated early in the twentieth century, at the same point that the sibling rivalry concept began to be introduced. Both terms began to serve as regular index-words in prescriptive manuals. But it was in fact jealous rivalry that first caught parents up in the need for new strategies of emotional management.

The first parental manual specifically to take up the theme of sibling jealousy among young children was Felix Adler's *Moral Instruction of Children,* issued in 1893, which talked about "ugly feelings" taking root in the hearts of children treated inequitably.[36] It was in the late 1920s, however, that the subject of childish jealousy became a staple of American parental life. A government publication in 1925 trumpeted the view that "Few emotions are experienced by man which from a social point of view are more important than jealousy."[37] And this disastrous emotion was, so the new wisdom held, characteristically developed early in life, most typically as a result of badly managed reactions to the arrival of a younger sibling. The message, as ultimately with anger, was two-fold: first, jealousy was much worse as a character flaw than had once been argued. Only a few developmentalists had anything positive to say about the role of jealousy in usefully spurring competition, as most noted how disliked the jealous person was, how deprived of the power to form stable business or family relationships. Second, the seed of jealousy sprouted early, in the child of two to four; and so its treatment was an issue of pressing parental concern. The management of jealousy could no longer be left to the character development of a maturing adolescent, for by then it would be too late. And a young child's jealousy was virtually inevitable; differences related mainly to it visibility, but the alert parent should not be deceived by an apparently generous offspring for "the child whose jealousy is not as easy to recognize suffers more and has greater need for help."[38]

The management of childish jealousy, for the sake of family harmony and even the physical safety of siblings, but also for the successful adult personality of the individual child, became a key issue in American parental advice literature through the 1950s. Dr. Spock, for example, abandoned his usual live-and-let-live approach to urge that the problem of childhood jealousy was so menacing that a "lot of effort" must be expended to combat it.[39] For jealousy in the young child might readily fester—the same gangrenous image later applied to anger—and produce an adult not only incapable of true love but also barred from the cooperative interpersonal endeavor now required in business life.

Techniques for curbing sibling jealousy were varied. A host of mechanical procedures formed part of the arsenal: the older sibling should have his or her own things, should be warned of a new baby's arrival, should be protected from baby-cooing grandparents, should indeed be given the lion's share of attention during the early weeks of an infant's arrival. Beyond procedures was the need to allow the child to vent emotion, verbally, with complete freedom. Parents should not insist on an affectionate attitude among siblings. They should tolerate, even encourage, expressions of hatred and a demand for disproportionate parental love. "I know how you feel, dear. Come on over and I'll give you a hug and we'll see if that doesn't help." "I know how you feel; you wish there were no baby; I love you just as always."[40]

This approach went beyond mere ventilation of emotion, of course. Jealous children were to be lovingly reassured, and not just allowed to talk about their bad feelings. For jealousy, involving a perceived deprivation of love as well as hostility, could be not treated as coldly as anger was to be in the ventilationist strategy. There were marked similarities even so. Jealousy was another of those dreadful emotions that had to be aired without finding direct behavioral expression. It had to be rendered passive, not used to motivate. And despite the sympathetic concern that a good parent should use in identifying his young child's jealous feelings, the assumption was that with proper management a child would outgrow the need for reassurance. Jealousy was a dire problem but not a permanent one. Precisely because it could be confronted in early childhood it need not persist. The same prescriptive literature that urged anxious attention to young sibling rivalry turned a cold shoulder on the jealousy problems of adults or even adolescents, who were simply immature people who had not received proper socialization when young. The jealous adult deserved none of the sympathy that was part of the emotion's management among young children. Only some kind of special therapy could really be envisaged for a person so badly out of step with the emotional norms of twentieth-century America—the psychiatrist or, for yuppies in the late 1970s, one of the burgeoning "jealousy workshops" that would help troubled individuals find out where they had gone wrong.

One of the reasons that adult jealousy could be so readily dismissed as aberrant was the obvious fact that the emotionological campaign against festering sibling rivalry had reached such a large audience. Few middle-class people could grow up after 1930 without some awareness of the battles being waged against the emotion. *Parents' Magazine* was deluged with letters dealing with the problem of sibling rivalry, with many parents concurring that jealousy was "by far the most troublesome, the gravest issue I've met so far in my career as mother."[41] Parental anxiety may indeed have triggered as much of the expert attention to jealousy as the converse, in what was clearly a widely popular area of concern. A poll taken in the mid-1940s drives the point home: in a survey of 544 families, jealousy was rated the most serious of all issues relating to children's personality and temperament, and the third most serious problem overall.[42]

The striking parallelisms in twentieth-century approaches to jealousy and to anger sketched a new suppressive style, despite some interesting variations in timing and precise response. Anger and jealousy alike became thoroughly bad, with no redeeming qualities. They both became synonymous with unacceptable childishness, emotions to be shed as part of growing up. They both demanded explicit attention during early childhood, to prevent incorporation into basic personality and drive home the lesson that distinctions must be drawn between feeling an emotion and giving it any but verbal expression. Bad emotions could no longer be gilded with assumptions of childish innocence or entrusted to purely moral injunctions; but they could be rendered passive. Avoid situations productive of bad emotions where possible even when this took effort: ventilate unpleasant emotions verbally when they did appear; socialize children early to label unpleasant emotions—here was the new strategic trinity directed at anger and jealousy alike.

The contrasts between this new suppressive style and the dominant emotionology of the nineteenth and early twentieth centuries were numerous. The new style allowed, at least in theory, for no gender distinctions. Men had no more natural right to anger than women, women no more leeway for romantic jealousy. The public-private distinction was also eroded, most obviously in the case of anger. The mid-twentieth century emotionology urged that attention to targeting emotions be dropped in favor of across-the-board defusing. Emotional life outside the home came to be viewed increasingly as a series of interpersonal relationships in which more consistent levels of emotional restraint were essential; hence the extension of suppressive norms once more exclusively directed at family life. The idea of directing risky, in some ways unpleasant emotions toward some explicit functions, as well as earlier ambivalence about what emotions were really unpleasant, vanished. Jealousy, which might be viewed as a reinforcer of family unity, was now a menace; anger still more obviously lost its entrepreneurial or reformist motivational role.

These redefinitions focused attention on the need for new strategies for control. Neither anger nor jealousy could be wished away; both emotions existed, and indeed their manifestations in early childhood served as the basis for the suppressive approach. Children were to learn from their first years a distinction between labelling a reproved emotion and admitting it was felt, on the one hand, and experiencing the emotion in any full sense. It was all right to say "I feel anger," much as one could denote a mild physical disturbance. It was not all right to let one of the reproved emotions intensify, to act on its base, or to express it with any pattern or frequency. These childhood lessons well learned, emotional suppression in adulthood could then rely on the sense of infantilization inherent in any serious, admitted recrudescence. This would be combined, of course, with normative rational controls in the nineteenth-century sense, but the combination was novel and many people might be more intimidated by their acute realization that anger or jealousy were childish, rooted as this realization was in their own socialization, than by more abstract ideas that the emotions were wrong. In this emphasis on childishness lay also the American interest in concealing reproved emotions, rather than either denying or acting on them outright.

Reliance on guilt, and mechanisms to emphasize guilt, declined in this atmosphere. Unpleasant emotions were no longer to be channeled, for emotions themselves, and not resulting behaviors, provided the key focus. Isolation of children and threats of loss of love, basic constituents of the guilt regime, were now downplayed. Suppression was to be accompanied by reassurance of affection, particularly of course in the case of childish jealousy. Early childhood now received new attention, as a prime target for appropriate emotional directions, and this was why emphasis on childishness replaced injunctions toward character-building in guiding control of undesirable emotions in adolescence and adulthood. The image of festering emotions and the strategy of talking them out, rather than denying or redirecting, completed the shift away from the nineteenth-century approach.

The unifying mechanism in this new suppressive system was an enhancement of acute embarrassment at feeling, and even more at openly expressing, a reproved emotion such as anger or jealousy. The instillation of the bases for the embarrassment reaction in early childhood was reminiscent of a guilt regime, but unlike guilt the embarrassment mechanism was not intended to provoke strong reactions. Evisceration of intensity, not passionate judgment—even self-judgment—was the goal. In these senses the new, suppressive use of embarrassment differed from both the Victorian and the more traditional systems of emotional control developed earlier in American history. Linked to the new scrutiny of early childhood, based on a newly-demanding definition of emotional maturity, emotional suppression twentieth-century style coexisted misleadingly with a sense that older control devices had been relaxed in favor of a more honest venting of impulse.

Embarrassment, to be sure, is not entirely distinguishable from shame, which recalls Ruth Benedict's judgment cited earlier. However, embarrassment differed from shame in being more internalized, not simply evoked by the judgments of others even as the importance of peer interactions rose. Fewer institutional mechanisms were set to produce embarrassment, unlike the community enforcement of shame; the force of the idea of childishness, whether invoked by an observer of emotional reactions or by oneself in judging one's own anger or jealousy, was meant to trigger the appropriate emotional response. This was thus a more directly emotional control over emotions labeled undesirable. Finally, the control itself, at least during the socialization process, was cushioned by reassurances of affection, which the starker uses of shame had not entailed. Not entirely separate from earlier suppression regimes, the reliance on embarrassment emerged nevertheless as a distinctive emphasis from the 1920s onward.

What caused the new suppressive approach to take shape during the first half of the twentieth century? The nineteenth-century replacement of shame with guilt, situated in a sufficiently remote past to allow explanatory perspective, seems to flow fairly logically from new ideologies of childrearing (the improvable child) and the decline of earlier community structures and religious sanctions. The unfolding of the new emphasis on suppressive embarrassment, if only because it is both recent and less familiar, requires more open-ended scrutiny. Explanation, even at this early stage, in fact divides into two segments: why a new approach was seen as necessary, and why a particular set of mechanisms answered perceived need.

What caused American standard setters to develop new discomfort, at roughly the same point in time, with certain forms of public anger and with sibling rivalry? Part of the explanation must attach to particular settings and emotions. Workplace anger drew attention after a period of rising labor unrest; suppression had obvious social control functions. Sibling rivalry among young children may have increased by the late nineteenth to early twentieth centuries as a function of heightened maternal intensity and decreased family size (even in the 1940s larger families reported fewer jealousy problems, as children banded together more readily, depended on a particular parent less). But there were more general factors at work as well.

First, earlier attempts to identify unacceptable emotions, though part of a different approach to suppression, fed newly shocked disapproval in the twentieth century. Because jealousy had been attacked, and the ideal innocence of children vaunted, parents reacted more desperately to new incidence of sibling rivalry than was in any sense inevitable—or even, so more sober assessment would later argue, objectively warranted. Middle-class personnel specialists like Frederick Taylor or Elton Mayo were truly appalled by the amount of open anger they found among workers, not simply because of their concern for employer interests but because of the familial standards of anger control built into their own nineteenth-century childhoods. They therefore amended their own original agendas, particularly in the case of Mayo, to build in explicit attempts to banish anger from the workplace. Twentieth-century labeling of emotion, and even more the heightened concern about control, thus evolved from the growing internalization of standards projected earlier in the nineteenth century, but only gradually assimilated into actual middle-class upbringing and therefore available to evaluate apparent lack of restraint. Images of familial love, promoted so actively in nineteenth-century emotionology (see the preceding chapter in this volume), worked increasingly into actual efforts to dominate emotions viewed as contradictory.

For the heightened disapproval of jealousy and anger resulted also from the growing idealization of love and affection as positive emotional norms. Family life had long been seen as damaged by undue anger, judged the opposite of love; now childhood jealousy, which related so convolutedly to familial love—symbolizing an understandable need for love but a breakdown in its conveyance—joined the reproved list. Even outside the home a desire for some positive affect in human relationships, though short of love, led to the growing attack on emotions seen as contradictory to a friendly stance: Many Americans looked for signs of warmth in part because past values became more widely accepted and applied; they turned against certain emotions also on the basis of past definitions that placed these in opposition. Defense of love was hardly new in American history, but it took on new salience and was extended to a growing desire for at least superficial friendship in work or customer relationships; and with this change the need for more blanket attack on jealousy and anger seemed obvious.

New expert opinions unquestionably entered the mix as well. Popularized Darwinism and, though only gradually, Freudianism were filtered through the advice literature available to the middle class, toward growing recognition that the human animal, even in its infant versions, contained strong and frightening impulses. The gloss of innocence so pervasive, following on the Enlightenment, in mid-nineteenth century materials faded, and this helped prompt new concerns about emotional control. Experts unquestionably guided middle-class opinion toward increasing equation of anger and aggression, by the 1940s, while the concept of sibling rivalry stemmed directly from Freud as mediated by a number of well-publicized American experiments in the 1920s.[43] The role of expert formulation should not be exaggerated, however, in its causal as opposed to labelling role. Freud's ideas about Oedipal sexual jealousies, though faithfully mirrored in much advice literature, fell largely on deaf ears, if only because they clashed too defiantly with still-pervasive family ideals. Experts, in sum, could cause new emotional concerns only when other factors predisposed.

In the case of jealousy, particularly, one must be impressed by the partially fantasy qualities of the twentieth-century concern. Sibling rivalry existed, and almost certainly in fact increased; there was an empirical base. But it was also greatly exaggerated. And while expert promptings may have played a role here, one must also wonder whether adults generally were displacing toward children a number of emotional concerns in their own lives. Thus: children should be jealous as a sign they properly love their mothers, even though this jealousy should then be combated. Thus: anxieties about new levels of sexual jealousy, and also jealousy provoked by tensions in management hierarchies that could not be directly acknowledged as jealousy, could easily be translated into attacks on imagined levels of childhood passion.

In addition, then, to the steady internalization of previous emotionology, supplemented by some new empirical problems and a new round of expertise, the intense efforts to leech out jealousy and anger, particularly in young children, may have stemmed in part from complicated reactions to new emotional stress. Adults found themselves tempted toward jealousy or anger in some new ways—for example, when they served as middle managers with frustrations in dealings both with supervisors and underlings—and found the effort to inculcate suppression through embarrassment a good way to express their own disapproval of these impulses. Thus it is striking that the new socialization strategy toward children, while meant to be implemented primarily by mothers, departed vividly from the reliance on the idealized maternal model so prominent in nineteenth-century emotionology, as described by Jan Lewis in the previous chapter. This shift may have reflected women's new public

SUPPRESSING UNPLEASANT EMOTIONS

activities and less inhibited sexuality, which could have roused new jealousies on the part of men and women alike—reactions sublimated in turn through a new zeal in combating sibling rivalry among children.

Finally, and more measurably, a strong functionalist ingredient entered into the adoption of new suppressive strategies that, through embarrassment, reflected heightened sensitivity to peer interactions. The most important causal factor stemmed from a shift, led by middle-class parents, in the kinds of personalities regarded as economically functional and therefore sought in child development. By the 1930s and 1940s, alterations in business climate that stressed bureaucratic or sales skills over entrepreneurship placed a growing premium on the kind of emotional control that could assure smooth personal relationships outside (as well, at least ideally, as within) the home.[44] Hence new patterns of socialization against anger and the new concern for controlling jealousy and competitiveness peaked as issues among families invested in management or professional life, rather than among blue-collar workers or even older segments of the middle class;[45] hence also the strictures about anger at work were applied most firmly to middle-level bureaucrats, rather than the assembly-line operators who had first provoked the concern. The new, service-sector middle class proved most zealous in identifying novel emotional issues and recognizing their seriousness; they also led the way in adopting control strategies that deliberately shifted from past patterns toward a more anxious interest in verbal ventilation of anger or jealousy. Here too it is possible that pressures for new business personalities meshed with some troubling impulses on the part of middle-class parents, exposed for example to increasing possibilities for romantic jealousy in adult life or to new tensions as work hierarchies became more subtle, that further heightened the desire to attack the emotion in others. Efforts to instill embarrassment about anger in children might reflect anxieties a middle-manager parent felt about new emotional tensions at work, when a pleasant face had to be turned to all comers. New concern for jealousy could easily reflect new levels of sexual temptation, in a fairly obvious displacement pattern. These effects could conjoin with the more readily-expressed demands for friction-free personalities in modern corporate and sales operations.

Prior standards, new ideas, new adult stresses, and above all new organizational demands pushed for reconsideration of prior suppressive practices, and toward greater rigor against anger and jealousy alike; but why did the response turn from guilt to a new utilization of embarrassment? Here again, past precedent played a role. The use of guilt had already extended the possibility of confusion at certain acts or feelings, in a process Norbert Elias has aptly dubbed a lowering of the threshold of embarrassment.[46] Expert advice, while only ancillary in prodding the middle class to identify new emotional issues, had greater impact in pushing toward new mechanisms, particularly in denoting very early childhood as a key point in which undesirable impulses might take root unless firmly countered. It was the focus on diluting anger and jealousy among young children, in turn, that set the basis for the continued reliance on embarrassment, as in the finding that a repetition of angry grievance could produce a sheepish emotional retraction.

At the same time, guilt declined in utility just as shame once had. The advent of new emphasis on consumerism, by the 1920s, played against continued stress on guilt, as the idea of pleasure gained approved recognition. The related shift to the notion of forming personality rather than building character denoted a move away from instilling guilt, which in turn forced a new strategy for dealing with emotions judged more thoroughly reprehensible than before.[47] This did not guarantee use of embarrassment, any more than the decline of community controls and shame earlier predicted a turn to guilt. It set the stage for innovation, however, which was then guided by the growing role embarrassment had played in middle-class emotional life and the promptings of experts about manipulating infant emotion, translated in turn into more durable, internalized strictures against infantile emotional expression.

Reliance on embarrassment—which unlike guilt does require an audience—followed as well from the new preoccupation with interpersonal relations. The same organizational concerns that help prompt a new suppression thus also conduced, along with expert advice on infant management, to the choice of strategies.

The campaign against reproved emotions, and the turn toward new uses of embarrassment, formed a particularly explicit theme in the emotionology and socialization efforts in the middle decades of the twentieth century. This was precisely when many people had first to adjust to the expectations of a corporate and service economy and when new expert advice about young children gained its growing audience. After the 1950s, however, the attacks on jealousy and anger progressively lost their pioneering tone. Family manuals talked of allowing expressions of anger in marital fights. Parenting experts cut down the space devoted to sibling rivalry and occasionally derided parents and authorities in the prior generation who had approached childish jealousy with a crisis mentality. The inevitability of jealousy was indeed talked down, and the level of parental concern, as measured by polls, dropped as well.[48] In the workplace, retraining sessions to dampen anger trailed off after 1960, and formal statements about the unacceptability of anger on the job became more cursory. Here too the sense of imminent disaster waned somewhat.[49]

While this new tone was significant, and reflected some specific changes in tactics worth monitoring, it revealed a widespread acceptance of earlier strategies and goals, rather than a real shift in direction. Foremen no longer had to be retrained, because they recognized their job as human relations experts. Parents well beyond the middle class knew by heart the tactics that defused sibling rivalry. Emotionology continued to urge against both jealousy and anger, and to assume that embarrassment could be used as a counter. Some prescriptive literature indeed echoed the old advice in full, like a 1987 sibling rivalry guide warning parents that dealing with childish jealousy for a parent's love posed an "incredibly difficult task."[50] And still the key tactics involved encouraging children to express their jealousy or anger verbally, without emotionally-motivated follow-up; those children were most troubled who bottled up feeling, because (as the manuals noted) they would intensify and solidify the emotion as a result and because (though this the manuals only implied) they would not learn to be embarrassed, to link jealousy and childishness, as a means of suppressing the emotion in later life. Guidance literature that talked of expressing anger, rather similarly, did so amid carefully bounded conditions and always with assumptions that the venting would remain hollow, an essentially private scream that a civilized adult would remain too embarrassed to bring into public view. At work, arguments against anger on health grounds extended the attack on this emotion for groups like flight attendants.[51] The suppressive framework newly sketched in the middle decades of the century had, in other words, won sufficiently wide acceptance for those who set emotional standards to drop a missionary stance in favor of more confident assumption of agreement, which in turn allowed briefer sketches of the basic suppressive strategies and some small margin of experimentation within the accepted boundaries. The new tone, in other words, suggests the success of the earlier efforts to win agreement on anger and jealousy as emotional problems and on tactics to defuse both.

Assessment of the actual impact of the new suppressive strategies, as opposed to experts' growing confidence, is inevitably difficult, the results uneven. American society, even middle-class society, was far too diverse and far-flung to expect any general set of emotional norms to win full acceptance. Thoroughly suppressive strategies, which drive basic emotions into virtual nonexistence save in indirect displacement, depend on small, tightly knit and homogeneous settings such as those of tiny tribes or, possibly for some Victorian women, the nineteenth-century household for those confined to domesticity. Furthermore, the suppressive goals and strategies that emerged in the twentieth-century were almost inherently inexact, whatever the complexity of the setting. The new emotionology that urged against anger and jealousy admitted that both emotions would appear and could legitimately be labeled and expressed. It argued that the expression should be verbal only, controlled by its very articulation and the embarrassment it would produce. The approach assumed that jealousy, at least, could largely be controlled in childhood, so that people properly raised would not have to confront the emotion very seriously. But the new suppression did not pretend to guard against all manifestations of reproved emotions, even in adulthood. Hence, even aside from continued disagreements and countercurrents, it was hardly surprising that anger and jealousy remained part of actual emotional experience for many Americans.

In the case of jealousy, the suppression approach launched in early childhood had a number of loopholes, despite intense parental hostility to the emotion itself. First, though jealousy was to be defused, the process entailed reassurance of love, not punishment. This could set an adult model in which embarrassment at the infantile qualities of jealousy would be modified by an expectation that nevertheless, when jealous, the equivalent of mommy would give the equivalent of hugs. This scenario may have been played out by many American adults by the 1960s, when efforts to deny jealousy broke down amid urgent appeals for assurance of love.

The second loophole was even more interesting. In defusing jealousy among young children great care was urged to protect children's identity as established through material objects. Jealousy was bad, but clear claim to toys, clothes, room and so on was quite legitimate. Jealousy might later find outlet in passions for material acquisition, a result obviously congenial to a society dependent on consumption and prepared by a childhood-jealousy nexus itself reflecting lessons in material self-definition.

Finally, the attention given to jealousy, though formulated in terms of the need to avoid the adult emotion lest it hamper both business and personal life, could cue children into unusual awareness of their need to pay attention to rivals' backstabbing and to further their self-interest as a means of avoiding a need for admission of outright jealousy. This trait, somewhat different from outright aggressiveness or self-aggrandizement, could be translated into maneuverings amid corporate hierachies in which jealousy would play an unacknowledged role. There may, in sum, have persisted some ambivalence about jealousy-based achievement and jealousy-free activity as a corporate team player. Ambivalence toward anger remained as well, for American culture had not fully renounced a rewarding, make-my-day anger. Complexities of this sort clearly warrant further analysis.

Yet the new suppression did have effects. The tendency of Americans to criticize and attempt to conceal the emotions they were taught to reprove, to an unusual extent when compared to other contemporary nationalities, has already been noted; a similar reaction would not have been found fifty years ago when many fathers, for example, openly encouraged channeled anger in their sons. While workplace anger hardly vanished, it did decline, with results extending to the decline of collective protest.[52] New embarrassment about jealousy helps explain institutions newly designed to minimize its incidence, such as steady-dating or more recently peer-group social emphasis where jealousy is particularly controlled; it also fed a variety of efforts to demonstrate maturity by striving to avoid traditional reactions to blatant sexual infidelity.[53] Americans, in sum, learned from the new suppressive campaigns not simply what emotions to claim to shun, but also how at least in some settings these emotions might be put aside.

The impact of new suppression on overall emotional experience forms a vital agenda for further research, in which scholars concerned with contemporary emotion and those interested in processes of change over time may conjoin. Suggestions about growing uses of embarrassment and consequences in actual emotional experience invite testing by social psychologists and sociologists of emotion as well as historians; they form indeed one of the areas in which a mutual interdisciplinary agenda might take shape.

It remains easier to speculate than to prove, for in dealing with results of the new suppressive strategy one moves obviously from emotional standards, and practices designed to implement them, to changes in emotional experience itself. Arlie Hochschild thus has persuasively argued that suppression of anger at work, particularly for many service-sector women, through new strategies of embarrassment and manipulation distorts general emotional life even off the job; but her work to date has not fully demonstrated this impact. The present analysis suggests that it may be fruitful to seek ways in which anger and jealousy are consciously avoided in some settings, or denied or evaded, and there is some evidence on these points.

Several other outcomes merit inquiry. The new tactics of emotional control involved a partial redefinition of emotional maturity, now seen in terms of keeping childish impulses in check. In the area of jealousy, at least, one must be impressed with the extent to which later twentieth-century American adults have have often seemingly wished to test themselves (not always successfully) to demonstrate their mature cool. Efforts to damp down jealous reactions even in cases of sexual infidelity, plus the embrace by certain middle-class groups of therapy workshops to enhance their control, serve as an interesting illustration of the wider new norms.

More generally, the effort to control anger and jealousy alike in certain settings, invites inquiry into a search for new outlets, where embarrassment is less salient than in normal circumstances. Anger at sports events or in furious driving habits are two obvious candidates, and suggest that contemporary suppression patterns raise new issues of targeting, a need to choose relatively anonymous or symbolic settings, where outbursts cannot be prevented altogether. Channels for suppressed jealousy may also be traced, for example in consumer acquisitiveness (prepared indeed by childhood diversions of sibling tension through new toys) or even the growing intensity of interest in the mechanics of sexuality.

It also seems likely that the twentieth-century stance toward reproved emotions produces a distinctive approach toward selecting appropriate audiences, spurred by the need for outlets though no longer directly sanctioned by emotionology itself. The emotional control regime of the nineteenth and early twentieth centuries, particularly though not exclusively where men were concerned, built on a public-private distinction, with emphasis on the emotional sanctity of the family but with the need for somewhat different drives in the messier public sphere. The new suppression regime of the twentieth century leads toward a tripartite private/familiar public/strangers division. The familial sphere still calls for extensive control over bad emotions, but with some leeway given the need for emotional reassurance when anger or jealousy do crop up (a complexity built into early childhood socialization). Strictest control is now sought when dealing with a known public, at work, in neighborhood, at school. Among outright strangers, occasionally encountered, a certain leeway is sought precisely because such freedom is no longer permitted, without embarrassment, either in family or at work. Angry rudeness toward strangers, then, in crowds or on the road, or even liaisons designed to vent sexual jealousy may increase in part as unintended results of a powerful new suppressive system. Ritual settings where anger can be exposed without embarrassment also of course involve strangers.

The results of the twentieth-century suppressive style, if still demanding further measurement in terms of shifts in actual emotional experience, suggest relationships to the wider efforts to sketch normative changes in the American character noted at the outset of this essay. Embarrassment, though partly internal, does link to new peer sensitivities and a certain other-directedness; indeed the shift to a service economy, involving more people-skills, helps explain changes both in suppression and in wider personality style. The suppressive shift outlined here differs from Lasch's invocation of narcissism, but it touches base with some of the phenomena he cites including new problems in expressing jealousy and difficulties in targeting anger.

The change in suppression demands evaluation in its own right, however, as a first step toward further understanding of the contemporary emotional framework. The relationship between a new kind of suppressive embarrassment and other, more casual forms of embarrassment set up obvious research questions about evaluating intensity and impact, in which a historically generated hypothesis can be subjected to empirical tests common in other emotions research fields.[54] Reduction of sexual embarrassment and of gender specificity—embarrassed blushes as charmingly feminine—is an assessable feature of the new emphasis on embarrassment in controlling emotional reactions especially amid a familiar public, but the full equation must be further explored.

The very existence of a suppressive approach deeply rooted in our socialization practices and applied in essentially consistent ways to at least two reproved emotions continues to require emphasis, for the decline of guilt can be misleading.[55] We too often believe that suppression has been jettisoned, for good or ill, in favor of an emotional laissez-faire, whereas in fact a system has taken root that subtly, in some ways insidiously, allows Americans to believe they can express emotion freely while in fact confining expression to articulation alone—again the distinction between being allowed to say I felt angry and actually indulging in the experience of being angry—or driving toward a limitation of the emotional range because of fear of embarrassment. Confused reaction to the adult experience of anger or jealousy, not a willingness to let either freely emerge, constitutes the real result of twentieth-century emotional norms.

This result may be good, of course. It certainly seems to fit a variety of expectations in family and sexual life and in work settings. Yet the campaign against jealousy and anger has one final probable consequence that certainly should be further explored, and might be deemed unfortunate. Strategies to defuse anger and jealousy may have tended, as against more standard Victorian experience, to have created some anxiety about emotional intensity in general. The relationship between the new definition of emotional maturity and the popularity of "being cool" is obvious, and not necessarily trivial. Affection may be conditioned by the worried desire not to appear possessive or jealous. Protest loses an edge when the emotional basis for righteous indignation is curtailed. Many

Americans, in sum, may have developed a blander emotional life than they realize as a result of a suppressive strategy that urges a separation between sophisticated ability to label emotion and real experience—a strategy that encourages an essentially passive stance toward key ingredients of emotional life. As embarrassment has extended its range over recent decades, it has certainly affected more than a few specific emotions. It may, indeed, in its use of early childhood lessons and aversions, have redefined what it means to be an emotional adult.

NOTES

1. Carol Tavris, *Anger: The Misunderstood Emotion* (New York, 1982).

2. Historians attuned to interdisciplinary work in the social sciences may be surprised—and I would expect pleased—at the finding that in the behavioral sciences area their research compass seems ambitious and broad. The practical result, aside from undeniable complexities in interdisciplinary collaboration with researchers accustomed to rather narrow but laboratory-replicable bands of data, is that historians do more agenda-setting in dealing with topics in emotions research than has been the case in some of the more conventional social science interactions.

3. Shula Sommers, "Adults Evaluating Their Emotions: A Cross-cultural Perspective,"in *Emotion and Adult Development,* ed. Carol Zander Malatesta and Carroll E. Izard (Beverly Hills, 1984), 319–38.

4. Arlie Russell Hochschild, *The Managed Heart: Commercialization of Human Feeling* (Berkeley, 1983).

5. See for example N. O'Neill and G. O'Neill, *Open Marriage: A New Life Style for Couples* (New York, 1972).

6. David Riesman and others, *The Lonely Crowd: A Study in the Changing American Character* (New Haven, 1973). Some of Riesman's insights concerning new anxieties about anger are particularly noteworthy in this context.

7. Christopher Lasch, *Haven in a Heartless World: The Family Besieged* (New York, 1977).

8. Jesse Battan, "New Narcissism in Twentieth-Century America: The Shadow and Substance of Social Change," *Journal of Social History* 17 (1983): 199–220.

9. For a fuller discussion of the emotionology (standards)/experience relationship, see Peter N. Stearns and Carol Z. Stearns, "Emotionology: Clarifying the History of Emotions and Emotional Standards,"*American Historical Review* 90 (1985): 813–30.

10. Ruth Benedict, *The Chrysanthemum and the Sword* (Boston, 1946), 223–24. See also, for its various insights including several which helped guide the present essay, E. Goffman, "Embarrassment and Social Organization," *American Journal of Sociology* 62 (1956): 264–71.

11. John Demos, "Shame and Guilt in Early New England," in *Emotions*

and Social Change: Toward a New Psychohistory, ed. Carol Z. Stearns and Peter N. Stearns (New York, 1988).

12. Carol Z. Stearns, " 'Lord Help Me Walk Humbly': Anger and Sadness in England and America, 1570–1750," in *Emotions and Social Change,* ed. Stearns and Stearns.

13. Lawrence Stone, *The Family, Sex and Marriage in England, 1500–1800* (New York, 1977): Demos, "Shame and Guilt"; Carol Z. Stearns and Peter N. Stearns, *Anger: The Struggle for Emotional Control in America's History* (Chicago, 1986).

14. Natalie Zemon Davis, *Society and Culture in Early Modern France* (Stanford, 1975).

15. Jean-Louis Flandrin, *Families in Former Times* (Cambridge, 1979); Randolph Trumbach, *The Rise of the Egalitarian Family: Aristocratic Kinship and Domestic Relations in Eighteenth Century England* (New York, 1978); Philip J. Greven, Jr., *The Protestant Temperament: Patterns of Childrearing, Religious Experience, and the Self in Early America* (New York, 1977).

16. For a ringing indictment of jealousy, see Michael Ryan, *The Philosophy of Marriage in Its Social Moral and Physical Relations* (London, 1839) and Max Lazarus, *Love vs. Marriage* (New York, 1854), 24.

17. Demos, "Shame and Guilt."

18. Catharine Sedgwick, *Home* (Boston, 1841).

19. Jean Briggs, *Never in Anger: Portrait of an Eskimo Family* (Cambridge, Mass., 1970).

20. William G. McLoughlin, "Evangelical Child-Rearing in the Age of Jackson: Francis Wayland's Views on When and How to Subdue the Willfulness of Children," *Journal of Social History* 9 (1975): 20–39.

21. Stearns and Stearns, *Anger.*

22. American Institute of Child Life, *The Problem of Temper* (Philadelphia, 1914); G. Stanley Hall, "A Study of Anger," *American Journal of Psychology* 10 (1899): 615–91.

23. Leigh Minturn and W. W. Lambert, *Mothers of Six Cultures* (New York, 1964), 143ff; Margaret Mead and Martha Wolfenstein, eds., *Childhood in Contemporary Cultures* (Chicago, 1955); Robert B. Sears, Eleanor Maccoby, and Harry Levine, *Patterns of Child Rearing* (New York, 1957) 231–48.

24. Arnold Gesell, "Jealousy," *American Journal of Psychology* 17 (1906): 484.

25. T. S. Arthur, *The Young Wife* (Philadelphia, 1846); Kingsley Davis, "Jealousy and Sexual Property," *Social Forces* 14 (1936): 395–405; David R. Mace, *Success in Marriage* (New York, 1958).

26. Mrs. E. B. Duffy, *What Women Should Know* (Philadelphia, 1873), 64.

27. See for example *Little Women*, where jealousy emerges only when sisters reach the age of courtship, and then not in the form of sibling rivalry so much as jealousy at the intruder's inroads on sororal affection.

28. Peter N. Stearns, "The Rise of Sibling Jealousy in the Twentieth Century," in *Emotions and Social Change,* ed. Stearns and Stearns.

29. T. S. Arthur, *The Mother's Rule* (Philadelphia, 1856), 20, 25.

30. Mrs. Theodore Birney, *Childhood* (New York, 1904).

31. Hills family papers, Amherst College, letters of 1887 and 1888. For comparison to twentieth-century teenagers, Arnold Gesell, Francis Ilg, and Laura Ames, *Youth: The Ages from Ten to Sixteen* (New York, 1956).

32. Peter Gay, *The Bourgeois Experience: Victoria to Freud,* vol.1, *Education of the Senses* (New York, 1984).

33. W. Lloyd Warner, *American Life: Dream and Reality* (Chicago, 1962), 108.

34. Hochschild, *Managed Heart;* Stearns and Stearns, *Anger.*

35. Stearns, "Rise of Sibling Jealousy."

36. Felix Adler, *The Moral Instruction of Children* (New York, 1893), 213–14.

37. D. A. Thom, *Child Management* (Washington, 1925), 9–12; see also U. S. Department of Labor, Children's Bureau, *Are You Training Your Child to Be Happy?* (Washington, 1930), 31.

38. Allan Fromme, *The Parent's Handbook* (New York, 1956), 93.

39. Benjamin Spock, *The Common Sense Book of Baby and Child Care* (New York, 1945), 272.

40. Edward Zilmer, *Jealousy in Children: Guide for Parents* (New York, 1949) 85; Joseph Pleck, *Your Child and His Problems* (Boston,1953), 101; Dorothy Baruch, *New Ways of Discipline* (New York, 1949), 122–23.

41. "Family Clinic," *Parents' Magazine* (June 1955): 26.

42. Arthur T. Jersild and others, *Joys and Problems of Childrearing* (New York, 1949), 28–30, 87, 94.

43. For a summary of the 1920s–1930s jealousy experiments, see Judy Dunn and Carl Kendrick, *Siblings: Love, Envy, and Understanding* (Cambridge, Mass., 1982); Mabel Sewall, "Some Causes of Jealousy in Young Children," *Smith College Studies in Social Work* 1 (1930–31): 6–22.

44. Abram de Swaan, "The Politics of Agoraphobia: On Changes in Emotional and Relational Management," *Theory and Society* 10 (1981): 373.

45. Jersild and others, *Joys and Problems;* Daniel Miller and Guy Swanson, *The Changing American Parent* (New York, 1958). Both studies point to the leading role taken in newly intense concern for combatting jealousy and anger, respectively, by managerial and professional families in the suburbs. See also Paul J. Woods and others, "A Mother-Daughter Comparison on Selected Aspects of Child-Rearing in a High Socioeconomic Group,"*Child Development* 31 (1960): 121–28; Ruth Staples and J. W. Smith, "Attitudes of Grandmothers and Mothers Toward Child-rearing Practices," *Child Development* 25 (1954): 91–97.

46. Norbert Elias, *The Civilizing Process: The History of Manners,* trans. Edmund Jephcott (New York, 1978).

47. Warren Susman, *Culture as History: The Transformation of American Society in the Twentieth Century* (New York, 1985), 271–85.

48. Goffman, "Embarrassment," 264–71.

49. Stearns and Stearns, *Anger;* Stearns, "Rise of Sibling Jealousy."

50. Adele Faber and Elaine Mazlish, *Siblings Without Rivalry* (New York, 1987), 15.

51. Hochschild, *Managed Heart.*

52. Barrington Moore, Jr., *Injustice: The Social Bases of Obedience and Revolt* (New York, 1978), 500-502.

53. Gordon Clanton and Lynn G. Smith, eds., *Jealousy* (Englewood Cliffs, N. J., 1977), 35.

54. The need for further study of embarrassment again relates both to historical and to contemporary perspectives. Changing social relations are often productive of new forms of embarrassment, as Goffman has pointed out in suggesting that more democratic contacts on the job created new embarrassment potentials by the 1950s. I am more impressed with the new, suppressive use of embarrassment, which gives the emotion a decided new twist, deepening its personal and social impact and the discomfort it causes, and linking it to feelings less of status inferiority than of infantilization. Parallel to this, it seems to me, has been an effort to ease more minor, conventional forms of embarrassment, by making interview situations less stiff, insisting on less punctilious sexual decorum, and so on. Embarrassment shifted from a "use" primarily to enforce hierarchy in social relations (plus sexual decorum), to a role in disciplining emotional repression; thus focus on embarrassment as part of institutional hazing declines in favor of concentration on the emotion's role in enforcing personal standards. But the nature, causes, and uses of embarrassment clearly deserve much more exploration than they have received in any kind of emotions research, for the change sketched in this chapter sets an obvious (and in my view important) agenda for further research.

55. It is also important, obviously, to extend consideration of the twentieth-century suppression pattern to other emotions. Grief, in the twentieth century, has been subjected to new pressures from embarrassment, and the same may hold true for certain types of fear. There is certainly an agenda item to flesh out our understanding of reproved emotions and their treatment in our own time.

— 12 —

Historical Emotionology: From a Social Psychologist's Perspective

Margaret S. Clark

As a social psychologist long interested in how social factors influence emotional expression but previously quite uninformed about historical approaches to this area, I found many of the ideas included in the Lewis and in the Stearns chapters to be fascinating. The arguments they have made regarding how one's social context can have an important impact on one's beliefs about the nature of emotions such as love, anger, and jealousy fit well with a large literature in social psychology in which complementary claims about the influence of social context on emotion are made. However, social psychologists have typically only investigated how moment-to-moment, hour-to-hour, or, at most, day-to-day changes in social context might influence the experience and expression of emotion. These historians' emphasis on how very slow changes in the nature of societies can influence how people think about emotions and when and where they will be willing to express these emotions was entirely new to me.

While reading the papers and thinking about how to comment upon them, my thoughts fell into three categories, each of which may be summed up by a question: (a) first, what might the historical study of emotionology in general and these two papers in particular have to offer to social psychologists interested in emotion? (b) second, what might social psychologists' work on emotion have to contribute to a social historical approach to understanding emotion? Finally, (c) what impediments might there be to intellectual contributions flowing in each of these two directions? Consider each question in turn.

Contributions to Social Psychology. First, what does social history in general and these two chapters in particular have to offer to social psychologists? Quite a bit, I think. One general type of contribution that work such as this can make to social psychology (and to those of us interested in emotion in particular) is that it can make us more sensitive to a very neglected class of variables that seem to influence the experience and expression of emotion. The most obvious class of variables in this regard are ones that have to do with *the passage of time with its accompanying changes in culture.* Although a few social psychologists have attended to potential moderating effects of culture[1] and while an even smaller group has pointed to likelihood of historical changes in our findings,[2] the amount of actual work addressing these issues in social psychology must be described as minuscule.[3] Yet, the present historical papers clearly make a case for the importance of such variables. For example, Jan Lewis's paper makes it evident that time and accompanying changes in culture can alter people's view of maternal love from something that is not innately determined and not absolutely central to the development of adult moral fiber into something that is. Moreover, Peter Stearns shows how time and culture seem to have changed society's view of anger and jealousy from something that, for the Puritans, was expected and acceptable, but controlled by shame to something that, in the eighteenth century, became less acceptable particularly for women and particularly in the home, and began to be controlled by guilt, and finally, to something that was even more suppressed and has come to be controlled by embarrassment in current times.

Second, both papers should serve to make psychologists more sensitive to how *macrolevel variables* as well as microlevel variables can influence emotional expressions and change. As Stearns observes, social historians tend to examine the macro determinants of social behavior while social psychologists tend to focus on more microlevel variables. I agree with his observation. Compare for instance, Lewis's emphasis on "republicanism, liberalism, evangelical Protestantism," and "sensationalist psychology" as determinants of how people conceptualize family roles with many developmental psychologists' emphasis on modeling one's parent as a determinant of such roles.[4,5] Or, compare Stearns's emphasis on "alterations in business climate that stressed bureaucratic or sales skills over entrepreneurship" as a determinant of people's negative reactions to others' displays of anger and jealousy with my own emphasis in a recent paper on the type of relationship one particular person desires with a particular other as a determinant of negative reactions to that other's display of irritability.[6]

Third, and not unrelated to either of the prior two points, both Lewis's and Stearns's chapters can serve to make us more aware of *distal* as well as proximal causes of willingness to express emotion and reactions to others' display of emotion. The historians in this collection have placed their emphasis on distal causes. For example, to identify a change in the economic basis of a society as a cause of suppressing emotion in relationships (as Stearns does) is to identify a rather distant cause of that effect— one that must be mediated by many intermediate effects. To say that the type of relationship a person desires with another influences reactions to emotions (as I have in some of my own recent research) is to identify a more proximal cause. These are clearly complementary approaches, but there is no reason why psychologists do not stand to have much to gain by not only looking at proximal causes but also more distal ones.

Aside from making us more sensitive to certain broad classes of variables as determinants of social behavior, papers such as those of Stearns and of Lewis can also be of service to psychologists in a quite different manner. Specifically, it was immediately obvious to me, upon reading these papers, that they can *serve as a rich source of hypotheses* which psychologists can test using their own methodologies. Because Stearns makes claims about the emotionology of our own current culture perhaps the most obvious examples of hypotheses that could be tested by psychologists in the present come from his essay. There are many, many examples of hypotheses expressed in his paper that could be tested using social psychological methods, but consider just one. He states that the twentieth-century approach to emotion he has laid out suggests, "a tripartite private/familiar public/strangers division" in which anger and jealousy are not considered acceptable in private or with familiar public figures but are acceptable with strangers whom one never expects to see again. That is certainly an idea which psychologists have the skills to answer. For instance we might conduct observational studies of interactions between representative dyads of each of these three types in controlled settings to see if, indeed, the amount of anger and jealousy expressed falls in the predicted pattern. Or, if we wished to conduct a true experimental study, we might randomly assign subjects to be led to desire one of the three types of relationships with a another, have that other behave in such a way as to provoke anger or jealousy and record whether or not (and to what extent) the subject displays evidence of anger or jealousy.

While the most obvious set of ideas to be tested in the case of these two papers comes from what Stearns postulates is going on today, that certainly is not the only source of ideas. These historians have also made claims about one type of variable influencing another in the past, and some of these claims could be tested in the present. For instance, consider Stearns's claim about shifts to a service economy having led to an increased emphasis on suppressing emotions such as anger or jealousy. If that claim is valid, should not it also be the case that anger is expressed less often by service workers than by other types of workers in the present? And, would it not also follow that parents who aspire for their offspring to enter service professions should make more attempts to suppress expressions of anger in their offspring than should others? Finally should not a person interviewing for a service job be less likely to express anger when provoked by an interviewer than one interviewing for a nonservice job? While Stearns's ideas relate to a shift that occurred in the past, these other closely related ideas could be tested in the present.

In sum, it seems that social psychologists could gain much from attending to what these social historians have done both in terms of attending to a broader class of variables than they have to date and treating the historians' work as a rich source of ideas regarding the interrelations between emotion and social behavior. Let me turn now to contributions that might flow in the reverse direction.

Contributions from Psychology. What might the discipline of social psychology have to offer to social historians interested in emotion? There are several types of contributions we might make. Before discussing them, however, let me first say that they are not exactly the mirror image of the contributions that I think the work of historians might make to psychologists. For instance, while social psychologists should probably focus more on changes in culture as a causal determinant of emotion as well as on macrolevel and distal events as causal determinants of social behavior, practical considerations have led me to conclude that it does not make much sense to say that the sort of work which social psychologists have done should inspire social historians to attend more to microlevel or proximal events as causal variables than has heretofore been the case. Conceptually it might make sense to suggest this, but practically it does not. That is because there is presumably very little historical data available on proximal and microlevel variables that would allow for this.

Still, there are some contributions to historians that I think we can make. First, by *combining knowledge* about emotions that has been gained by social psychologists with that which has been reported by social historians, I think social historians could extend conclusions they have drawn in ways that would otherwise not be possible. Let me give an example using the two chapters at hand. Both Lewis and Stearns make a case that advice about expressing and controlling emotion has changed over the course of history. Further their chapters strongly suggest that actual expression and control of emotion has changed along with this advice (although perhaps not to extent suggested by the advice). However, to their credit both authors are very cautious about taking their arguments one step further to argue that the actual experience of emotions such as maternal love, jealousy, and anger have changed over the course of history. What recent social psychological work on emotions can tell them is that they need not be quite so cautious. There is some clear evidence in social psychology that how a given state of emotional arousal is experienced depends importantly on how others in our environment and our socialization in general teach us to label that state.[7] There is also some clear evidence that choosing to express an emotion or to cognitively rehearse it may intensify or even create the actual experience of that emotion[8] while choosing to suppress it or not think about it may have opposite effect.[9] The former type of finding certainly suggests that cultural advice regarding what emotions are appropriate to experience when and where will influence actual experience of those emotions. The latter type suggests that choosing to follow that advice or not will also influence the actual experience of these emotions. What all this adds up to is the conclusion that the work of people such as Lewis and Stearns may be more important than even they have suspected. That is, they may be discovering historical changes not only in advice about and in willingness to express emotion but also in emotional experience itself.

A second type of contribution that social psychologists might make to historians is linked to a point made above regarding what contributions historians can make to psychology. That is, while historians can provide us with a rich source of hypotheses to be tested using our methodologies, by actually testing those hypotheses we can *provide them with additional evidence for the plausibility of those ideas.* For example, if psychologists actually did conduct experiments demonstrating that service workers do express less anger than do other workers, that parents aspiring for their offspring to enter service professions do make more attempts to suppress their offspring's expression of emotion, and that people interviewing for service jobs are less easily provoked to anger than are those interviewing for a different sort of job, then Stearns's claims about a historical shift to a service economy having led to an increased cultural emphasis on suppressing anger and jealousy would gain credence. In contrast, if no evidence could be obtained for such hypotheses, those claims would seem less plausible, although we would not be able to rule them out altogether.

Finally, what about psychology suggesting hypotheses/ideas regarding why cultural shifts in the treatment of emotions might have taken place?

Might this also be an area where social psychologists could contribute to social history? Here my feelings are a bit equivocal. Since many of our theories and findings have to do with the effects of proximal and relatively microlevel variables and since, as already noted, historians generally do not have access to data regarding such variables, productively transporting theory and ideas from social psychology to historical analyses may prove to be quite difficult. But I am not ready to conclude it cannot be done. In a few cases the causal determinants of emotional behavior in which psychologists have been interested are at a level at which there may be some historical data available. For instance deindividuation theory[10] has received considerable support within psychology. It suggests that feelings of close group unity, increasing levels of anonymity and a focus on external events and goals will lead to decreases in self-focus, increased sensitivity of one's current emotional states along with lessened concerns about other's evaluations and consequently more expression of emotional states. Certainly, one can imagine finding historical indices of such things as feelings of a close group unity, feelings of anonymity, and a focus on external events and goals. If so, it would be reasonable, on the basis of psychological data, to hypothesize that historical changes in these indices might be paralleled by historical changes in emotional expression as well.

In sum, social psychology might contribute to the social historical study of emotions by: (a) providing data which, when combined with knowledge gained from historical studies might considerably broaden the implications of the historical work; (b) by providing methodologically converging tests of some of the historians' claims regarding mechanisms assumed to have brought the changes about; and (c) perhaps by providing hypotheses for historians to explore using their own methodologies.

Impediments to Cooperation Between the Disciplines? As should be evident from my comments to this point, I do not see any great conceptual disagreements in the ways in which many social psychologists think about social context influencing emotion and the ways in which the social historians think about the same thing. Indeed, I believe the approachs taken by the two groups were quite compatible and complementary. Yet, for the most part, emotions researchers on both sides seem fairly unaware of one another's work. In part this is obviously due to the segregation of psychologists in psychology departments and at psychology conventions and the historians in history departments and at history conventions. Interdisciplinary groups such as a recently formed emotions society and symposiums such as the one where these contributions are presented can help in this regard.

However, I personally feel that a much larger impediment to cooperation between these fields has to do with the methodological differences between the two areas as well as differences in preferred styles of reporting results. Being a social psychologist, I can best explain this from a psychologist's viewpoint. As mentioned early in these comments, one reaction that I had to these papers was that they contained many fascinating (and seemingly quite plausible) ideas. Moreover, the ideas seem compatible with many psychologists' approaches to emotion. However, I must admit to having had feelings of skepticism too. As I read these contributions I kept thinking the sorts of thoughts that skeptical social psychologists interested in empirical research often think. Why should I believe the conclusions these authors have drawn? Where did they get their data from anyway? Were those data quantified in any way? Just how were they analyzed? Are there converging sources of information that independently tend to verify the conclusions? Would a different historian with a different theoretical perspective be driven to the same conclusions from the same data? Are there alternative explanations for the conclusions that are drawn? The information presented in these papers and attendant discussions is insufficient to answer these questions. Of course, this may be a bit unfair since these are syntheses, not original empirical pieces. Nonetheless, I was left with some skepticism.

Not only did I feel that way myself, I also feel confident that a social historian would be similarly skeptical of many social psychological studies on emotion. I can just hear their criticisms of a report of a social psychological, lab-based study on the social functions of emotion that utilizes college students. How do we know that the behavior of such students will generalize to other populations? How do we know that they will generalize to real life settings? How do we deal with students' desires to present themselves in a favorable light in the laboratory? I could address such concerns and I'm sure that the historians could address many of mine. However, I think in large part because we are all used to presenting our work to colleagues who share our own methodologies and philosophical assumptions, we tend not to explicitly address these issues in our papers. As a result, when talking with members of other disciplines skeptical attitudes remain and chances for collaboration are diminished. For these reasons, I would endorse a suggestion that other participants in the volume have voiced. That is, I think we need small, intense workshops including both psychologists and historians interested in similar questions which allow for lots of debate and exchanges of methodological assumptions as well as ideas, if the two disciplines are to truly cooperate in discovering the effects of social context on emotion.

NOTES

1. See, for instance, K. J. Gergen, P. Ellsworth, C. Maslach, and M. Seipel, "Obligation, Donor Resources, and Reactions to Aid in Three Cultures," *Journal of Personality and Social Psychology* 31 (1975): 390–400.

2. K. J. Gergen, "Social Psychology as History," *Journal of Personality and Social Psychology* 20 (1973): 309–20.

3. E. Sampson, "Opening Address," paper presented at the 1988 International Conference on Social Justice and Societal Problems, The University of Leiden, Leiden, The Netherlands, 1 Aug. 1988.

4. A. Bandura, "Social Learning Theory of Identificatory Processes," in *Handbook of Socialization Theory and Research,* ed. D. A. Goslin (Chicago, 1969).

5. W. Mischel, "Sex-typing and Socialization," in *Carmichael's Manual of Child Psychology,* ed. P. H. Mussen (New York, 1970).

6. M. S. Clark and C. Taraban, "Reactions to and Willingness to Express Emotion in Communal and Exchange Relationships," manuscript submitted for publication.

7. S. Schachter and J. Singer, "Cognitive, Social, and Physiological Determinants of Emotional States," *Psychological Review* 69 (1962): 379–99.

8. J. D. Laird, "Self-attribution of Emotion: The Effects of Expressive Behavior on the Quality of Emotional Experience," *Journal of Personality and Social Psychology* 29 (1974): 475–86.

9. M. S. Clark and A. M. Isen, "Toward Understanding the Relationship Between Feeling States and Social Behavior," in *Cognitive Social Psychology,* ed. A. H. Hastorf and A. M. Isen (Elsevier/North Holland, 1982), 73–108.

10. E. Diener, "Deindividuation: The Absence of Self-awareness and Disinhibition," *Journal of Personality and Social Psychology* 37 (1979): 1160–71.

Index